The Ambitious Generation

W9-DCA-515

the Ambitious

America's Teenagers, Motivated but Directionless

generation

Barbara Schneider and
David Stevenson

Yale University Press   New Haven and London

Copyright © 1999 by Barbara Schneider.
All rights reserved.
This book may not be reproduced, in whole or in part, including illustrations, in any form (beyond that copying permitted by Sections 107 and 108 of the U.S. Copyright Law and except by reviewers for the public press), without written permission from the publishers.

Printed in the United States of America by R. R. Donnelley & Sons.

Library of Congress Cataloging-in-Publication Data

Schneider, Barbara L.

The ambitious generation : America's teenagers, motivated but directionless / Barbara Schneider and David Stevenson.

p.   cm.

Includes bibliographical references.

ISBN 0-300-07982-6 (cloth : alk. paper)
ISBN 0-300-08275-4 (pbk. : alk. paper)

1. Teenagers—United States—Social conditions—Longitudinal studies.   2. Adolescent psychology—United States—Longitudinal studies.   3. Motivation (Psychology) in adolescence—United States—Longitudinal studies.   I. Stevenson, David, 1951–   .   II. Title.

HQ799.U65S27   1999
305.235′0973—dc21   98-52033

A catalogue record for this book is available from the British Library.

The paper in this book meets the guidelines for permanence and durability of the Committee on Production Guidelines for Book Longevity of the Council on Library Resources.

10 9 8 7 6 5 4 3 2

To our parents, wise nurturers of dreams, and our families,
Lewis, Dana, Joshua, and Lisa, and Phoebe and Andrew

contents

Preface [ix]

one. Ambitious Adolescents [1]

Part I

Voices from the 1950s and the 1990s

two. Imagining the Future [15]

three. Trying to Make It with a High School Diploma [56]

four. The Importance of Aligned Ambitions [79]

Part II

The Formation of Aligned Ambitions

five. Channeling Ambitions in High School [113]

six. Families and the Shaping of Aligned Ambitions [141]

seven. Teenage Work and Internships [170]

eight. Being Alone and Being with Friends [189]

Part III

Defining a Pathway

nine. The Ambition Paradox [215]

ten. Supporting the Development of Aligned Ambitions [245]

Appendix A

The Alfred P. Sloan Study of Youth and Social Development [265]

Appendix B

Logistic Regression Models [269]

Notes [277]

Index [309]

preface

In the spring of 1989, we began conducting the first analyses of a new national longitudinal study of American eighth-grade students. These analyses formed the basis of a national report, *A Profile of the American Eighth Grader*. Initial analyses can be a source of surprising results, and one of the most intriguing was the very high ambitions of middle school students. Large numbers of them expected to become college graduates and to work as professionals. At first we were unsure how to interpret these findings. We did not know if the ambitions of these teenagers would become more modest as they progressed through high school or whether today's adolescents are indeed more ambitious than previous generations. We had to wait until the next data collection to find out. Two years later, when these students were high school sophomores, the findings began to suggest that their ambitions were not declining as they moved through high school. But were they more ambitious than previous generations of adolescents? We compared the ambitions of this generation of teenagers with results from similar studies in the 1970s and 1980s. The answer that began to emerge was that there had been a significant rise in the ambitions of American adolescents.

When we told colleagues of these findings, their first reaction was usually one of disbelief, because the ambitions of adolescents had been often studied and there had been only a few signs of change. The magnitude of the change we were describing was dramatic, and it appeared to be occurring among both males and females as well as adolescents from different racial and ethnic groups. These rising ambitions were not limited to students from high- and middle-income families.

The rising ambitions of American adolescents raised for us some important issues. The ambitions of adolescents are fundamental to sociological models of social mobility—that is, who gets ahead and why. But with rising ambitions occurring across all students, adolescents are beginning to look more alike in terms of their educational expectations and occupational aspirations. We suspected that this similarity might make it more difficult to tease out the effects of ambitions on social mobility. Therefore, we set out to see if there were other ways to think about the ambitions of today's adolescents that might be of value in understanding social mobility. We hope that the ideas in this book are a step in that direction.

We gratefully thank the Alfred P. Sloan Foundation for supporting the Sloan Study of Youth and Social Development. Without the Sloan Foundation's financial support, it would not have been possible to collect and analyze the longitudinal data reported in this book. We were fortunate to have the advice and good counsel of Dr. Hirsh Cohen, vice president of the Sloan Foundation. His questions pushed us to clarify our arguments, reanalyze our data, and keep to a reasonable timetable. We believe this book was qualitatively improved and completed sooner because of his attentiveness. We would like to thank Dr. Patricia Graham, president of the Spencer Foundation, for her continuing interest in the project, and the foundation itself for its financial support for the writing and manuscript preparation for this book.

We are very grateful for the comments and suggestions of our colleagues Professor Mihaly Csikszentmihalyi of the University of Chicago and Professor John W. Meyer of Stanford University. Our work has benefited from ongoing conversations with them over the past five years, and parts of this book have been stimulated by those conversations. We would like to offer special thanks to Jennifer A. Schmidt, study director of the Alfred P. Sloan Center on Parents, Children, and Work, who with a light touch and a wonderful smile was willing to run and rerun our data models. Ms. Schmidt has been an invaluable colleague and we thank her for her thoughtful criticisms and suggestions on drafts of the manuscript.

Graduate students at the University of Chicago have also assisted us with data runs, table and figure preparations, editing, and helpful commentary. We especially thank Fengbin Chang, Christopher Swanson, Julie Kochanek, Robert Petrin, and Rustin Wolfe. Lisa Hoogstra has been an invaluable editor and we greatly appreciate her careful rereading of the manuscript. Several undergraduate students also helped us with the preparation of the manuscript and references; we wish to thank Benjamin Axelrad and Sunny Chang. We also wish to thank the graduate students in our spring seminar on adolescents and social policy, who gave us helpful comments on the case studies. We also thank the sociology of education brown-bag group for listening to our preliminary ideas. Special thanks to Professor Charles Bidwell, who has been a helpful and supportive colleague throughout the development of this project. We also appreciated constructive conversations with Professor Kathryn Borman of the University of South Florida and Professor Aaron Pallas of Michigan State University.

Two professors at the University of Chicago, Robert Dreeben and Casey Mulligan, spent considerable time with us discussing our arguments and findings. We thank them for their insightful and challenging comments. Selected sections of the book were read by thoughtful and supportive colleagues and friends, including Sue Betka, Cory Heyman, Christine Li, Kay Kahler Vose, and Betsy Wittleder. We thank them for their comments and suggestions. We also extend our deep appreciation to Susan Arellano, senior editor at Yale University Press, for helping us sharpen the focus of our findings and make them more accessible to parents and school personnel. Her confidence in the importance of our work helped us make those final deadlines. We thank Phillip King for his careful and comprehensive manuscript editing. Finally, we would like to thank our very capable and gracious agent, Katinka Matson, for guidance.

We would like to especially thank Professor Robert Dreeben, of the department of education at the University of Chicago, for arranging for Dr. David Stevenson to be a visiting scholar at the university during the period he worked on this book. We also are indebted to Dr. Marshall S. Smith, acting deputy secretary of education of the U.S. Department of Education, for his support and his interest in the book's implications for educational policy. The views expressed are those of the authors, and no official support by the University of Chicago or the Office of Science and Technology is intended or should be inferred.

Several colleagues at the National Center for Education Statistics were extremely helpful to us in obtaining longitudinal data and checking our numbers against other federal data sets. We thank Dr. Pascal D. Forgione, Jr., commissioner of the National Center for Education Statistics, Dr. Martin Orland and Dr. C. Dennis Carroll, associate commissioners, Dr. Jeffrey Owings, director of elementary and secondary longitudinal studies, and Dr. Thomas D. Snyder, director of the annual reports program. We also appreciate the time and information that Professor Karl Alexander, at Johns Hopkins University, gave to us. Professor Alexander's knowledge of the National Science Foundation's Study of the 1955 Senior Class was invaluable, and without his codebooks we would have been unable to prepare our trend analyses.

We are very grateful for the encouragement and support of our colleagues at the National Opinion Research Center who answered our seemingly endless queries. We would like to give special thanks to Dr. Phillip DePoy, president of the NORC, and

Dr. Norman Bradburn, director of research at NORC and professor of psychology at the University of Chicago.

We owe a special thanks to Professor Mihaly Csikszentmihalyi for suggesting the use of Robert Havighurst's River City data, and to Dr. Daniel Meyer, associate curator and university archivist of the department of special collections at the University of Chicago Library, for making the data archives available to us. We thank the mayor, high school principal, teachers and students, community college president, and college administrators in River City for allowing us to interview them.

Finally, we would like to acknowledge a debt to James S. Coleman, teacher and colleague, for his work in describing how adolescents make choices as they move through adolescence into adulthood. We hope that he would see this work as a contribution to that tradition.

chapter one

Ambitious Adolescents

Ted and Sue Marshall have three children; their eldest, Sarah, is a junior in college. Sarah was a good student in high school and according to her teachers had shown "some real talent in writing and art design." Sarah's dream was to become the fashion editor for a chic, international publication like *Elle*, her favorite magazine. For Sarah, however, it was little more than a dream. She had not taken any steps to learn more about the worlds of fashion or publishing. She had not pursued an internship at Arnold's, a local book publishing company, volunteered to do costume design for the high school play, submitted articles for the school newspaper, or enrolled in art classes outside of school.

Sarah did, however, spend a lot of time deciding which college to attend. The decision process had been lengthy and costly. In the fall of her junior year, Sarah took the Princeton Review course to prepare for the college entrance examinations, the SAT and ACT. She carefully followed the high school's guidelines for preparing for college and went to the school's special programs for college admissions, including the college fairs. She met with the school's college counselor, who recommended several colleges based on her interests, listed some teachers to ask for recommendation letters, and handed her a pamphlet on how to fill out college application forms.

Sarah's parents spent little time talking with her about how to pursue a career as a fashion editor, what types of colleges offered appropriate programs, and what courses she should take in college. They did, however, spend considerable resources on helping Sarah select the "right" college. They hired a private college counselor, who recommended seven schools based on Sarah's SAT and ACT scores, her junior-class rank, and her interest in fashion and writing. Two of the colleges on the list were "reach schools," where Sarah was unlikely to be admitted, and two others were "safety schools," places that would be likely to admit her. The remaining three were considered "real possibilities."

In the spring of her junior year, Sarah, her mother, and her father visited seven colleges across the United States. During the trip, she "fell in love" with a college on the East Coast. Ranked one of the best liberal arts colleges in the country, the school had an outstanding reputation in the humanities. Sarah was especially interested in the college because of its close proximity to a major city. Following these campus visits, she made a personal ranking of the schools and began the time-consuming process of applying. Her second choice was not as competitive as the first, but it had a good program in English. She also applied to the remaining five colleges, but her hopes were set on attending her first choice.

The acceptance and rejection letters arrived in the spring of her senior year. Sarah received four of the dreaded thin letters. She had not been admitted to her first, second, or third choices and was wait-listed at her fourth. She was accepted at her two safety schools and at a large state university. Devastated by the rejections, Sarah decided to enroll in one of her safety schools, a small private college in Ohio, where she planned to major in English.

The costs of selecting and attending this college were significant. They included the private counselor ($2,500), college admissions preparation classes ($700), trips to visit colleges ($1,750), and college application fees for the seven schools ($280). The actual bill for attending the college for a year was more than the cost of a moderately priced car; to obtain a bachelor's degree in four years, the total would exceed $100,000. Because of her parents' middle-class income, Sarah was not eligible for financial aid, and she did not receive any scholarship assistance. Her parents were concerned whether she was "making the right choice," given the high costs of the college and her ambivalence about attending one of her safety schools. Their concerns were well founded.

When Sarah enrolled in the school she was unfamiliar with the college curriculum and soon learned that it offered few courses in art or fashion design. In her first semester, she found the English classes very difficult and changed her major to communications. But this decision also proved to be a mistake: the communications courses seemed uninteresting, so she changed her major again, to business. Now a junior, Sarah remains enrolled in the college but still is unsure what she wants to study. She has already changed her major twice and will need an additional semester to earn her bachelor's degree. Sarah feels she has made poor choices. She is not sure this college was the best one for her and worries that she will be unable to find a job after graduating.

Why Study Adolescent Ambitions?

Sarah's ambitions are similar to those of many American adolescents in the 1990s. Large numbers of them expect to become physicians, lawyers, and business managers; few want to work as machinists, secretaries, or plumbers. Such high ambitions are held by teenagers from all families—rich, poor, Asian, black, Hispanic, and white. More adolescents than ever expect to graduate from college, earn graduate degrees, and work in the white-collar world of professionals. They are America's most ambitious teenage generation ever.

Popular media images often portray adolescents as "slackers," drug users, and perpetrators of violent crimes. The overwhelming majority of teenagers, however, graduate from high school, do not use hard drugs, are not criminals, and do not father or have babies while still in their teens. Many of them are willing to work hard to get good grades and assume this will make them eligible for scholarships at the college they plan to attend. Most young people are worried about their futures and believe attaining a college degree is critical for finding a first real job. The bachelor's degree is seen as the necessary first step in moving up the economic and social ladder. Many consider graduate and professional degrees essential.

Although very ambitious, many adolescents find it very difficult to fulfill their dreams. They are unaware of steps they can take that may help them achieve their ambitions. Often their ambitions are dreamlike and not realistically connected to specific educational and career paths. Regardless of how hard they try, they may find themselves, like Sarah, "running in place and unsure where to go." In this book, we examine the ambitions of today's adolescents. We explore why adolescents are so ambitious and what influences the formation of their ambitions. We describe how some ambitions are more useful to them than others and the advantages of ambitions anchored in an understanding of the relationship between educational credentials and later labor market opportunities.

Ambitions are an important part of the lives of adolescents[1]. Whether realistic or not, they help teenagers make sense of their lives and their futures. They can use their ambitions like a compass to help chart a life course and to provide direction for spending their time and energy. Ambitions can increase the chances that adolescents will take schoolwork seriously, gain admission to the college of their choice, and view their success as a product of hard work. Ambitions developed during adolescence also have lifelong significance; they influence career choices and future earnings. Decades of research demonstrate that one of the most important early predictors of social mobility is how much schooling an adolescent expects to obtain.[2]

Young people understand that the jobs available to today's high school graduates are likely to be parking cars, filling orders, and moving boxes. Completing a college education is a gateway to more prestigious jobs and higher earnings. The ambitions of today's adolescents reflect these realities and raise some important issues. Why are ambitions rising? What are adolescents' views of their futures? How do the ambitions of teenagers influence the choices they make during high school and after graduation? What role do schools and families play in shaping their ambitions?

Today more than 90 percent of high school seniors expect to attend college, and more than 70 percent expect to work in professional jobs. Four decades ago, the picture was quite different, with only 55 percent expecting to attend college and approximately 42 percent expecting to work in professional jobs. This dramatic change in ambitions can be understood through studying the lives of adolescents. Using portraits of six of them, three from the 1950s and three from the 1990s, we describe these changes in the lives of teenagers. The social world of high school students in the 1950s helped to prepare them to take on adult responsibilities after high school graduation, and the transition from adolescence to adulthood was brief. Soon after high school, many teenagers assumed the social obligations of marriage and parenthood and, for most males, the responsibility of being the sole full-time wage earner in the family. These are not the concerns of the adolescents of the 1990s.

In the 1990s, the transition to adulthood takes much longer. Most young people do not take on full-time jobs after high school. Instead, they enroll in college, where many of them will remain for more than four years. They are likely to leave school later, marry later, and have children later. This elongated transition is filled with a series of decisions that will have consequences for their futures: What courses to take in high school? What college to attend? What type of work to prepare for? Making these choices opens up new opportunities as well as closing off others. Without a coherent plan, adolescents can find such choices overwhelming and less than meaningful.

Are Today's Adolescents Too Ambitious?

Pursuing a college education is a pervasive desire of today's adolescents. It is fair to ask whether they want more education than is necessary. We find that almost half of these teenagers hope to get degrees that exceed the credentials needed for the occupations they want. It could be that these adolescents foresee a rise in the educational credentials required for today's jobs, and there is some evidence that jobs that are now available to high school graduates may soon require a bachelor's degree. Such a trend is apparent in police work, where the requirement for becoming a police officer in some major cities has increased from a high school diploma to a college degree. As a generation, today's adolescents desire to be professionals in numbers far greater than the number of jobs projected for professionals in 2005. Six times more adolescents want to be doctors and five times more want to be lawyers than there are projected to be openings in these professions.

Some high school graduates in the 1990s do not attend college immediately after high school. However, unlike those in the 1950s, today's high school graduates are not likely to obtain well-paying jobs that can lead to long-term, stable employment. The jobs they can get pay poorly and provide few opportunities for career promotion. Facing such job prospects, high school graduates who have entered the workforce hold on to their dreams of attending college and obtaining additional training and skills.

Some adolescents have educational and occupational goals that are complementary. We describe these teenagers as having aligned ambitions. Students with aligned ambitions know the type of job they want and how much education is needed to get it. Adolescents with aligned ambitions are more likely to select a path or construct a life plan that enhances their chances of reaching their occupational goals. Life plans are important for transforming ambitions from a dream to an everyday goal. Such plans vary in form, however. We have found that life plans that are coherent with detail and realism are especially useful for choosing a path that increases the probability of success in adulthood. They provide adolescents with a sense of order, encourage them to engage in strategic effort and to sustain high levels of motivation, and help them to use familial and organizational resources.

Most high school students are like Sarah: they have high ambitions but no clear life plans for reaching them. We describe these adolescents as having misaligned ambitions. These "drifting dreamers" have limited knowledge about their chosen occupations, about educational requirements, or about future demand for these occupations. Without such information, their life plans are not realistic and are often ill formed. Drifting dreamers are found among boys and girls and all racial and ethnic groups.

Why do some students have aligned ambitions and others misaligned ambitions? We look at two important influences in the formation of aligned ambitions: the school and the family. What role can high schools play in encouraging the development of aligned ambitions? Are some schools more effective than others? We compare three types of high schools and describe what actions they take to help students make the transition from high school to college or work. We also explain why some high schools are more effective in helping students develop plans than others.

Today's parents share their adolescents' high ambitions. Although many parents have high educational expectations for their children, they often fail to draw meaningful connections between educational credentials and future work opportunities. Sarah's parents expended considerable money and effort on the college application process. Are there better ways to spend time and resources? What role do parents need to take in helping to form their adolescents' ambitions, and how can they assist their teenagers in strategically organizing and managing their lives around college and work opportunities? Contrary to popular descriptions of teenagers as uninterested in the opinions of their parents, we find that they desire support and direction from their parents in planning their futures. But many parents do not see it as their responsibility to actively help their adolescents form plans for their futures. Parents are willing to depend on the high schools and colleges to assume that role.

Nearly all adolescents have a paying job during their high school years. What role do teenage jobs, such as fast-food server, salesclerk, and grocery bagger, play in the formation of ambitions? What types of work experiences influence the development of ambitions? What jobs influence the decisions adolescents make about their futures?

Unlike teenagers in the 1950s, these adolescents do not have long-lasting peer group friendships. They spend considerable periods outside of school alone; they have few friends for longer than several months; few have steady girlfriends or boyfriends; and some even claim not to have a best friend. The social groups they belong to are very fluid, and teenagers move easily from group to group. What effect does spending time alone have on teenage ambitions? What influence do peer groups have on the shaping of ambitions? Are there teenage peer activities that can help the formation of ambitions?

A basic choice today's adolescents face is whether to begin college at a two-year or a four-year institution. More students who expect to obtain a bachelor's or graduate degree are deciding to begin their college studies at two-year institutions. Unfortunately, this decision creates what we describe as an ambition paradox—students with high ambitions choosing an educational route with low odds of success. Students with misaligned ambitions are more likely to be caught in this ambition paradox. We describe how these students adapt to this problem and discuss what parents, high schools, and colleges can do to prevent students from being caught in this paradox.

To understand how the ambitions of today's adolescents are formed and are different from previous generations, we draw upon many different data sources. The stories of today's adolescents are taken from the Alfred P. Sloan Study of Youth and Social Development. The Sloan study is the most detailed and comprehensive national study of adolescents in the 1990s. More than a thousand adolescents in twelve different geographical locations around the country participated in this five-year longitudinal study of their daily lives and their plans for the future. These adolescents from all regions of the United States were followed as they changed schools or residences, graduated from high school, and went on to work or college. The sampling frame for the Sloan study was designed to assure a racially and ethnically diverse sample that was representative of American teenagers nationwide. In addition to the students who were followed for five years, information was also collected from other students in the sample schools. All together, more than seven thousand students participated in the study.[3]

The Sloan study collected many different types of information about adolescents and their lives. This information was gathered through multiple interviews conducted over five years with the adolescents and their parents, teachers, and school administrators; field studies of their schools and communities; questionnaires surveying adolescents' perceptions and attitudes toward their schools, friends, and futures, ascertaining their school performance, including grades and courses taken, and assessing their knowledge about the world of work; and measures of how adolescents spend their time. When the study began in

the early 1990s, the adolescents were in middle school and high
school; by now most have made the transition from high school
to college or work.

The rich, comprehensive qualitative data from the Sloan
study were used to create the 1990s case studies in this book.
What is perhaps most unusual about these data is that the in-
depth interviews are longitudinal and conducted at key transitional points. From the cases we see how students weighed their
postsecondary choices, whether their experiences in college met
their expectations, and how they are planning for their futures.
The dreams and life plans of these thousand adolescents, woven
into a shared biography, form the story of this book.[4]

The Sloan Study of Youth and Social Development is part
of the University of Chicago tradition of studying the lives of
adolescents. During the 1950s, several researchers at the university carried out landmark community studies of adolescents and
published their findings in important books, including Robert
Havighurst's *Growing Up in River City* and James Coleman's *The Adolescent Society*. These two studies are elaborately detailed, and they
helped us to describe what the world was like for an adolescent
in the 1950s. The Havighurst study was particularly rich in case
materials on selected adolescents when they were in high school
and five years later. We were fortunate to uncover many of the
original case materials from the Havighurst study in the archival
collection of the University of Chicago's Regenstein Library.
From these case materials we created our portraits of adolescents
in the 1950s. We relied on the Coleman data to contrast the values and friendship ties in high schools of the 1950s and the
1990s.

Another major study of adolescents in the Chicago tradition was conducted by Mihaly Csikszentmihalyi and Reed Larson in the 1980s. The resulting work, *Being Adolescent*, introduced
a new methodology—the experience sampling method—for
studying the daily lives of adolescents. This methodology was

used in the Sloan study and made it possible to compare how young people spend their time, how they perceive the quality of their experiences, and what they wish they could do in the future.[5]

To trace changes in adolescent ambitions, we conducted new analyses of data from national longitudinal studies from the 1950s, 1960s, 1970s, 1980s, and 1990s. Sponsored by the National Center for Education Statistics and the National Science Foundation, these comprehensive studies used rigorous sampling techniques and were based on samples of tens of thousands of adolescents. Results from these data sets serve as benchmarks for comparing the findings from the Sloan study. It is this combination of multiple data sources—current and historical and qualitative and quantitative—that we use to make our case about the importance of adolescent ambitions.

Today's teenagers see their future work lives as filled with promise and uncertainty. They believe in the value of technology, in the importance of being flexible, and in the need for specialization; they also believe that they will change jobs frequently and change careers occasionally. Teenagers accept the volatility of the labor market and believe that the way to create a personal safety net is to obtain additional education. This focus on postsecondary education as a form of security helps to explain the dramatic rise in ambitions. It also makes more apparent the importance of the choices that teenagers make for reaching their dreams. Small choices, such as which courses to take in high school, can influence their preparation for college, and other choices, such as whether to enroll in a two-year or four-year college, can influence their chances of earning a bachelor's degree. Unfortunately, many adolescents make uninformed choices, and the costs of making poor choices can be great. Sarah chose a college that did not offer what she wanted to study; she changed her major several times; and she is about to finish college with little idea of what she wants to do. Sarah and many other adolescents do not have meaningful life plans to help guide them in making choices. Many, like Sarah, believe that college is necessary to obtain a decent job. The time and energy young people put into going to college and the resources and effort their parents and schools expend in helping them make the transition can be substantial. Many of these efforts, however, focus on a single objective—getting into college—without attention to the formation of ambitions.

Voices from the
1950s and the 1990s

I

c h a p t e r   t w o

Imagining the Future

Adolescence is a time for imagining. It is a time when teenagers dream about what their lives will be like in the future; what it will be like to go to college, to have an adult job, to fall in love, and to become a parent. These images are shaped by adolescents' experiences, by what they see happening to their parents, siblings, and friends, by the messages of the media, and by their understandings of what is possible. The content of these dreams and the lives of teenagers have changed significantly from the 1950s to the 1990s.

The experiences of teenagers in the 1950s provide an interesting contrast with the experiences of adolescents today. We chose the 1950s for several reasons. As a generation, adolescents of the 1950s did not have their lives dramatically disrupted by large historical events such as the Great Depression or a world war. They were the last generation to leave high school before the rapid expansion of higher education in the 1960s. Also, there are numerous high-quality studies of adolescents in the 1950s that create a valuable and accessible historical record of their lives. We describe the lives of six adolescents, three from the 1950s and three from the 1990s, following each for five years. These cases were selected to be representative of the choices adolescents face after high school and to illustrate the dominant patterns of transition from adolescence to adulthood.[1]

Teenage Life in the 1950s

Adolescents in the 1950s belonged to a transitional generation. Their early childhood years were bound to the Second World

War as their fathers left home for military service and their mothers went to work in the war production factories or served as volunteers supporting the war effort. By their elementary school years, the war was a fading memory for most of these children, and they were growing up in an age of unprecedented prosperity. The 1950s was a time of relaxation, recreation, and family stability.

In their adolescence, members of this generation found themselves in a world of expanding occupational opportunities, steady employment, and increasing consumerism. Mass marketing through the new medium of television created a youth market and promoted a youth culture. Teenagers had their own tastes in music, clothes, cars, and movies. Such popular teenage songs as "Venus in Blue Jeans" and "Johnny Angel" promoted idealized romantic images of male-female relations. Teenage marriage and motherhood became a common and accepted part of the social landscape.[2]

Parents and older siblings of these teenagers were purchasing single-family homes and moving to the suburbs at a faster rate than ever before. The mass production of suburban housing modeled after the successful Levittown development skyrocketed. More than one and a half million new houses were built each year during the 1950s. By the end of the decade, more than 80 percent of newly constructed homes had been built in the suburbs.[3] Fields of potatoes, corn, and grazing pastures were quickly transformed into miles of winding roads and hundreds of houses. Spurred in part by low-interest mortgage rates to veterans and loans subsidized by the Federal Housing Authority, the suburban development changed the nature of America's neighborhoods. Ownership of a suburban home came to represent personal fulfillment, contentment, and well-being.

The growth of suburbs with mass-produced small houses on small lots and strict community building and maintenance codes was seen by critics as marking the decline of American individuality.[4] But others stressed that, in these new suburbs, community associations flourished and brought together people to solve common problems and became vehicles for building strong community ties.[5] For millions of adolescents in the 1950s, the new suburbs helped to foster the belief that home ownership was not beyond their reach.

A prominent feature of many of these suburban homes was the television set. The explosion of television into the living rooms of American families occurred during the 1950s and brought to the American family a barrage of consumerism packaged in commercials, game shows, and an idealized portrayal of the American family. Television sales averaged five million per year during the 1950s, and by the end of the decade fully 90 percent of American households owned at least one set. Early television provided viewers with a limited number of channels and the television schedule was dominated by Lucille Ball, Milton Berle, Jackie Gleason, and Red Skelton. Families gathered around the television to watch comedies like I Love Lucy or dramas featured on such shows as Studio One. Since there was no capacity to videotape programs at home, the television schedule could dominate the organization of family leisure time.[6]

For suburban families, the time needed to commute to work, shop, and transport children greatly expanded as communities grew farther and farther from urban centers. The automobile quickly became one of the family's most valued possessions. This was especially the case for adolescents, who viewed ownership of a car as a ticket to freedom and as a symbol of autonomy and status among their peers. Cars were relatively simple to repair, and working on them became a prominent part of male teenage life. To the teenager, a car was seen as essential for taking in the latest drive-in movies, fast-food restaurants, and new shopping centers.[7]

The most significant demographic change in the postwar period was an increase in the birth rate. During the 1950s, the number of adolescents in high school grew dramatically from six million to nine million. This rise in enrollment reflected an increase both in the number of students entering high school and in the number remaining in school. The influx created a demand for more classrooms, and in the 1950s more than one thousand new high schools were built.[8]

Life for most adolescents in the 1950s was a time of optimism, economic security, and clearly defined career and gender roles. The comprehensive high school of the time, with its differentiated curricular programs, provided basic knowledge and skills for the majority of students who planned to enter the labor market directly after graduation and offered selected academic programs for those who planned to attend postsecondary school.[9] The job choices available after high school were tied to specific gender roles; most young men went to work full time, and most young women worked for a short period before marrying and having children. Early marriage for females and entry into the labor force after high school graduation for most males established clear boundaries between adolescence and adulthood.

To compare the lives of young people in the 1950s and the 1990s, we were fortunate to find comprehensive records of Robert V. Havighurst's well-known study of adolescents in the 1950s in the place he called River City. After reading the materials and visiting the actual town, we began to form a picture of how adolescent life there had changed over the past four decades. To highlight these changes and provide a backdrop for analyzing the experiences of students in the 1990s, we developed portraits of three adolescents—Mary Fuller, Tom Becker, and Ray Powell—who attended public high school. These young people are representative of the students who graduated from River City High School in 1958.[10]

Mary Fuller enjoyed high school and strongly believed that a diploma was important for obtaining a good job, but her ma-

jor goal after graduation was to raise a family. Tom Becker and
Ray Powell were good students who had thoughts about attending college. All three of these young adults considered graduation from high school as an important passage from the adolescent world of bobby socks, high school sports, and school dances
to the world of adult responsibilities. For them, the carefree days
of high school ended with a diploma, and a more serious life
with adult responsibilities began.

Life in River City

Located along the banks of the Mississippi River, River City is a
medium-sized midwestern town. Like many river towns, it is situated on a bluff with a panoramic view of the great waterway. In
the 1950s, the economic and social life of the residents was tied
to the river. The lumber yards, docks, and train tracks stretched
along the wide banks of the water below the bluff. Fishing and
boating were popular recreational activities, and many people
had summer homes built on one-story stilts along the banks or
set up summer lodgings in "camps" along the often flooded flats
by the water. The city was divided into neighborhoods, with
large homes and mansions on the broad avenues close to the
country club and the smaller homes of skilled and unskilled
workers near the bluff by the river. By the 1950s several new suburban developments had begun to emerge on the edges of
town.[11]

River City was first settled in the early 1800s as a trading
post and grew to become the commercial center for the surrounding agricultural counties. Shortly after the Civil War, ferry
service was provided on a regular basis across the Mississippi and
was soon joined by a railway bridge that opened up the commercial routes to the west. At that time, large numbers of German immigrants settled in River City along with migrants from
bordering states. The population of the city remained stable
throughout the first half of the twentieth century. By the 1950s,

the local economy had diversified from a strong agricultural and shipping base to one that included light manufacturing industries. Many of the small industrial firms were locally owned and operated, and River City had a growing number of very prosperous families.

River City had one large public high school. Built as part of the Works Progress Administration in the 1930s, it was an architectural landmark with deep-carved facades and intricate brickwork. The town also had a small Catholic high school and several Catholic elementary schools. In the late 1950s, to handle the increasing number of students in the public school system, the town built a new high school and converted the old one to a junior high school. River City High was known for its award-winning band and orchestra and its athletic programs in baseball, golf, and marksmanship. A survey of the academic programs in the state's high schools in the 1950s ranked River City High about average for the state. Nearly a third of River City High's students went on to college, business school, or nursing school, roughly a third went directly to work, and around a third did not graduate.

Mary Fuller

In 1963, five years after her high school graduation, Mary Fuller appears at the door in an apron and a clean housedress. A large and physically strong woman, she is visiting her mother and helping to prepare a casserole for the church's Lenten potluck dinner. Mary lives in Evanville, a small farming community about fifteen miles from where she was raised in River City. She is married to Gil, and they have two daughters, Susie, five, and Annie, two. Five months ago, Mary and Gil purchased a somewhat dilapidated farmhouse in which they have been gradually making repairs to the furnace and plumbing. Gil works his father's eighty-acre farm and has also been employed for the past four years at a local rug factory, where he cleans, patches, and repairs rugs. Mary feels that the combination allows them to have a steady income from his factory job and if all goes well the extra income from the farm will allow them to make gradual improvements to their home.

Mary had started dating Gil in 1952, when she was twelve; they were married when she was sixteen. As she says, "I was about fourteen when I decided that Gil was the man I would like to marry. I have never had any regrets." Early marriages were not uncommon in River City, or in the rest of the United States, in the 1950s. Almost half of the new brides in the decade were teenagers. In River City, marriage was often viewed as an acceptable reason for girls to drop out of high school. These early marriages were often quickly followed by having children, making this the decade with the youngest new mothers and fathers of any in the twentieth century.[12]

Gil joined the navy after graduating from high school; while he served out his term, Mary continued to live with her mother and father. Her parents lived in a modest house, and her father worked as a janitor. Being married gave Mary additional autonomy, as she explained: "Now that I'm married, my folks let me decide. My folks want me to finish high school, if possible. I never thought of quitting, but if something should come up this year that I can't go back to school in the fall, I might go out to River City College and take a point test [for an equivalency degree]. My brother did that and he got his diploma that way."

Mary did return to high school in the fall. "I told my daddy that I wouldn't quit unless I had to. I think kids who quit school are foolish. They're going to regret it sooner or later. Anyway, it's the first thing they ask you when you go for a job, 'Do you have a diploma?'" Mary's belief in the importance of a high school diploma as an entry pass for a better-paying job was widely shared among her high school classmates. By the time of their graduation, most of the students in Mary's class had received more formal education than their parents had. In fact, the size of the seventeen-year-old population that had graduated from high school increased from 6.4 percent in 1900 to 50.8 percent in 1940 and 63.1 percent in 1956.[13]

Mary was an average student who generally enjoyed her teachers and classes. When she had academic troubles, she was careful to judge herself responsible. As she explains, "I just couldn't understand history. It wasn't the teacher's fault. I just hated it and couldn't get it." Mary liked her courses in general business and retail selling but disliked one teacher because he failed to perform an essential responsibility, job placement. "I liked retail selling but not the teacher. He wouldn't help me get a job for the distributive education class. I wanted to take it next year, and he said I couldn't because I got married and he didn't know if I'd get pregnant right away." At River City High School girls who had married could continue to attend school, but not if they were pregnant. Mary considered the teacher's assumption that she would become pregnant unfair.

Like most teenage girls in River City, Mary's work experiences were limited. One summer, she worked in the dairy bar at a local grocery store where she wrapped cheese and ground coffee. The job did not last long. "I was supposed to work three days a week, and I only got to work two days. That way I wasn't making much money, and when I went to work there I thought I could make enough to buy clothes and help out on my spending money. It didn't work out like that." After high school, Mary went to work doing general cleaning for a local medical clinic. While working at the clinic, she continued to live at home and was able to save money to buy a car. Soon after her husband left the navy, Mary quit her job and gave birth to her first daughter.

Mary had definite opinions about women working. "I think it is all right for women to work if it's a necessity to help out in the family. If not, I believe they should be with their kids. I would like to be a beautician and someday I am going to take the training, [even] if I have to go back to work to get it. But I would like to have a beauty shop in my basement. We have got a cement basement and it's big enough. And a lot of women around our place and at our church say they would come to me if I had a shop." Like many young married women in River City, Mary's focus was on her family and on supporting her husband. Work outside the home was not desirable, especially when there were young children. One acceptable way for young mothers to work was to create a viable cottage industry, as Mary planned to do.

When asked four years after graduating from high school what life would be like in another five to ten years, Mary replied, "I don't think it will be much different. Of course, we will have our house paid for a little more and that will be nice. If the crops are all right that would help. We are very happy. I can't say that I want many changes." At twenty-two, Mary had set a firm course for her adult life, a path she both desired and was comfortable traveling.

Mary was typical of many young women in the 1950s. Earning a high school diploma was an accomplishment and provided better employment opportunities. Employment for females was limited to "female" occupations—secretaries, clerks, maids, waitresses, teachers, and nurses. For the most part, young women did not consider pursuing careers other than teaching and nursing, and few thought about working permanently in even these occupations. Marriage, however, was seen as permanent, and fulfillment was to come through being a wife and raising children.

The decade of the 1950s was a time of domesticity and distinct gender roles. Young husbands were the main, if not sole, wage earners. Caring for children, cleaning, and cooking formed the expected full-time occupation of young mothers. Parenting and attending to the needs of the household were often seen as the "joy of young motherhood," and studies show that the amount of time spent on housework increased during this period. Both females and males considered it undesirable for mothers to work outside the home. Childbearing outside marriage was undesired and uncommon. This clarity of gender roles helped to foster uncomplicated images of adolescents' futures.[14]

Tom Becker

Across the downtown park bordered by small specialty shops and Prangle's, the town's only department store, comes Tom Becker on his way to work. It is 1958 and Tom has been working as a stock boy and window trimmer at Prangle's since the beginning of his senior year. Dressed in slacks and a long-sleeve white shirt and with a crew cut, this slender young man appears very much at ease. This is not surprising since Tom has spent his entire life in River City and his family has been here for several generations. Close familial ties are common in River City. Tom's mother and grandmother live on the same block and see each other almost daily. Tom's father sells chewing gum for a distributing firm, and his mother does not work outside the home.

Schoolwork has never been difficult for Tom. The opinions of his teachers and the grades on his school record suggest that Tom is an adolescent of above average ability. He is in the general education track and has taken a full load of academic courses, maintaining better than a B average. Tom's scholastic record is matched by his athletic accomplishments on the high school's golf team. Golf is a favorite sport at River City, and more than once the school's golf team has been the state champion.

Like many other teenagers in River City, Tom enjoys working on cars. After school and on weekends, one can find Tom and his friends under the hood of a Chevy tuning it up. Cars are an important part of the lives of boys in River City, and most aspire to own one. Several of Tom's friends own used cars, usually bought at a bargain price from their fathers; others are working as stock boys and laborers to earn enough to buy a car of their own.

A few of Tom's friends are planning to enlist in the military after high school. Military service is often seen as a viable way of gaining the training and skills needed for a well-paying job. It is also a way to leave River City and see more of the world under the protective branches of the service. Because many young men are eligible to be drafted, some have the attitude that it is "better to get it over with." Tom's desire is not to enlist after high school but to attend college.

In the spring of 1958, Tom was accepted at Bradley University, where he planned to prepare to become an industrial arts teacher. His aspirations to attend college were not typical. By the late 1950s, a little less than a third of the high school students in River City went on to college, business school, or nursing school. Tom did not attend Bradley though. The early death of his father and the family's serious financial problems made going to college nearly impossible. After graduation, Tom decided to stay in River City to financially support and care for his mother. He continued to work full time at Prangle's in the same position he held while he was in high school. Describing this job, Tom says, "There wasn't too much to the job. It was mostly stock work and trimming windows. I didn't make much there. The clerks are paid pretty well but I didn't get much." After more than two years on the job, Tom left the department store to take a job with the city pouring cement and driving a truck. This job had no opportunity for promotion, and Tom received just one raise in two years.

Tom is married to a local girl, "the joy of my life." He has reservations about early marriages, he says. "A lot of young ones are married and divorced right out of high school. I think it is better to wait myself." Tom was married at twenty-one, and by the time he turned twenty-three he was the father of a five-month old baby boy. Although Tom felt he had "waited" to marry, most adolescents in the 1990s would view this as an early marriage.

Tom views his future prospects for work in River City as limited. Only four years after graduating from high school, he sees his current job as a dead end with no opportunities for advancement. As he explains, "Well, I don't mind the work but I would like to find a better job, something with a future to it." One path to a better job is obtaining additional education and training, and Tom is exploring some options. "I was just down to St. Louis to talk to my brother-in-law to see about a trade school down there. There is a technical school that you can go to, and my brother-in-law works for IBM and they hire a lot of the graduates from that school. Of course, guys who don't get hired by IBM maybe get jobs as TV repairmen." Thinking about where he will be in five years, Tom says he hopes to "see myself in a different place than I am now, but where that is—is a different question. If I had the money, I would take up going to St. Louis. Of course, I would have to sell my house and go to night school. The training down there is for a full year, but I couldn't go without working. That means I would have to go to night school for about eighty weeks."

Tom's wife is supportive about moving to St. Louis, but this option has high personal costs for the entire family. Tom is reluctant to leave his mother, who is unable to support herself financially. He also knows that he would have to sell his house and face the challenge of finding a job in another city. Close family ties appear to keep Tom in River City despite the limited local opportunities for work. Tom explains, "Well, I think River City is a fine town but it needs industries. That is why a lot of young people cannot find work. I would really like to stay here—I have never worked away from here—and I would rather stay here than move. I have friends and relatives and everyone else is here."

Tom and his wife appear more fixed in their present circumstances than Tom's educational aspirations or occupational expectations would suggest. Although his city job pays modestly, he and his wife have managed to buy a fourteen-year-old, four-room bungalow only four years out of high school. The frame house, in good condition and surrounded by a well-landscaped yard, is located in a recently developed suburb of the city. A new Chevy sports car sits in the driveway. The reluctance to leave River City, even though Tom thinks good jobs are difficult to obtain, reflects a belief widely held among adults there, that it is a good place to live and raise a family.

Tom continues to look for the "right job," a search he began after graduating from high school. The right job is one that pays enough to comfortably support his family without having his wife work, offers security with few chances of being laid off, and is personally satisfying. It is his belief that he can find such a job in River City and he won't have to move to another town. The expanding economy here gives him confidence that such a job does exist and that he will find it if he continues to look.

Ray Powell

While listening to a rich, soulful recording of Charlie Parker playing the saxophone, Ray Powell imagines what it would be like to be a famous musician. He is pulled back to reality by the sound of his mother opening the front door, returning home from her full-time job as a punch-press operator at a local factory. Ray belongs to a family that enjoys music. His father and grandfather were musicians, and his mother hopes he will follow in that tradition. With limited financial means, Ray and his mother live in a very modest section of River City. Despite their straitened circumstances, Ray's mother has made considerable sacrifices to pay for musical training to develop Ray's talent.

Ray stands slightly less than five feet eight inches tall and has a medium stocky build. With his short haircut, dark-rimmed glasses, and pleasant smile, he is, according to one of his teachers, "the kind of person one enjoys spending time with. He does not impress you as an intellectual as much as a fellow with a fine personality, relaxed style, and a great deal of poise. He gives the appearance of being an all-around guy." A very good student, Ray is interested in more than music. "I always had an interest in science as a kid. I used to tinker around with Erector sets and that sort of thing." In high school, he took the standard academic load of subjects, including biology and plane geometry, but not higher-level mathematics and science courses.

By tenth grade, Ray had decided that he was going to go to college and become a music teacher. He had considerable talent, and his teachers encouraged him to continue his education. With a college scholarship and some financial help from his mother, Ray left River City to attend a state university. The financial assistance he received, however, was not sufficient to cover his expenses, so he took on a variety of part-time jobs. During the first two years at college he worked as a waiter, played his trumpet at dances every weekend, and gave private music lessons to high school students. In his senior year, he worked as a desk clerk at the YMCA.

It was not unusual for students in the 1950s to work their way through college. There was limited financial assistance from government programs for students who did not have veterans' education benefits. Attending college usually required significant personal costs for students from families with limited resources. For later generations of adolescents, the opportunities for postsecondary schooling would be much greater. The creation and expansion of federal student loan programs provided needed financial assistance. The growth of higher-education institutions, in particular the creation of community colleges, permitted more students to attend college as commuting or part-time students.[15]

As a college student, Ray studied hard but not in all areas. "A lot of my friends were in applied music and they worked harder on their particular instruments. I spent more time on book work. In the last two years of school, I probably worked harder." After his junior year, Ray married Diane, a nineteen-year-old River City girl. Following her graduation from high school, Diane moved to the university town and worked as a stenographer for the music college. According to Ray, the couple "held off about as long as we could, but couldn't have afforded to get married any earlier because of finances. By the end of my junior year we were ready." Diane shares Ray's strong interest in music; she plays the piano and is active in community choirs. Diane's family background is similar to Ray's. Her family owns a small repair shop in downtown River City, and, having prospered through the years, they recently moved to a new suburban residential area where they own a small ranch-style house.

After graduating with a bachelor's degree, Ray began to work on his master's. Before he finished, however, he was offered a teaching job in Oakdale, a wealthy suburban community outside Chicago. His responsibilities the first year were the elementary and junior high school bands. The music director, a thirty-year veteran, was eligible for retirement in four years. When he retired, it was expected that Ray would assume his duties as director of music for the community and leader of the high school music program. As Ray describes the opportunity, "I was looking for something where I could start in a small school system and build it up. Actually, this program is already built up, but I think the music there hit a plateau and I will be able to move it up another notch."

Before they moved to Oakdale, Ray and Diane returned to River City for the summer and stayed with Diane's parents. Diane was in the last term of her pregnancy, and Ray worked in the high school's summer music program. When asked about his future, Ray described his Oakdale job as a step toward something else. "After six or eight years, I would like to have moved the music program up to another level, and then I would like to move on and try it again someplace else. This is what I see as successful teaching." When asked about future schooling, he said, "I will finish my master's and then at Oakdale you have to go to school every three years until you have finished the classwork through a doctorate. You don't have to get a doctorate, but you have to get the classwork."

Ray's life revolved around music. He purchased a used saxophone as part of his interest in repairing and playing old instruments. When asked about clubs and organizations he belongs to, Ray replied, "I haven't gotten my permanent membership in the national music fraternity. The only reason is that it takes twenty dollars and I haven't had that amount, but I will apply for a life membership. You are selected for this fraternity on the basis of your undergraduate scholarship."

Reflecting on his life after high school, Ray said, "Things have gone real well, I think. Financially, we have made it all right. We haven't lived high on the hog, but things have gone real well and should do a lot better with this job. The work this summer has been a real good experience for me, working at the school with Mr. Huebner, because it is the type of work I will be doing at Oakdale this fall." Before beginning his first full-time job after college, Ray has an intimate knowledge of what his job responsibilities will be as a school music teacher.

Ray's life after graduation from high school does not fit the dominant pattern for young people in River City. He left to go to college and completed his bachelor's and master's degrees. He deliberately delayed his marriage until he believed it would not interfere with his education. Ray's interest in attending college was not to obtain a liberal arts education but to meet the requirements to be a music teacher in a public school. Like some adolescents in the 1950s, Ray wanted a professional education.[16] Being a public school teacher would enable him to be the sole wage earner for his family. Ray and Diane maintained strong ties to River City and eventually returned there to raise their children. Ray became the music director at the high school, and under his leadership the school won several more championship competitions.

Teenage Life in the 1990s

The social world of adolescents in the 1990s is more complex than it was in the 1950s. An indicator of this complexity is the number of choices that adolescents make in their schooling, careers, and entertainment. Schooling is more complex because students can choose to study a wider range of subjects, to earn postsecondary degrees in more fields and at more institutions, and to select among numerous financial aid programs to support their efforts.[17] Career choices are more complicated because there are a greater number of jobs, more new types of jobs, and many jobs without well-established career lines. Adolescents also have many more choices in mass entertainment, including movies, television shows, and music.

The family circumstances of adolescents in the 1990s also are different. In the 1950s, being married was highly desirable and the proportion of people who never married was low, as was the divorce rate. In the 1990s, marriages are less permanent. Whereas 90 percent of children under eighteen lived with their father and mother in 1960, by 1993 this number had declined to 70 percent. Among some of these two-parent families are blended households with children from previous marriages.[18] It has been estimated that in the next decade, because of the rise in single motherhood and divorce rates, 53 percent of children under eighteen will spend some time in one-parent families.[19] If an adolescent does live in a two-parent family, it is likely that both parents work, most often full time.[20] These adolescents see their worlds changing quickly. In general, however, they assume that they will marry later, have children later, be part of dual-career couples, and change jobs more often than their parents.[21]

Today's adolescents are more ambitious than those in previous generations. Most high school students plan to attend college, and many of these aspire to jobs as professionals or managers. Typically, many adolescents imagine futures very different from

the lives of their parents. The following are portraits of three ambitious adolescents in the 1990s who live in different geographic
regions of the country, and whose families vary in the resources
available to help them make the transition from high school to
college. Although the three students do not share similar family
backgrounds, the problems they face are exemplary of the many
issues confronted by most adolescents in the 1990s. (We have
changed the names and physical descriptions of the students to
protect their anonymity.) They also were chosen because they are
illustrative of the major themes of this book—how ambitions
help adolescents organize their lives and how ambitions are
shaped by families and schools.[22]

Jake Roberts

Nestled on the shore of a small inland lake in southern Florida
is the Roberts home, a single-family ranch house similar to others in the New Shoreline development. Jake Roberts, a tall, slim
twelfth grader in 1994, is busily drawing pictures of characters
from a recent science-fiction movie that he intends to sell at the
local mall for a small price. Drawing and rappelling are the two
major activities that occupy Jake's time when he is not in school
or "hanging out" at the community theater.

　　Jake, the youngest in the family, lives with his father,
mother, and grandfather. His older brothers and sisters have
moved out and set up their own households. When Jake was in
elementary school, his family experienced a period of severe financial hardship and lived in a trailer camp in Arizona. Later their
financial circumstances improved. Jake's mother became a sales
manager for a mobile-homes office, and she is working toward
a degree at a community college. Jake's father, whose formal education never went beyond eighth grade, is employed as an elec-
trician. Jake has already gone to school four years longer than his
father did, which is a source of pride to his parents. All but one

of Jake's brothers and sisters graduated from high school, and none of them are working toward or planning to obtain a post-secondary degree.

Similar to most parents of teenagers in the 1990s, Jake's mother and father would like him to go to college, but they do not offer explicit advice about where he should go or how he would pay for it. While they are supportive of his plans to attend college, they are concerned that he may push himself too hard. "I would say that my parents' expectations of me are a bit lower than the expectations I have for myself. I really push myself a lot more than they say I should. They don't want to press on me because they're afraid if they press on me too much then I won't want to go" to college.

Explaining his major reason for planning on postsecondary schooling, Jake says, "I want to go because I probably need the education. And especially now that you have to work so hard to get a decent job with decent pay." Jake is well aware of the types of jobs that are available with only a high school diploma, for one of his brothers parks cars and the other is unemployed. The view that college is the route to a better job with a higher salary is a common assumption of teenagers in the 1990s. So strongly is this opinion held that many believe a college degree is required for nearly all jobs, including those of security guard or actor.[23]

The growing concern for most students in the 1990s is not whether to attend college but how to pay for it. With rising tuition and room and board costs, the expense of attending a state university is a financial stretch even for middle-class families with both parents working full time. It will be difficult for Jake to afford college because his family does not have the extra re-sources to pay his tuition. "I need to do well in school because we haven't got a lot of money, we're not mongrel rich. My family isn't really a high-income family. We're not even really a mid-dle-income one, we kind of teeter on the edge, in the low to middle income. We got a nice house and all of that, but there is no way my family is going to be able to foot the bill for something like a $13,000 a year college note."

For Jake, the way to afford college is an academic scholarship or a student loan. "I have to keep my grades up or I'm not going to get a scholarship. And I need a scholarship to go to college. Either that or I'll just go ahead and get a loan." The loan alternative is not the preferred choice, because "even if you get a loan, yeah, you're going to be paying off that money for twenty-five years." Facing such a financial burden, many students believe that high grades will make them eligible for scholarships awarded on the basis of academic merit or special talent. Earning good grades is a major objective of many high school students. It is not unusual to find students willing to do extra-credit work or imploring their teachers to let them retake a test to keep their grades up.[24] Grade inflation may result less from teachers lowering their standards than from the efforts of students to improve their grades to be competitive for college admissions.

Jake works very hard in school. He is taking a typical high academic course load with several honors classes. With a 3.8 grade point average, he was selected in his junior year to become a member of the National Honor Society. Active in community service, such as working at a senior citizens home, he is also a member of the lacrosse team and the theater club. Currently, he has the lead role in the school play, and his performance has received glowing reviews from friends and teachers. A perfectionist who takes his craft very seriously, Jake was dissatisfied after reviewing his performance on videotape and planned to audition for roles at the community theater to improve his skills.

Jake believes his desire to go to college was instilled by his tenth-grade geometry teacher, who actually seemed "so interested in the students and what happened to them. He gave me reasons why college was important for me and he is the one who finally made up my mind to definitely go to college." As for his guidance counselors, Jake expresses both resentment and anger at their advice and interest level. During his first semester in high school, his academic performance was not very good, although he kept saying he planned to go to college. His teachers and counselors were not as optimistic. He says his counselor told him that "I would never be able to make it into college. In fact, they told me I wasn't going to graduate, and I could always go to night school and get a GED." These remarks had a dramatic effect on Jake's performance. "After that comment by Mr. Smith, I got really mad and decided to get a straight-A report card in the next nine weeks, and I did." Perhaps it was their initial negative assessment or the lack of personal attention from his counselors that led Jake to take upon himself the task of researching what different colleges offer.

Jake's educational and occupational plans are ambitious and influenced by his understanding of the realities of the labor market. He has special talents in art and writing, but he recognizes that pursuing academic work in these areas may not lead to desirable employment. "I want to get a master's degree. I just haven't decided on my major. I might go to a special graduate school. I don't know. I like a lot of stuff, especially right now there are so many things that I like doing. I like art. But, that's not really something I'd take as a career choice because it's not very stable. Writing isn't either. I love writing stories, but that's not a very stable career."

But his dream, first communicated as a sophomore and reiterated over the next two years of high school, is to produce and direct films. "I love working with all aspects of films. I would like to produce films, but that's really going to take a lot of work to get to do that, because you have to establish yourself first and then work yourself up." Getting established, in Jake's view, requires planning and then starting a long upward march on a bumpy road. "You really can't start off as a great, or good, producer. You have to start off in these little B films and nobody hears about them. And if they become really successful, even if they are B films and people like them, that will help you to get established until you can find somebody to finance a good movie."

For Jake, learning to be a director or producer requires going to college to learn about the technical aspects of filmmaking. College, he says, "is where you learn how to spend $140 million to make a film. If one is going to be a producer or director, one needs at least a master's." Jake thinks that a college degree in filmmaking will separate him from others who are not as well trained: "The film industry has always been very selective of people. Since it is so selective, more highly trained people are not going to have to compete with all the low-level people. Only the more highly trained people are going to get in."

Jake does not know anyone who is a producer or director, but with his wistful imagination he fantasizes about having a big producer looking over his portfolio and deciding to give him a job. Steven Spielberg is his role model, and Jake reads everything he can about him and sees all his movies. Through this in-depth study, Jake concludes that in many ways the successful director's life mirrors his own. "Did you know, he started out as a child who was in a mediocre-income family? He made a few short films when he was in high school. He got his first job directing the first episode of *Columbo*, the TV show. And then he went on to make films like *Jaws* and E.T., major, big, huge blockbusters, and he's now raking in big bucks. He seems to have the perfect balance of family life and enjoys doing what he does, which is the most important thing in your life."

Jake worked very hard in school as a sophomore and junior, but less so as a senior. His decision to expend less effort is a calculated one. "Colleges don't want to look at your senior year because they know that seniors are going to goof off a bit. But they know your junior year is your hardest year. And what I did last year was put all my effort into my junior year. I have an overall 3.8 out of a 4.0 so I'm not worried." It appears that Jake's efforts paid off, for he has received more than thirty letters from colleges inviting him to apply. Because his major interest is film, he is looking at schools in California and Florida. "The way it looks right now, it seems that the best place for school is Florida. Florida and California are really big on film. Both states have really big film programs. But the way the industry is in California and the way the industry is growing in Florida, it seems that the best place for school would be Florida."

To make his dreams a reality, he also is developing a plan to obtain an internship in the film industry. He explains that Spielberg and David Geffen are opening a new studio, "So I have decided I'm going to write a letter to them telling them what I want to do. I want to let them know I'm an aspiring actor and director, screenwriter, blah, blah, blah, who would love an internship or a job or anything related to the theater industry. And I would really appreciate the chance to show you my portfolio. Hopefully, they will say, 'I like this kid! Let's give him a job.'"

Jake's perspectives on other life decisions sound a little less scripted than a Hollywood movie. Marriage and having a family is something he is thinking about for after college. "If you marry before college, then it means that either the husband or the wife is going to have to drop out of college to support the family. And that is something I wouldn't want to do to her or me. Because I wouldn't like to ruin both our lives. I would like to wait until after college."

In many ways Jake has two faces, similar to the Euripides mask of Greek theater. There is a pragmatic side that expects most likely to become a college teacher, although this is certainly not his first choice. The other side desires a chance to work in the film industry. Making a career in film a reality is the focus of Jake's strategic energies. His primary career choice however, cannot be dismissed as merely a passing notion of an adolescent. Jake has the lead in the senior play, takes his acting very seriously, and is working on perfecting his skills. He continually seeks information about the film world and carefully weighs which college program is likely to maximize his chances at fulfilling this dream.

In early 1997, we spoke with Jake again. After graduating from high school in 1995, he enrolled in a major state university in Florida but did not find college to be as he had expected. Upon arrival, he discovered that he could not take theater classes as a freshman. He considered his living arrangements less than desirable, as his roommate was a third-year engineering student. Family problems contributed to his unhappiness, and his grades suffered. He left college after a semester, returned home, and began paying off his student loans. In the fall he enrolled at a local community college, but this also proved to be a mismatch between his interests and the academic offerings, so he decided not to return the second semester. He is still working on paying off his loans. As for the future, Jake is considering attending a fine-arts college where he can "major in film and minor in drawing." The theater continues to be an important part of his life. "I am auditioning for plays at several civic theaters," he says. Surviving a misstep in his transition from high school to college, for now, Jake continues to hold on to his dream of working in the film industry.

Jake's life after graduation illustrates some of the difficulties in creating a viable plan for the future. Jake worked hard in high school. He was a good student, took advanced-level courses, and expended considerable time and effort acquiring acting and directing skills. His choice of a college, however, was uninformed, and he was disappointed at not being allowed to study theater in his first year. Selecting an appropriate college required information that Jake did not have. His experiences in high school led him to distrust his teachers, and he was reluctant to ask them for advice. Unfortunately, he did not have information sources in his family. None of his siblings had gone to college, and his father and mother had not graduated from one. Although his parents had reasonably high educational expectations for Jake, they did not have sufficient background or knowledge to help him select an appropriate school. The lack of familial resources can be a major barrier to young people as they plan for the future, especially if they are selecting a career, as Jake did, in which the path to success is not clearly defined. In such instances, the role of the high school takes on special importance in guiding students' plans for the future.

Grace Park

It is Saturday morning, and Grace Park is hurrying to catch the subway for work at the family restaurant in Lower Manhattan. Recently, her mother opened a Korean restaurant, and Grace will spend the day waiting on tables and working alongside her mother and sister. Her father is disabled and does not work.

As a young girl, Grace emigrated from South Korea with her family. Neither of her parents have received much formal education. Grace is enrolled at a well-known public high school that draws students from the five boroughs of New York City. It has a stringent competitive admissions policy, and only students with high test scores and elementary school grades are considered for acceptance. Specializing in science and mathematics, the school has a reputation for high-quality students and faculty, a demanding curriculum, and a large number of graduates who matriculate at competitive universities.

Since her freshman year, Grace has achieved a B-plus average, which places her in the upper fifth of her class. She is a member of the school's fencing team and belongs to a student financial club that makes mock stock investments. At about five feet five inches tall, with dark black hair, Grace is slim and physically trim from her training for competitive fencing.

Planning for the future is a preoccupation of Grace and her friends. They talk, she says, "all the time" about what they would like to do and where they want to go to college. It is not unusual to sit down in the lunchroom and hear about who is thinking of applying to a certain school, whose brother, sister, or friends went to that school, and considerable speculation about what type of student one has to be to get accepted there. They quickly form opinions that a certain college is interested only in students with high scores on the college entrance examinations, while another may accept those with high grades but low test scores.

By her sophomore year of high school, Grace has made some decisions, she explains. "I'm already set on trying to get into the naval academy. I kind of really know what I want to do from then on. You know, after the four years of schooling, I'll have to serve like five or six years. And then, after that, I want to continue to like serve as an officer. I don't want to [be on a ship]. I don't want to do that kind of service because I want to major in economics." Grace's interest in the naval academy began after a visit to her high school's college office, where extensive information on different college programs is easily available to anyone who walks in. Originally, she was interested in the coast guard academy, but after looking at some promotional brochures, she decided she would prefer the naval academy.

Her mother supports her decision, especially because it is a demanding school. "I know my mother would be thrilled if I did get into the naval academy. She knows that it's very tough and she'd be very proud of me if I did make it. My dad, he just wants me to go to college, stick to my education, and do well in school." Her father is less concerned about which school she attends, but he still wants her to excel in her studies. Grace does not know anyone at the naval academy, but she likes the idea of the navy because she expects it to be intellectually and physically challenging. She also anticipates that it will provide a path for a secure career. "I think it's really because it's very secure, secure for the future, and I like that. I like to be very secure about something. If I succeed at the end, it's something I can be very proud of because it's very tough. It's very challenging." But by her junior year, Grace has discovered that her eyesight may not be good enough for admission to the academy, and she is less certain about her plans. "Oh God, I don't even want to talk about that anymore," she says. "Because I just found out that I might medically disqualify for a school I want to go to. I really wanted to go to the naval academy and I still do."

Grace's desire to join the navy reflects her view that it will provide a secure and challenging career, one that is well structured with lots of opportunity. The transition from high school requires students to make strategic choices about which path to choose, and sometimes they feel overwhelmed by the options. With a naval career, Grace has a fairly clear idea what she will be doing in ten or twelve years. Knowing this is important for her, in part because not knowing seems nightmarish. "The worst thing I think I could ever be, which I think there's like a slight possibility, is like becoming one of my sister's friends, or even like her, in New York in some expensive school but without a stable career or a stable job. I mean, a lot of the older people that I know in their twenties are still in school. They're paying a lot of money for school, but you can't imagine them with very stable jobs because [of] the kind of degrees that they're getting, the kind of things they're studying. It just doesn't provide a stable career. Like I don't want to wind up going to NYU studying English. I mean it might work out, but it's not what I want to do. It scares me to think about it, actually." Grace does not believe that simply going to college will provide her with a sufficient sense of direction and purpose.

Grace thinks it is important to have a firm picture of the future in order to be certain that her postsecondary education will lead to an adult job. "I was at this reception once, it was from Wharton. A lot of these women were talking about how they still didn't know what they wanted to do. They went to different schools, studied different things, and they just kept changing. I'm determined. I really don't want to be in that position when

I'm forty-two and I've started a new study. Or I might be like, 'Well, I've done this and this but I really don't know what I'm gonna be when I grow up.' I don't want to be that kind of person."

Adolescence for Grace is a time for making decisions about the future. As she explains, "This is a time when I'm really trying to get myself together. I think this is like the most important part, especially about my future, because it's like the building point of it. Like where I put everything together to prepare myself for later on. It's tough, but I'm having fun." Although Grace is actively engaged in planning her future and is enjoying the challenge, she feels vulnerable in making these decisions. "I can screw up a whole lot. I mean, like I said, at this point I'm making all these decisions about college and my future. What I want to do later on. But I don't really know if the choices I'm making are the best or if they're going to have like the best outcome later on. So that's the scary part of it. It's like maybe the college I choose to go to will be completely wrong for me, and I'll just be totally miserable later. I mean you never know." She is more aware than Jake of the consequences of making a bad decision, such as selecting the wrong college, which can result in the costs of tuition for courses never completed or credits that do not transfer. There also can be personal costs in questioning one's capacity to make important decisions and in explaining to others why the wrong choice was made.

Adolescents are concerned about making the right choices partly because they see it becoming more difficult to earn a living and to enter the ranks of those with well-paying jobs. In the past, Grace explains, "those in high schools thought City College would be enough or getting a high school diploma. But now it's not even a high school diploma. If you want to be guaranteed to be middle class, you have to have like a doctorate in this and that. It's getting harder, not only because society's advancing, but there's a lot more expected from people." Grace, like most adolescents these days, sees a college degree similarly to the way adolescents in the 1950s viewed a high school diploma—the necessary ticket for an entry-level job.

The ambitions of adolescents are shaped in their families and schools. While Grace's mother has limited financial resources to support her daughter's ambitions, she has many conversations with her daughter about her dreams. "I've already told my mother everything, about what I really wanted to do. We've actually been talking about my future a lot. Well, I've been talking about it a lot." At school, the encouragement comes not from the college counselor's office but from her classroom teachers. "I have a college mentor, but I don't really [talk to him]. Guidance counselors are not very accessible in this school. There is one counselor I speak to some times. One of the reasons why I think my physics teacher [is] so great is because he gives a lot of advice; he knows a lot. He was like a college counselor once, too. We talk about the future a lot. My economics teacher I suppose because he wants me to go to Wharton. He was ragging on me about that."

In her senior year, Grace learned that she was medically unqualified for the naval academy and decided to attend a competitive eastern university. Her major is international relations, and she plans to obtain a master's degree in economics or business administration. She finds her college courses slightly more difficult than those in high school, mainly because the subject matter is covered more quickly. Her freshman grades were very good, so she decided to take a full-time job at a bookstore, not for the additional money but for the challenge of being a full-time student and full-time worker. As she says, "I just want to see if I can do it."

Some adolescents, like Grace, are life planners. They hope that when they reach adulthood they will have a stable, well-paying job. They can foresee potential problems in being an adult and still being uncertain about the kind of work they want to do.

To make sure that they are not asking themselves at twenty-four, "What am I going to do now?" they choose college programs that they believe will give them skills for future employment. They work hard in college and plan on acquiring additional education to be competitive in the labor market.

Even these life planners, however, face disappointments. Planning cannot always protect one from the vicissitudes of life. But by being a planner Grace is more purposeful and resilient. When faced with setbacks, she quickly takes new steps to help her find a path toward becoming an economically independent adult.

Elizabeth Houghton

Pencil and paper in hand, Elizabeth Houghton charges down the corridor, intent on covering the latest breaking news story in her high school. As editor-in-chief and founder of an alternative student newspaper in her sophomore year, Elizabeth tries to offer students a different point of view from the two other student papers. Having worked for both, she concluded that "a fair number of people were dissatisfied with them." The source of this dissatisfaction, she feels, is the lack of an objective student voice in reporting the news: "We have one paper, which is basically given press releases by the administration, and the other paper that is given press releases by a very conservative faction of local politics. This makes it difficult to avoid editorializing the news."

Elizabeth's high school is located in a northeastern community surrounded by small colleges and prestigious universities, and some of the students' parents are faculty members or administrators at these institutions. The high school was built to resemble a small college and offers an open-campus policy. It maintains strong ties with the community, and extensive opportunities are available to take courses at local colleges and work on local and state policy initiatives. Allowing Elizabeth to begin a third student paper is consistent with the intellectual environment of the community, reflected in school policies that encourage scholarly excellence, leadership development, and civic participation.

Elizabeth's deep interest in journalism can be traced to the careers of her parents, who have stressed throughout her life the importance of intellectual accomplishments. Elizabeth's father is a documentary journalist for a major television station. According to Elizabeth, his job entails "becoming an expert on a given topic, spending a few years researching about it. But, once he's finished he really knows all there is to know about that particular subject . . . and his product is really enjoyable, and he lectures all over the world." His job requires considerable travel, and often Elizabeth and her younger sister accompany him. Elizabeth enjoys this aspect of her father's work and the opportunity it provides to be involved in the projects he is working on. Her older brother also makes historical documentaries, and her mother was a writer and a photojournalist. Through the work experiences in her family, Elizabeth is learning firsthand what it means to be a documentary journalist.

Standing five feet four inches tall, with a mass of curly black hair partially tucked under a baseball cap, Elizabeth characterizes herself as "a good writer, I'm interested, I'm ambitious. And I tend to be persistent and to do what I can do." Her interest in writing, Elizabeth believes, is a consequence of her upbringing, in which television watching was limited to the news and educational programs. "I like to write a lot and taught myself to read when I was very young, partially because we were only allowed to watch Channel 2 news and PBS. I think writing is derivative of reading and I like to read a lot."

According to Elizabeth, her family situation has helped her develop a strong sense of being in control of her own life. "My mother died when I was thirteen, and, you know, there are unfortunate things and they certainly do affect you. But in the end, it is your decision of whether or not you want to look at yourself forever as somebody who was sort of set off on the wrong track as a child and therefore never has any chance to come back. I had to decide that I could survive." After her mother's death, care of Elizabeth and her sister was taken over by her father and an au pair who works in the home and periodically stays overnight.

The time Elizabeth spends with her family is both personally supportive and intellectually challenging. She and her sister are emotionally close to their father and enjoy spending time together sailing, reading, and playing board games. One of the family's favorite activities is sitting around the living room debating political issues. Although they share many of the same views, "my father usually plays the devil's advocate to kind of get us thinking." Elizabeth thinks that what she expects of herself, being reflective and able to discuss almost everything, is "pretty much the same thing" as what her father expects of her.

An excellent student, Elizabeth pushes herself and takes "a pretty hard course load" of higher-level science and mathematics and advanced-placement courses. She has taken economics and history at a highly competitive private university while still in high school. By her junior year, she admits, "I may be pushing it, I may not. I figure I'm running on empty. If I make it to the end of the year, I'll be fine, but then there's a chance I'll crash and burn before the year ends." Her experience in her physics course demonstrates the intensity with which Elizabeth tackles her schoolwork. "I never liked science before, but I have managed to keep up and teach myself little basic things like derivatives." Recognizing that math could be a potential weakness, Elizabeth developed a plan for mastering more mathematical skills before taking the next level of physics in the fall of her senior year. "I am planning to take Physics 2 advanced placement as a senior, and I'll probably work a little over the summer to make sure the math is up there."

Elizabeth is fluent in French and is taking the highest-level course offered by her high school. She feels qualified to make an assessment of her French teacher: "I think I have the first competent French teacher I've had in a long time and that's good." Judgments about her teachers are fairly common, and Elizabeth is extremely critical of those who are not knowledgeable about the subjects they teach. But, for her, doing well in school is primarily her responsibility; the teacher's role is more ancillary than central. Her determination and excellence in school have earned Elizabeth recognition and several awards. She was selected to join the school's highly competitive academic decathlon team and a school debate society. She was also elected to several key leadership positions, as a member of the student council and chair of the school legislature.

Elizabeth has two major career interests, journalism and politics. "Journalism, news, if not anchoring, at least doing the research. I'm not that interested in doing the sort of TV full-face job. I'd be more interested in the research and the politics." There are two reasons Elizabeth is attracted to a career in journalism. "The first is how much fun I've had doing it here, starting my own paper. The second is it's very important for me to know what's going on and it's always been that way. I watch the news usually; I read the paper almost always; and I travel a lot." Traveling, she believes, helps one develop a world perspective: "You find when you see that the rest of the planet doesn't have stars and stripes and then things change."

In discussing how much education is needed to become a journalist, Elizabeth concludes that it is more than a college degree. "Actually, I've been arguing with the people I'm familiar with in journalism about it, in that it used to be a kind of an apprenticeship job, now almost everybody there has at least a bachelor's in something. I think I'll be spending a lot of time in school. I'll definitely go beyond four years, I think." Elizabeth, like Jake, believes that additional education beyond a bachelor's degree will give her a competitive advantage in the labor market.

Elizabeth is less confident that she will have a career in politics. "I would like to be an ambassador dealing with strategies.
I have a bizarre little quirk that I would really enjoy military
diplomacy, working as a liaison between two governments." This
interest in politics inspired her to apply to a summer school at
Georgetown University that offers a college course in government studies and foreign policy. Accepted from hundreds of applicants from all over the country, she went to Washington the
summer after her junior year. "It was very intense. It's a kind of
crazy, psychotic, sleep-deprivation type of thing. We had eight
hours of classes a day and then two hours of debating at night.
The days that we didn't have classes, we were on speakers' programs, which have like eighteen senators come in one day, for a
half an hour each." In addition to her Georgetown experience,
Elizabeth worked as an intern in the office of her U.S. senator during the summers following her junior and senior years of high
school.

Having in mind more than one future job is something Elizabeth considers an asset. She is confident that she will change
jobs and is "hoping that this is the case. I think I'll probably try
a few things. On the other hand, I don't think any of the stuff I'm
doing is mutually exclusive. It all just kind of feeds off each
other." Facing a changing labor market, many adolescents like
Elizabeth assume that they will have more than one job or career
during their adult lives.

Elizabeth plans to marry, have a family, and continue her career. She sees this as possible and describes how her parents could
be both professionals and parents. "You know, my parents were
probably the first generation that actually managed to work it out
and that there was pretty equal responsibility. There was a time
when they both worked part time and spent half their time taking care of us. If the woman cannot have it all, why should the
man be able to? I mean it doesn't make sense to me. Maybe I
won't find someone who agrees with me, but that's how I feel."

The distinctively different roles of men and women in the 1950s have disappeared. Young women of the 1990s do not believe they will need to make a choice between marriage and child-bearing or a career. It is assumed that they will pursue a career regardless of whether they marry and have children.

The primary purpose of high school for Elizabeth is preparing for the next stage of one's life, college. "The thing about high school is there's sort of a basic recognition that it is a transition process." She views the courses she takes and the teachers she selects as strategic decisions to maximize the chances of being admitted to the college of her choice. Every small step in her high school experience is calculated in terms of how it will ultimately affect the admission process. "It's hard to justify saying why should I take the really hard teacher who is going to give me maybe a C over an A, even if it's in the interest of furthering my education, because my grade point average matters. I just have to think about balancing. I can afford different courses, if I think about it, calculate it, I can afford to have an A-minus in advanced-placement history and bring up something else."

After grade point average, the next most important factor in the college admission process is doing well on the entrance examinations. As colleges have increasingly come to rely on these tests in making admissions decisions, students have intensified their efforts to be successful on them. By their sophomore year many begin intensive preparation for the entrance examinations through practicing with old test items, learning tricks about how to guess without penalty, using computer programs, and hiring private tutors.[25] As Elizabeth explains, "I've been through it for a while, even working on my Pre-Scholastic Aptitude Tests. I have been working toward it so that none of what is on the test comes to me as especially new because I've been thinking about it."

Then comes the application process itself, including the decision of how many colleges to apply to, obtaining the right letters of recommendation, and learning about financial assistance.

Elizabeth is considering applying only to "a good school, a prestigious school simply because I value the selection process, and
I want to be with kids who are equally interested. I know that for
my own track classes, there are some kids who don't care—that's
fine. It's high school, it is part of what you learn. But in college,
I want to be with people who are really interested." She is applying to fourteen universities, including Harvard, Yale, Stanford, Princeton, Northwestern, and Brown. The costs of applying are considerable—sometimes as much as fifty dollars each.
Elizabeth is unsure about applying to so many colleges, but her
father thinks it is a good idea. In reality, the cost is negligible: "In
the face of what he's going to be paying, it's peanuts to do all
these applications."

Like Jake, Elizabeth has received many letters from colleges
inviting her to apply, and some have waived their application fee
or offered "to let her come there for free." She is unfamiliar with
most of these institutions and would not consider attending
them. "You would have to pay me," she says "to come there." Her
sights are set on being admitted to the most elite universities in
the nation.

Elizabeth was admitted to several highly competitive
schools but was wait-listed for admission to Harvard University.
Through the spring of her senior year, she tried not to commit
to another institution in the hope of eventually being admitted
to Harvard. As the days passed and the possibility became increasingly unlikely, she decided to accept a four-year merit fel-
lowship at another prestigious university, which would pay her
tuition, room and board, and a travel stipend. Admitted as a liberal arts scholar, she can finish her bachelor's and master's degrees in four years. Although Elizabeth did not end up at her first
choice, she is "extremely happy," studying politics, and thinking
about attending law school.

Elizabeth's admission to a highly competitive university

cannot be attributed solely to her high scores on the college entrance examinations or the occasionally idiosyncratic admissions process. It took sustained and focused effort for her to become a highly competitive applicant. Her success is due, in part, to her willingness to take extra steps to achieve her goals and her consciousness about the significance of her decisions. Before taking action, Elizabeth carefully weighs the consequences. Even in selecting her high school courses, for example, Elizabeth faced trade-offs. The advantages of taking a difficult advanced-placement course, which would be more challenging and improve her transcript, had to be weighed against the additional studying time required and the lower chances of receiving a very high grade. Each grade is important to Elizabeth because it affects her overall average, and that may subsequently affect her competitiveness in applying to college. Elizabeth thinks about the time and effort she is willing to spend on activities in and out of high school in relation to the consequences it may have on reaching her ambitions.

The Social Transformation of Adolescence

During the past four decades, adolescence has undergone a sharp transformation. Adolescence as experienced by Mary Fuller, Tom Becker, and Ray Powell was very different from that of Jake Roberts, Grace Park, and Elizabeth Houghton. Among the major differences are their expectations of what life will be like after high school and their perspectives on how they will make the transition to adulthood.

Replacing the High School Diploma with a College Degree

In the 1950s, adolescents believed that a high school diploma was the necessary qualification for work, and they could expect an employer to ask whether they had graduated from high school, as Mary Fuller mentioned. A high school diploma made it possible for young men to find jobs that would allow them to marry, have children, and support a family. It also enabled women to find work in retail sales and offices.

In the 1990s, adolescents believe the college diploma is the basic credential needed to obtain meaningful work. In many ways, this attitude is similar to that of adolescents in the 1950s toward the high school diploma. A college degree is considered necessary to be competitive in the job market and to signal one's employability. For many, such as Jake Roberts, Grace Park, and Elizabeth Houghton, it is the minimum needed, and advanced degrees are seen as important and valuable. Postsecondary educational credentials are thought to separate winners from losers in the job market. There is little concern for being too educated or too qualified.

High School: From Preparation for Adulthood to Preparation for College

In the 1950s, adolescents quickly and willingly assumed the social obligations of marriage and parenthood. Their orientation toward adopting adult responsibilities was reflected in what they valued about the high school experience. One of the most well known studies of adolescents in the 1950s was conducted by James S. Coleman. Coleman was interested in the development of an adolescent society that was increasingly independent from parents and adults and whose values and norms were often different from those of parents and schools. In Coleman's view, this adolescent society undercut the norms of academic achievement promoted by schools.

Coleman found that adolescents in the 1950s were more likely to value things other than academic performance. Female students were likely to place most importance on being physically attractive and socially popular, while males valued athletic accomplishments and popularity. Although females and males acknowledged the importance of doing well academically, this was not critical to being socially accepted and popular. To be popular at school one needed to be active in its organized social life. This social life was part of the preparation for taking on adult roles through marriage and civic participation. Adolescence was a period of intense courtship. With half of females being married by the time they were twenty, they were likely to meet the person they would marry during their high school years. Mary Fuller, for example, dated her husband in school and married before she graduated. Ray Powell courted his wife while he was in high school, although they waited until after his junior year of college to get married.

Adolescents in the 1950s were intensely interested in extracurricular activities, such as sports, school newspapers, social service, and the arts. Through joining and leading these high school clubs and teams, they learned how to interact with their peers, to recruit their friends to participate in these activities, and to manage their time and commitments to various organizations. The skills and abilities needed to maintain student-run extracurricular activities were similar to those they would need as young adults participating in community life, especially in the new suburbs.[26] The intense focus of high school students on social life and their highly differentiated gender roles reflected their social futures as adult males and females.

The sociological critique of adolescent society in the 1950s was that high school students were not sufficiently interested in their academic performance and that they valued being popular and athletic more highly. But for many adolescents, high school was preparation for the adult work, marriage, and parenthood that soon followed their graduation. For many of them, attending college was not seen as possible or even necessary for taking on the obligations of adulthood.

The high school experience in the 1990s is significantly different. High school as described by Jake Roberts, Grace Park, and Elizabeth Houghton is preparation for college. It is in high school that teenagers build an academic record that will make them strong college applicants. Participation in their school's student organizations is one way of building a portfolio of extracurricular interests and activities that may make them a more attractive candidate for college admissions. The organization of the curriculum, with its honors and advanced-placement classes, allows students to decide which courses to take and which skills to develop for college.

Expanding Postsecondary Opportunities

In the 1950s, avenues for additional education and training were limited. There was not an extended community college system, nor were there large financial assistance programs except for those with veterans' benefits from service in the Korean War. Obtaining additional education and training after high school usually came with significant social costs—moving the family, having the wife return to work, going to school at night, and so on, as Tom Becker explained.

The opportunities for postsecondary education in the 1990s are so numerous that for many adolescents the question has shifted to where to enroll and how to pay for college. The expansion of financial assistance, particularly federal grants and loans, has made postsecondary education more accessible to more students. Increasingly, however, students are paying for college by going deeper into debt.[27]

Redefinition of Gender Roles

During the past four decades, there has been a substantial shift in adolescents' perceptions of appropriate gender roles. In the 1950s, these roles, particularly parenthood, were different for males and females. Husbands were expected to be the primary wage earner for the family, and in many cases the sole wage earner. Wives expected their responsibilities to revolve around domestic work and tending to children. These gender-specific definitions of family life were widely shared, even if at times the roles seemed confining. Unlike in the 1950s, adolescents in the 1990s do not hold sharply different images of the social obligations of husbands and wives.[28] Females as well as males expect that when they are married both wife and husband will work. And this is reflected in the similar occupational and educational ambitions of boys and girls. These adolescents, male and female, also share the view that building their human capital will provide a personal safety net beneath them as they face the uncertainties of the labor market. Such a human-capital perspective undergirds their educational ambitions.[29]

chapter three

Trying to Make It with
a High School Diploma

y the middle of the 1950s, American companies were producing large volumes of consumer goods, and the mass production system assured high school graduates jobs with relatively stable futures. Like Tom Becker, the majority of them entered the workforce full time, since large numbers of good jobs were available for semiskilled workers. The workforce they joined was predominately male and in some industries unionized. Male high school graduates could find work as machinists, carpenters, factory workers, or other manual laborers. Many of these workers had jobs with union protection, pensions, and reasonable expectations for rising wages. Female graduates were likely to take jobs as secretaries, bookkeepers, salesclerks, nurses, and beauticians.[1]

These jobs offered a sense of security and stability. Workers assumed that they would remain in their jobs and that their jobs would continue to exist. These assumptions were often reasonable in the 1950s. In the major companies and on the union shop floor, workers were not likely to be fired, and their jobs were not likely to be abolished. Most jobs did not require advanced education and training, because the technology used in the workplace was relatively simple and familiar. For many jobs, the technology had not changed significantly in the previous three or four decades. Work as a clerk, an operator in a lumber mill, a laborer, or a schoolteacher had not been technically transformed.

The work of a secretary still involved typing and taking short-hand as it had for decades. The retail clerk was likely to count the inventory manually and write receipts longhand. Workers did not receive or need long periods of training because the work did not require special knowledge or skills and used very simple technologies.

By the end of the decade, the labor market for these graduates showed signs of change. Growing international competition and technological advances were undermining the production system, and once viable manufacturing industries, such as textiles, mining, lumber, and steel, began experiencing periods of slower growth while newer industries like electronics, plastics, and chemicals started to rapidly expand. More married women with children began entering the labor force as jobs in such fields as teaching, nursing, and retail sales increased. American businesses needed more skilled workers, and managerial, professional, and technical workers were increasingly in demand.[2]

In stark contrast, today's graduates who go directly to work after high school enter an economy that offers diminished job opportunities. The increasing reliance on computers and technology, the demand for highly skilled workers, and the decline of manufacturing jobs have decreased the choices available to these graduates. There are now relatively few blue-collar jobs, and those are difficult to obtain. The ones that are available tend to be low-skilled, low-wage, service-sector jobs with limited possibilities for stable long-term employment. During the past two decades, the wages paid to high school graduates have declined dramatically, while the wages of the most-educated workers have increased substantially. The ambitions of today's adolescents are, in part, a response to the work opportunities and wages available to young people with only a high school diploma.[3]

The high school graduates who entered the labor force in the 1950s were different from those who go directly to work today. These young people did not find their high school courses difficult and when they graduated were unlikely to have aspirations to become white-collar workers, such as engineers and teachers. They were likely to participate in school activities and perhaps to serve as leaders in athletics or social service clubs. After graduation, even if not pursuing the career they dreamed of, they were optimistic about their future employment possibilities. The high school graduates of the 1990s who enter the labor force full time after high school are more likely to have found their coursework in high school difficult, are less likely to participate in school activities, and are more uncertain about future employment.[4]

The four cases that follow illustrate the differences in the work experiences and future plans of young people who entered the labor force full time after high school. George Wilson and Jeanie Cole graduated from River City High School in the 1950s, and Calvin Norris and Lorna Peters graduated in the 1990s. George's and Jeanie's are representative of the paths followed by the majority of high school graduates in the 1950s; Calvin and Lorna are typical of the minority in the 1990s who went to work immediately following high school.[5]

Work After High School in the 1950s

George Wilson

After graduating from high school in 1958, George Wilson began working full time as a shipping clerk for a local manufacturing firm. As a high school senior, he had worked part time in this job to meet the requirements of his distributive education program. A tall, muscular young man with ambitions, he became discouraged with his position when he realized that it offered him "no future, no money, and lots of work." Eight months later, he left the job and began working as a machine operator at the local paper mill. George enjoyed this job, but less than two years after he began it the production line was reorganized, and he was "bumped from his job" by workers with more seniority. For three months, George was on unemployment and looking for a "good job." He found work with a roofing company, but the work was not steady; he worked only a day or two a week during the winter season.

George quit the job as a roofer to begin working at a veterans' home. His first job there was working on the grounds at $250 a month; later he was placed in charge of the cemetery burials. Soon after, George was hired to work in a power house. Through his membership in a local civic association, he had become acquainted with several men from the machinist's union who told him about the job opening. There were sixty applicants for it, but George won the job, a union position. "I help run the boilers," he explains. "Actually, there is more learning about the power equipment than there is firing the boiler. We work on the ashes and the grades, but it is more sort of a training. There are six engineers, six firemen, and six coal passers. That is what I am, a coal passer, but there is a chance for advancement. I like it real well. There is a future to it. It gets pretty dirty down there, and you have to do a lot of cleaning up, but it seems like there is going to be some security down there, and something to work up to. I can just about make fireman in three years and engineer here in twelve years without moving away." As a coal passer, George made $525 a month; as a boiler engineer he would earn $680 a month.

Although George is convinced that being a high school graduate made a difference in getting the job, he thinks he took the wrong courses in high school and should have taken more in the industrial arts program rather than being a distributive education major. When he entered high school, George thought he might go to college and become an engineer. By his senior year he was thinking about attending a business administration school. Upon graduation, George did not think that he could afford to go to any type of postsecondary school. Despite his lack of additional training, George is well established five years after high school. He is earning more than $6,000 a year, is married, and has a fifteen-month-old daughter. His wife, Anne, works as a bookkeeper for a small firm, earning two dollars an hour. Currently, a relative takes care of the baby while his wife works, and they are saving money to purchase a house. After that, Anne plans to quit her job and stay home to take care of their daughter.

Jeanie Cole

Five years after graduating from high school, Jeanie Cole lives in a two-story apartment with her husband, four-year-old daughter, and infant son. After graduating in 1958, Jeanie worked for a year before giving birth to her first child. She worked first as a clerk at Woolworth's, a local dime store, and then as a secretary at an insurance company. The new Woolworth's opened at the same time Jeanie finished high school. To qualify for a position as a clerk, one needed to be a high school graduate. The training program at Woolworth's lasted a few days, and by the end of it, according to Jeanie, one knew everything one needed to know to be a clerk. After becoming dissatisfied with that job, Jeanie took a position as a secretary, which she particularly enjoyed. If she did not have children, Jeanie says, she "would be working full time as a secretary."

Jeanie believes that her high school training adequately prepared her for the jobs at Woolworth's and as a secretary. In reflecting on her high school career, however, she wishes "that I had knuckled down and studied harder. I just felt when I got out on the job that I would have been better on the job if I had worked harder. Then a lot of times kids from the downstairs apartment come up here and I try to help them out with their studies. I could have worked a lot harder in school." As a high school student Jeanie had taken commercial subjects, including typing and accounting, as part of the distributive education program. Approximately a third of the girls in her senior class were in commercial or business education, and about 85 percent of the commercial and business students were female.[6]

Jeanie's husband, Ben, works at an electrical supply store, where his responsibilities include selling equipment, bookkeeping, and managing the store when the owners are away. Last year Ben wanted to go to a training school, but his bosses gave him a large raise and he decided to stay at his job. The owners would like to open another store in a different location and have Ben manage it. Even though it would mean more money, Jeanie is concerned that they would have to move away from River City. Both are lifelong residents, and neither wants to leave behind family and friends.

Finding a job immediately after high school graduation was not difficult for most females in the 1950s, although the type of work that Jeanie and many of her friends did was not highly skilled, and there were few chances for promotion. This type of employment, which adolescents in the 1990s would consider undesirable, was seen as an acceptable and reasonable choice for young women who expected to marry soon and have a family. Most female high school graduates in the 1950s did not aspire to managerial or professional jobs. When asked what she would most like to see for herself in the next ten years, Jeanie answered, to "own my own home. Gee, I want it so bad I can taste it. We even have our plans drawn up."

George and Jeanie exemplify how adolescents viewed work and education in the 1950s. Both could find employment after high school and were willing to change jobs to find better opportunities. George looked for a position where there was opportunity for advancement and some security; Jeanie left the labor force to raise her children. Five years after graduating, they were optimistic about their futures and could imagine job promotions, George for himself, and Jeanie for her husband.

Work After High School in the 1990s

The American economy has grown significantly since the 1950s, from one employing 65 million workers to one employing 120 million. It has changed its primary emphasis to producing services, mainly in the medical, business, and personal fields. In the 1950s, about 35 percent of the labor force was involved in the production of such services. By the middle of the 1990s, the service sector employed more than 65 percent of the labor force, and projections indicate a continuing growth in these types of jobs.[7] The shift in what people produce also means a change in the kinds of job opportunities and skills required. By the 1990s, many jobs in the manufacturing sector, such as those for machine operators, fabricators, and laborers, were disappearing. So were jobs as furnace operators, railyard engineers, metal pourers and casters, electrical assemblers, and typesetters.

While the work opportunities for many high school graduates today are easily accessible, they are generally low-wage and low-skill jobs in the service sector. Much of this work is similar to the kinds of jobs teenagers have while in high school: fast-food workers, cashiers, waitresses, child care providers, retail sellers, house cleaners, and general laborers.[8] The expectations of what these jobs can provide are low. The working high school graduate is not likely to earn enough to live independently, much less support a family. Some high school graduates do fill these jobs, but many aspire to leave them for better opportunities.

Calvin Norris, Jr.

When Calvin Norris was a sophomore, he was a starting forward on the junior varsity basketball team. He was especially proud that his team lost only three games that season. Basketball was a central focus of Calvin's life and a major topic of conversation with his friends. His dream as a high school sophomore was to play in the National Basketball Association, get on "some sorry team and make them winners." Calvin practiced almost every day, playing in slam-dunk contests and after-school pickup games.

In contrast to basketball, schoolwork was not a passionate interest. His grade average was about a C as a sophomore, and during his junior year he was almost declared academically ineligible after receiving two Ds in the last grading period. Despite his academic performance, Calvin and his parents hoped he would attend college and get a good job. As a junior, Calvin was uncertain whether he would attend a two-year or a four-year college, but he thought he probably would go "through another four years of school." He said he would like to study marketing, accounting, and business law. When starting college, "you should be able to decide on your own career," but he thinks that will be difficult because "there are so many types of jobs that are available now."

Calvin worked part time at a fast-food restaurant for one semester during his junior year; it is one job that he would never want to have again. "It's too hard. I couldn't see myself doing that every day." After being hired "on the spot" and being trained for an hour and a half by watching a videotape, Calvin felt inadequately prepared for the job. He worried about "messing up" and having to deal with complaining, impatient customers. After a few months he actively began searching for a job as a stock boy or a salesclerk.

During his junior year several college recruiters came to watch Calvin play basketball. "I would like to [play professional ball] but I doubt I would go that far. I really don't want to play college ball because it's a lot of hard work. You have to play every day." On the other hand, if he were to get a college scholarship to play basketball then things might be different. "If I could get a scholarship, I'll accept it and play. If I could get on the team, I'll play." By his senior year, Calvin had definitely decided not to play college basketball, and the sport no longer held the same passionate interest for him. "I think I just played myself out. I played too much. I was thinking about going to college and playing but not now. I will play for the team this year but that's it."

After graduating from high school, Calvin expected to join his father's heating and air-conditioning business and enroll in a junior college to earn an associate's degree. Calvin's father also worked on the night shift at a unionized automobile factory, and during the day he operated his small business. His father suggested that Calvin attend the local community college to learn more about the technical side of the business. Calvin liked the idea and soon envisioned himself "owning and managing my own business, something the size of a Wal-Mart store."

In the spring of his senior year, Calvin's days were divided between classes at the high school and at the area vocational school, where he studied heating and refrigeration to give him a "head start" in his father's business. Calvin enjoyed these classes, but he had a difficult time describing them: "The math is hard. You have all this scientific part where you learn welding and electronics." He considers English his favorite class, because "it is after that class that I can leave and get out of school."

Calvin believes that a postsecondary degree will allow him to earn more money, as his father and his teacher at the vocational school have told him. "Well, my father told me about how people with degrees in engineering are getting twenty-two dollars an hour for just walking around the plant doing nothing most of the time." Calvin's views about his future job opportunities are somewhat pessimistic: "So many people are trying to look for a job, and so many people are trying to keep their jobs. And I know a lot of older people who didn't even plan for retirement or nothing, and they just are going to have to work for the rest of their lives."

A few months after Calvin's graduation from high school, his father took a day-shift position at the automobile factory and gave up his heating and air-conditioning business. Calvin decided to attend the community college as a full-time student while also working full time at a computer store. This was a difficult schedule to manage, Calvin explained: "When I started at the community college I started taking business courses and was a computer science major. But I could not make it working full time and going to school full time." He decided to give up going to college.

Calvin is presently working full time at the computer store as the supervising manager for the receiving department. It is his responsibility to make certain that the floor is well stocked and to check the inventory. His wages are $10.50 per hour with no fringe benefits. He is not satisfied with the job, as he feels he has too much responsibility and too little recognition. "I don't get a lot of credit for all the things that I do. We are understaffed, and it is tense. I will leave if they don't get more help. I cannot take on doing too many more things." In reflection, Calvin says, "I have no idea what direction I am going. I am sort of feeling my way around."

Lorna Peters

Lorna Peters is a strikingly attractive young woman with long black hair and green eyes. In her last year of high school, she lives at home with her mother and sister; her brother died last year in a car accident. In describing her family, she says she regards her mother more like an understanding sister. "If you saw my mom, you would swear she was my sister. She acts like a sister most of the time. We do things for each other all the time." Lorna rarely sees her father, who has remarried and lives not too far from her home. Lorna's mother wishes she had enough money to send Lorna to cosmetology school.

Although Lorna believed that it was important to do well

in school, she was not a good student. She frequently skipped classes, nearly failed her photography class, and often left school to spend time with her boyfriend. Reflecting on her high school career, she says she skipped school because of "sheer laziness." She also feels, though, that some of her academic difficulties could be traced to her teachers, who talked about everything but the subject matter, expected that the students knew things that they did not, and discussed events that had nothing to do with her future. "I had a geometry teacher who always talked about his tobacco farm, instead of teaching. Nobody did too good in that class." She found history irrelevant to her future and could not understand "why we spent so much time talking about how things were back then. I kept wondering, what is it going to do for me, you know, when I'm out of school." She did enjoy American government, however, and thought it would help her in later meeting her adult civic responsibilities, such as voting.

The only class she did well in as a senior was accounting, in which she received an A. She found it challenging because "you had to work hard and really concentrate." Despite her interest in accounting, she knew little about what accountants actually do at their jobs. "I guess if I were to be an accountant, I would be a tax teller or something like that. I think accountants have something to do with taxes. I'm just clueless." Lorna believed that it was important for an accountant to be precise and careful: "You have to know where to get certain information. I mean find the number for this problem, you need to know which page to look on, and . . . to get it off the worksheet, or the balance sheet, whatever." Unclear about how to get a job or what credentials were needed for employment, Lorna assumed that accountants could probably learn all they needed to know at the local community college.

When asked as a senior about her college plans, Lorna replied, "I don't really know. I mean, I know I probably will go to the local community college, but I don't really know what I'm going to do." Lorna is unlike many seniors in the 1990s in that she does not take school seriously and her academic performance matters little to her.[9] Her plans for the future are very unfocused, and she does not know what she will do when she graduates. At eighteen, Lorna has neither clearly defined educational expectations nor occupational aspirations.

During her senior year of high school, Lorna began working part time as a day care worker at a nursery in a local gym, where parents leave their children while they exercise. Several weeks after Lorna started working at the nursery, the supervisor quit, and she took over the position. At first, Lorna was overwhelmed by her responsibilities, hiring several new day care workers and creating a schedule of activities for the children. "I didn't know how to hire people. I didn't know how to interview people or to make a schedule. Before I just felt like an employee, you know, come to work, do my job, but then I was given all these responsibilities. I felt more like a leader."

As the supervisor of the day care center, Lorna had to talk frequently with the other girls and monitor their performance. One of her responsibilities was to ensure that other workers paid attention to the children and did not play video games. Making everyone feel they were part of the team was a major goal of Lorna's, and she often found herself asking the others "how things were going. If they had any questions, complaints, or anything to just let her know by leaving a note or calling."

Because she had always enjoyed children, Lorna found her tasks at the day care center reasonable—even cleaning up. She felt she was successful because "I know how to treat children and which ones you need to give special attention to. You kind of learn . . . you know, if this kid is crying, it might be because he's hungry; and this kid, if he's crying, it's because he needs his diaper changed or he misses his parents. You have to learn how to act and how to treat them. If they start crying when their parents walk out of the room, you have to hold them and act like it's going to be okay."

Even as the supervisor, Lorna earned $5.25 an hour—only twenty-five cents more than the two girls who worked for her. Lorna thought this was unfair. She stayed at the job because of the substantial debts to her friends she had incurred by borrowing money to buy concert tickets and clothes, as well as several hundred dollars she owed her mother for insurance payments on her car. She hoped to find a different job after graduating from high school, but she was unable to find one that would pay enough for her to live on her own. Her job as a supervisor provided only thirty hours of work a week. To earn extra money, Lorna would take home one of the gym owner's daughters and watch her until about three in the afternoon.

Despite her dissatisfaction with the pay and the hours, Lorna remained the supervisor of the day care center for two years. She did not attend college or take classes and continued to live with her mother. Her performance as supervisor was widely respected, and friends from the gym suggested that she apply for a job as a day care worker at the local elementary school. As she explains, "I really love working with kids, and I interviewed for the job to be a worker at the extended day care program at the elementary school." She was hired, and after working in this program for a few weeks, a job as a teaching assistant in a program for emotionally disturbed young children became available. Lorna interviewed for this job and was accepted.

The program is designed for preschool children and kindergartners. There are five children, the teacher, and Lorna in the classroom. According to Lorna, the children "have either been abused or their parents were taking drugs when they were pregnant. They are emotionally traumatized, and then, there are other children who have not been abused but they have other problems controlling themselves." Her responsibilities include talking with the teacher in charge and making sure that both are in agreement when interacting with and disciplining the children. Trust is what Lorna believes makes her job especially satisfying. "The teacher really trusts me. We work really well together, so basically the decisions I make are fine with her. And if they are not, she tells me. She's never really had to tell me that I was doing something wrong."

Lorna remained at this program until the end of the school year. The following fall she changed to a different elementary school, but in the middle of her second year there she left because of the low wages the county pays teaching assistants. She immediately took a job as a receptionist and warehouse worker at an air-conditioning and filtration company owned by the parents of a friend. Lorna's responsibilities include filling orders in the warehouse and answering the phone, for which she receives $6.75 an hour. Although the work is quite physical, Lorna is pleased because she has already lost the thirty-five pounds she had gained while teaching. She says now, "I feel much better about myself. When I am sweating, I feel as if I am accomplishing something."

Lorna is no longer committed to becoming a schoolteacher. Her learning problems throughout her school career have made her rethink her postsecondary plans because the effort she would have to put forth seems overwhelming. And she believes that the monetary payoff for becoming a certified teacher would not be worth the work. "I wasn't a very good high school student. I have what we now call learning attention deficit disorder. And it was not discovered, people at that time did not catch on to it. The whole time I was in school I had a hard time, it was so easy for me to get sidetracked. I would read a page and a minute later I would forget what was on it, and I would have to read it again. At one time I thought about going to school to become a teacher for the emotionally handicapped. I am not sure I can put on the challenge. I am not sure I am willing to take the challenge to become a teacher, and it pays so little."

Although Lorna enjoys her job and the people she works with, she would leave her present situation for one that pays more. She wishes that she could earn more money to pay her bills and save. Currently, she lives with her boyfriend but is not in a hurry to marry. She does not want to enter into a more formal relationship, in which she feels "you have to struggle for everything." She is not interested in planning for a different career or making any major changes in her life. "I don't plan for the future. I plan pretty much for the next couple of weeks. I just let things go easy."

Wages and Ambition

Both Calvin and Lorna had difficulty performing well in high school. For Calvin, the problem was mainly that he lacked the interest to do well in school. Lorna thinks that school was hard for her because of an attention deficit disorder that made concentration difficult. For both, work after high school was an attractive alternative to more education.

Calvin's and Lorna's poor performance in high school is fairly typical of students who enter the labor force directly after graduation. Fewer high school graduates today go directly to full-time work than did in the 1950s, and the characteristics of these students have changed over time. Analyses of national data indicate that a greater proportion of students who go directly to work after high school in the 1990s were low academic performers compared with their counterparts in the 1970s. Those who go directly to work after high school today are more likely to have had behavioral problems in school, such as skipping classes, getting suspended, and troublemaking.[10]

When we last talked with Calvin and Lorna, neither had plans to obtain a postsecondary degree. Although Calvin began studying computers and business at the local community college, he quickly decided that he preferred working full time to juggling a schedule of working and attending college. After two years as a day care provider and a teacher's assistant, Lorna wished to go to college to earn a teaching degree but was not certain she was up to the challenge. Both Calvin and Lorna now feel that going to college is undesirable and unattainable. They have had little success in school and limited financial support from home. Their uncertainty about the future and reluctance to make plans pushes further education beyond the sphere of their daily concerns.

Calvin and Lorna live in different parts of the country, but both are working at the same type of job, inventory control. The position requires working with a computer to enter information and to manage the inventory system. The work also includes manual labor in lifting and moving boxes of supplies. In the 1990s, males and females expect to work at similar jobs whether they involve entering numbers in a computer or lifting boxes. In the 1950s, such work would have been divided into gender-specific jobs, with females typing the numbers and males lifting the boxes. The occupational aspirations of teenage females and males are more alike today, and their employers are more likely to give them similar responsibilities, regardless of gender.[11]

Both Calvin and Lorna are dissatisfied with their current jobs. They consider their wages low and do not see avenues for advancement. They have little sense of commitment to their work, and both of them would leave their jobs immediately if presented with a better opportunity. The likelihood of recent high school graduates changing jobs is well documented. During their first ten years in the labor force, male workers are likely to change their jobs seven times.[12] The work careers of young workers are marked by frequent job changes and a search for better wages.

In the 1950s, adolescents viewed a high school diploma as

an important credential. It was regarded as a significant academic and social achievement, and when seeking employment
often the first question asked was whether the applicant had one.
About 25 percent of students never met the requirements to earn
one, and for almost two-thirds of the graduates a high school
diploma marked the end of their formal education. The importance and economic value of a high school diploma has greatly
diminished in the 1990s.

Students in the 1990s are very familiar with the wages paid
to high school graduates. They have not only their own experiences in the labor market to draw upon but also those of their
friends and relatives. They know the kinds of work available to
high school graduates and the difficulties of living independently on such low wages. They cannot imagine the world of
George Wilson and Jeanie Cole, in which it was possible to
marry, have children, and own a house on the income of a sole
wage earner with a high school diploma.

The wages such teenagers can earn have gradually declined,
creating a growing gap between those of high school and college graduates. In 1979, a male worker with a high school degree earned about 27 percent less than a male college graduate.
By 1995, the gap had grown to 44 percent. Most of the increase
in this wage gap was due to a drop in the real earnings of high
school graduates. In the 1970s, a twenty-four-year-old male
worker with a high school degree was able to earn $8.60 per
hour, approximately $18,000 a year (in 1995 dollars). By 1992,
a similar worker earned $6.20 per hour, or $13,000 a year.[13]

The wages of all groups of workers declined slightly between 1973 and 1979. After 1979, the wage profiles of workers
with different amounts of education began to diverge. From
1979 to 1995, wages for those with college degrees and advanced degrees began to rise, while the wages of workers with
less than a college degree began to decline (fig. 3.1). By 1995,
workers who were high school graduates and those with some

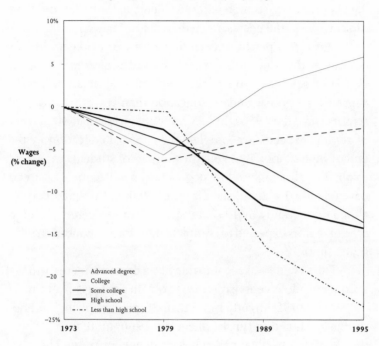

Fig. 3.1 Education Level and Hourly Wages

Wages in 1995 dollars
Data from Mishel, Bernstein, and Schmitt, *The State of Working America, 1996–1997*

college were earning about 13 percent less than they were in 1973, whereas workers without a high school degree were earning about 24 percent less. In contrast, wages for workers with college degrees were almost the same as in 1973, and for those with advanced degrees they were about 6 percent higher in 1995 than in 1973.

The attractiveness of additional schooling as an investment to improve earnings is widely recognized by teenagers in the 1990s. Employers consider the jobs of their workers to require more skills, and they are willing to offer higher wages to attract employees with adequate abilities. Adolescents are very aware of the economic benefits of the college premium. Many see the college degree today as high school students in the 1950s did their diplomas—as the necessary credential to obtain a job.[14]

During the period of declining wages for workers with less education, the educational expectations of adolescents began to rise. High school seniors in the 1990s plan to obtain more advanced-level postsecondary education than any other group of seniors since the 1950s. In 1955, slightly more than 40 percent of seniors expected to complete their formal education by the end of high school. By 1960, the number of students expecting to obtain only a high school degree began to decline. This trend continued in 1972 and stabilized in 1980, but the number declined significantly by 1992. In that year, only 5 percent of high school seniors expected to complete their formal education with high school (fig. 3.2).[15]

This decline was accompanied by a dramatic increase in the number of adolescents expecting to obtain a college or advanced degree. In 1955, slightly more than 30 percent of high school students planned to finish college. By 1960, more than 40 percent expected to obtain a bachelor's degree or more. This percentage increased through the 1970s and declined slightly by 1980. By 1992, however, nearly 70 percent of seniors expected to earn at least a college degree. The most significant increase has been in the advanced-degree category: seniors who intended to earn an advanced degree doubled between 1972 and 1992, from 14 percent to more than 30 percent.

This significant rise in educational expectations is not confined to any particular group of students. The increase is found among those from different racial and ethnic groups and also those from different socioeconomic backgrounds. The educational expectations of both males and females increased, with those of female students rising faster than those of males.[16] The increase in educational expectations occurs at the same time that more students are graduating from high school. The national

Fig. 3.2 Educational Expectations of High School Seniors, 1955–1992

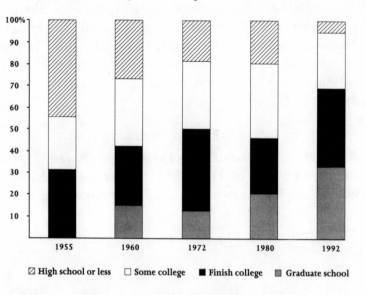

☑ High school or less   ☐ Some college   ■ Finish college   ▨ Graduate school

For the 1955 sample, there was not a separate category for graduate school.
Data from senior samples of the Educational Testing Service study 1955
(weighted); Project Talent 1960 (weighted); NLS-72 1972 (weighted); HS&B
1980 (weighted); NELS:88–94 (weighted)

dropout rate in 1972 was about 20 percent; by 1980 it had declined by almost half, to 11 percent, and by 1992 it had dropped
to less than 6 percent.[17] In addition to their staying in school,
the academic performance of high school students has been improving as well. Following a decline in the test scores of high
school students beginning in the 1960s and continuing through
the 1970s, performance once again began to rise in the late
1980s.[18]

 Over these years the occupational aspirations of adolescents also rose (fig. 3.3). Since 1955 there has been a steady increase in the percentage of seniors aspiring to jobs in the professional category. The greatest increase occurred from 1980 to
1992, when the percentage of students desiring professional

jobs increased from 54 percent to more than 70 percent. Nearly all other occupational categories, including those for salespeople, service workers, technicians, manual laborers, farmers, and homemakers, have declined over the past forty years. The percentage of high school seniors desiring clerical positions, manual jobs, or farm jobs declined by more than 50 percent between 1980 and 1992.

Too Ambitious?

Today's adolescents are the most ambitious ever. But are they too ambitious? Will all of them be able to reach their goals? How likely is Jake Roberts to make it as a film producer or Elizabeth

Fig. 3.3 Occupational Aspirations of High School Seniors, 1955–1992

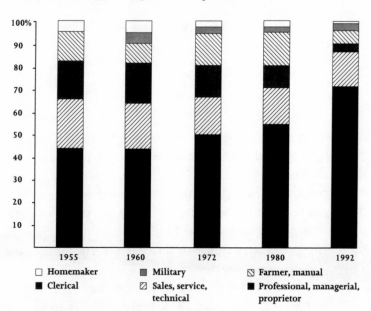

For the 1955 sample, there was not a separate category for military.
Data from senior samples of the Educational Testing Service study 1955 (weighted); Project Talent 1960 (weighted); NLS-72 1972 (weighted); HS&B 1980 (weighted); NELS:88–94 1992 (weighted)

Houghton to become a journalist? One way to assess their collective ambitions is to compare the occupational goals of these adolescents with the projected needs of the American economy in the near future. The rates at which tenth and twelfth graders expect to hold certain occupations, it turns out, are much greater than the actual prevalence of these jobs in the labor force in 1990, and often even more so than the projections for 2005 (fig. 3.4).[19]

Although the ambitions of a single adolescent may be reasonable, the collective expectations of this generation of students are probably not. One can readily see the potential mismatch. Teenagers like Jake Roberts, Grace Park, and Elizabeth Houghton want to be executives, engineers, health professionals, lawyers, athletes, and entertainers at a rate much greater than the number of such jobs currently in the labor force or projected for 2005. The number of adolescents aspiring to become lawyers and judges is five times the projected number needed; the number who want to become writers, artists, entertainers, and athletes is

Fig. 3.4 Adolescents' Job Choices and Prevalence of Jobs in the Labor Force

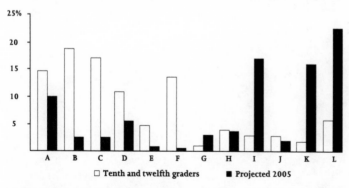

□ Tenth and twelfth graders   ■ Projected 2005

A Executive, administrative, and managerial
B Engineers, architects, natural and social scientists
C Health diagnosing, assessment, and treating
D Teachers, counselors, librarians, social workers, and religious workers
E Lawyers and judges
F Writers, artists, entertainers, and athletes
G Technicians and related support
H Sales
I Administrative support, including clerical
J Protective services
K Service, including food, cleaning, and personal
L Nonprofessional, including farming, mechanics, operators, fabricators, transportation

fourteen times the anticipated openings. High school students are much less likely to aspire to work in service and administrative occupations, and the number of jobs projected in these categories by 2005 exceeds the number of adolescents who want to fill them. There will be five times as many administrative and clerical jobs as there are adolescents interested in such work. The picture is also skewed for service jobs, with seven times as many jobs as there are teenagers interested in them.

It appears that many adolescents of the 1990s will not realize their occupational ambitions. When faced with the realities of the labor market, some may change their dreams about the kind of work they hope to do or for which they plan to prepare. When faced with the difficulties of obtaining a postsecondary education, some may also change their educational plans. Other adolescents, however, will fulfill their occupational aspirations. Why are some more likely to achieve their ambitions than others? One reason is because some adolescents are more knowledgeable about how to reach their goals. These adolescents are better able to visualize a future and to develop a useful strategy that will help them move toward their dream.

chapter four

The Importance of Aligned Ambitions

Adolescents in the 1990s are the most occupationally and educationally ambitious generation of teenagers. Many, however, lack basic information about how much education is required for the occupations they desire. Not knowing how much education is needed makes it difficult to construct realistic plans for reaching their goals. Other adolescents, however, have educational expectations that are consistent with their occupational aspirations. We describe such adolescents as having aligned ambitions. Adolescents with aligned ambitions know what type of job they want and how much education is needed for it.

Aligned ambitions reflect an adolescent's knowledge of the world of work and the educational pathways to different occupations. Such knowledge allows them to sustain higher levels of motivation and to make strategic choices about how to use their time and invest their efforts. Almost all adolescents can name an occupation that they would like to have as adults, but during their high school years many are likely to change their desired occupation. It is not, however, consistency of occupational choice that helps adolescents organize and manage their lives, but rather knowledge of the educational pathways to their desired occupations.

To determine how many adolescents have aligned ambitions, we examined the national base-year sample of the Sloan study. Every student in the Sloan study was asked what occupation he or she aspired to have as an adult and how much education he or she expected to obtain after graduating from high school. Unlike other national studies, which ask students to select the general type of field they plan to work in, the Sloan study asked them to list the specific job they expected to have as adults. These adolescents identified more than 470 different types of jobs. Using information from the U.S. Census, we determined the average years of education for people currently working in each of these occupations. For each adolescent we then calculated whether the amount of schooling he or she expected to obtain was more than, the same as, or less than the average educational level of individuals currently employed in those occupations.[1]

Our concept of alignment brings a new approach to continuing discussions among sociologists about the relationship between educational expectations and occupational aspirations.[2] First, we see these goals as related rather than independent of each other. How much education a student thinks he or she would like to acquire is associated with the type of job he or she would like to have. For some students, this association will be consistent—for example, the student who wants to be a neonatologist and knows she has to go to medical school and then receive additional training. For other students the association will be inconsistent—a student who expects to become a physician but does not know that he has to go to medical school, for instance.

Second, and perhaps more important, we use an independent criterion to determine whether the student's educational and occupational aims match. This criterion—how much education is needed for the job the student desires—helps us to gain a clearer understanding of how students think about educational attainment in relationship to their job choices. Some students will be aligned, while others will either underestimate or overestimate the amount of education required for the jobs they aspire to. Alignment involves more than simply selecting a job; it demonstrates how consistent the student's educational requirements are in relation to those of the job he or she desires.

The distribution of educational and occupational goals for high school students shows that 43.7 percent have aligned ambitions; these students expect to attain as much education as the average person who works in their desired job (fig. 4.1). More than half of the Sloan adolescents (56.2 percent), however, have misaligned ambitions, expecting to obtain either more or less education than the average person who works in their desired occupation. Among those with misaligned ambitions, most expect to obtain more education than the average worker in their chosen occupation. Only 16 percent expect to obtain less education than the average worker in the occupation they aspire to.[3]

It is not surprising that students would desire more rather than less education for their desired job. As discussed earlier, they recognize the earnings limitations of a high school diploma in today's labor market. The increasing need for further specializa-

Fig. 4.1 Alignment of Ambitions in High School Students

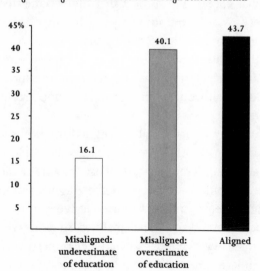

Data from Sloan study (*n* = 1,233) and United States Census

tion and technological skills also signals to them the need for more education. It is not unreasonable to suspect that certain companies will eventually demand more educated workers. There are also some occupations, such as teaching, where many practitioners already have more education—in this case a master's degree—than the job initially requires.

Aligned Ambitions and Student Characteristics

We are interested in whether certain types of students are more likely than others to have aligned ambitions. We examined whether the proportion of students with aligned ambitions varied by race and ethnicity, gender, and level of parent education. Our analyses did not reveal strong patterns of association between aligned ambitions and the social background characteristics of the students, with one exception. There is a tendency for adolescents whose parents have high levels of education—more than a college degree—to have misaligned ambitions and to expect to obtain more education than is typically required for their occupational choice. We suspect that highly educated parents may be very aware of the advantages of having more education in the future job market and convey that message to their children. In their interviews, these parents frequently mentioned how important a postsecondary degree was and expressed hope that their children would attend graduate school irrespective of their interests or job choices.[4]

Because any student can have aligned ambitions regardless of desired occupation, it is not surprising that we do not find strong relationships between student background characteristics and aligned ambitions. To learn whether aligned ambitions varied among students aspiring to different types of occupations, we conducted several additional analyses. Students who aspired to be doctors, lawyers, judges, and college professors were most likely to underestimate the amount of education required for their job choice. Students who underestimated the amount of education needed for the job typically chose the wrong type of advanced degree—for example, a Ph.D. for a doctor, a master's degree for a judge. Students who aspired to be engineers, architects, natural and social scientists, writers, artists, entertainers, and athletes were most likely to overestimate the amount of education they would need. For some occupations, such as athlete and actor, where the value of an educational credential is unpredictable and the routes to obtaining jobs are not widely known, adolescents are especially likely to overestimate the amount of education needed. We also examined whether the proportion of alignment within occupational categories varied by race and ethnicity, gender, and level of parent education. Few associations were found between alignment and occupations when these student background characteristics were taken into account.[5]

Constructing Life Plans

Adolescents with aligned ambitions are more likely to construct a life plan that increases their chances of reaching their occupational goals. A life plan is what an adolescent believes he or she needs to do to reach a desired occupation. Life plans are important for changing ambitions from a wish or a dream to an everyday goal. They provide adolescents with a valuable orientation toward the future. Jake Roberts hopes to be the next Steven Spielberg, Grace Park imagines herself working in international business, and Elizabeth Houghton sees herself as a prize-winning journalist. These three adolescents have different ambitions and different life plans for realizing their dreams.[6]

Adolescents construct life plans to help fulfill their ambitions, but these plans vary in their coherence, detail, and realism, and therefore in their usefulness. Sometimes the life plans of adolescents are not coherent: a teenager may wish to become a lawyer but not know that she has to attend law school after graduating from college. Her plan may lack detail: she may not know that in order to practice law she needs to pass the bar examination. And her plan may not be realistic: she may not know that many law school graduates do not practice law and even fewer make daily court appearances. Life plans that are coherent, detailed, and realistic are especially useful for choosing a path that increases the probability of success in adulthood.

Adolescents who choose paths with low odds of success are common. Jake Roberts was able to describe with some passion what he wanted to do—be a filmmaker—and was taking some steps in preparing for this dream by working at the local theater and studying film, but he had difficulty in selecting a pathway. Jake unknowingly chose a school that did not allow him to study theater his first year, and he dropped out of college. Grace Park wanted to work in the field of international economics, but her initial desire was to attend the naval academy even though she did not want to serve on a ship.

Planning for the future is a strategic process that requires both organizational skills and the willingness to commit to a course of action to achieve specific goals. By developing clear plans, students with aligned ambitions are able to orchestrate a set of actions to achieve their goals. Visualizing a desired outcome and a pathway serves as a personal standard to guide and regulate actions, mobilize personal resources, and sustain high levels of effort. A coherent life plan can help adolescents bring a sense of order to their social world, focus their efforts, and highlight the consequences of making particular choices.

Creating Order

Students with aligned ambitions are more likely to realistically describe how someone moves from being a high school student to obtaining the education and training necessary to acquire a desired job. They are more likely to place their lives within a historical context, to be aware of the changing technological demands of the labor force, and to describe the increasing demand for specialized training and educational credentials. The capacity to see the world as changing in predictable ways allows them to imbue their daily routines with the broader purpose of career preparation.

In describing their life plans, adolescents with aligned ambitions demonstrate a knowledge of how the adult world works and thus are more likely to be seen as adultlike by others. Their life plans often reveal an understanding of the institutional rules governing who is admitted to college, who is considered qualified for specific jobs, and who is likely to be hired. Perhaps the most significant feature of having aligned ambitions is that adolescents come to see life events as sequentially organized. They understand how doing well at something creates opportunities to do something else. A teenager who wants to become a physician is more likely to take advanced science courses in high school to increase the chances of being admitted to a competitive college. Or, as in the case of Paul, whom we describe below, he may seek employment in a local hospital rather than a fast-food restaurant because he wants to learn more about what it is like to work in a medical setting.

Viewing one's actions as having meaningful consequences helps to minimize the perceived importance of luck and increase the perceived importance of one's actions. Attending to the consequences of one's actions also makes trade-offs more apparent and provides adolescents with more opportunities to weigh alternatives and make choices. Elizabeth, for example, a high school student who wishes to attend a highly competitive university, faces trade-offs in managing her high school transcript. She needs to decide whether she is better served by choosing an advanced-placement biology course, with its more demanding workload and its more rigorous grading standards, or an honors biology course with a lighter workload and increased chances of earning a good grade.

Engaging in Strategic Effort

Adolescents with aligned ambitions are more likely to use their time and effort strategically. They are more likely to choose challenging activities that are of interest to them, that they are good at, and for which there is a reasonable probability of success. They have high levels of determination to accomplish challenging activities, and they are more likely to persist in their efforts even when the tasks become difficult. Such adolescents will seek assistance from more knowledgeable peers and adults and are likely to dedicate additional time to mastering the activity. This is true of Jordie, a student we discuss below, who sought out the tutoring center at his school library to get additional help with calculus, and also of Elizabeth, who took advanced economics at a local college because it was not offered in her high school.

Adolescents who have aligned ambitions are better able to provide explanations for how they spend their time and energy. These explanations are more likely to be judged acceptable by adults since they are oriented to the future rather than the present and focus on ways of joining the adult world. These generalizations are based on an examination of interviews with more than five hundred students, most of whom were interviewed at least twice. The cases we present here and in other chapters are representative of this broader sample of students.

To illustrate how adolescents with aligned ambitions organize their lives to increase the chances that they will achieve their goals, we present four new cases. Two are adolescents with aligned ambitions, one who aspires to be a physician and one an engineer. The other two are adolescents with misaligned ambitions who aspire to those same professions. We decided to examine students who selected the same occupations in order to highlight the differences in how those with aligned and misaligned ambitions construct their life plans and how their plans are influenced by their parents, teachers, and counselors. We specifically focus on how their life plans vary in coherence, detail, and realism. We chose the occupations of physician and engineer because they were among the most frequently mentioned choices of adolescents in the 1990s.[7]

Paul Cheng: An Aspiring Physician with Aligned Ambitions

At six feet three inches, Paul Cheng towers over many of his sophomore classmates. His height is the one advantage he has in playing basketball. Although he does not practice daily or play on his high school team, Paul's fantasy is to be a professional basketball player. This is not, however, what he aspires to do and is not what he is working toward. Paul wants to become a physician.

Paul attends a competitive academic high school in New York City. He has a long commute to school and seldom sees his high school friends in the afternoons or on weekends. His evenings are spent studying at home in his apartment building. On the weekends, he generally spends time with his parents, visits relatives, or helps out in the family business. The potential danger posed by adolescent street life to Paul's dreams is a continuing concern to his parents. "I'm usually not allowed out at night. They try to keep me in and make me study. They say, like, 'I don't care what you do at home as long as you don't go out with the bad people.' You know, hang out with the wrong crowd. There's a lot of gangs around the neighborhood. There's mostly Spanish and Puerto Rican gangs, but when I go to Chinatown, you also have to chance those gangs. I mean they try and recruit anybody to join."

Paul's parents immigrated to the United States from China and settled in New York, close to relatives. Both his parents graduated from college before they left China. His father is an engineer who owns and operates a small electronics shop, where he repairs radios, televisions, computers, VCRs, and other appliances. His mother occasionally helps out in the store. Since he knows little about electronics, Paul helps by being the cashier, picking up supplies, or answering the phone. He does not receive payment for his work and does not expect it. His parents, however, expect him to work in the store because his father needs the help.

His father does not expect Paul to take over the family business and actively discourages him from going into the electronics field because it is financially unstable. He is less forceful in encouraging Paul to become a physician. "My dad just wants me to succeed, he doesn't care about what I'm planning on doing. He just doesn't want me to go into his field, though." Paul's mother, on the other hand, is committed to seeing him become a doctor, a desire shared by his relatives. "My relatives always say, like, 'Be a doctor, it's a stable job, don't be in a field you get laid off any time and [they] force you into early retirement.' They're all usually telling me how their jobs are unstable. They can get laid off any second. Like usually they'll get rid of you if you start getting old. So, I guess, they all want me to go into something stable."

The family's concern about choosing an occupation that offers long-term stability has had a major impact on Paul's career choice. He is very aware of fields in which people are likely to be laid off and believes that physicians are unlikely to lose their jobs because of changes in the labor market. Instead, the chances of being fired as a physician rest on one's technical competence. "Since the economy's pretty bad, everyone's getting laid off here and there, and finding jobs [is] really hard now. I guess maybe the news can also influence me. Usually in the news, every day they'll be finding new things in medicine, which is very interesting, and then they'll be, like, over here this airline company laid off six hundred people and over there a company closed three factories. If I can tolerate another ten years of school, I guess I'd like to be a doctor. I like the doctor field 'cause its a steady job, 'cause basically doctors don't really get fired unless they really do something bad."

His mother's occupational ambitions for him are accompanied by attempts to organize his life around academic pursuits. She monitors his free time and discourages him from watching television. "When my dad has the ball game on he'll say, 'Come on, let's watch the game.' My mom will be like, 'Wait, he's trying to learn,' or something like that and my dad's like, 'Whatever he wants to do, it's up to him.'" To increase Paul's chances of scoring high on the college admissions tests, his mother has been sending him to preparation classes.

Paul's mother is very aware of the differences among colleges and universities and hopes that Paul will attend a highly competitive school. "My mom already knows which colleges she wants me to go to. And I started getting these letters from like other colleges, which I know are pretty good liberal arts schools; my mom is like, 'I never heard of it, you can't go. You have to go to somewhere that's established in something.' . . . She has the rankings of all the colleges for the whole United States, so I'll be like, 'Look mom, Carleton is like number six on the liberal arts schools. It's a very good school.' And she'll be like, 'No, you have go to Cornell,' or something like that."

Paul has organized his life around preparing for admission to college. At high school, he is taking advanced-placement courses in biology, mathematics, and English, and he has decided to develop a Westinghouse talent project, all in addition to taking the preparation courses for the SAT on and off over several years. According to Paul, this had changed his life: "Studying for the SATs, getting ready for college, well, it kind of changes your life completely because what you usually do is focus on recreation—now you have to focus mostly your time on studying." He is concerned about his high school grades and says his junior-year report card made him feel particularly good about himself, since his grade point average had improved.

Paul's focus on preparing for college also led him to change his friends. His new high school friends are academic achievers.

"The people who I mostly hang around with now are people I met this summer, even though they'd been to the school for a while. I've never really hung around them until the start of last summer. And the people I used to hang with I'd prefer not to be with them anymore, 'cause they've gone the wrong way, so to speak. They were into crime, taking drugs, they drink beer. So I'm trying to shy away."

Paul does not have friends or relatives who are physicians. In order to prepare for a medical career and to develop a better understanding of the medical world, he works as an admissions clerk at a local hospital. He can envision a path to becoming a doctor and can describe some of the difficulties ahead and the sacrifices he will need to make. His awareness of these future challenges are a source of motivation and perseverance. "The fields I'm pursuing almost everyone wants to pursue, so there's only so many jobs they can create, so more competition. I guess I'll need to give up my social life. Basically I'm going to have to hit the books for the next few years and basically I have to give up a lot of recreation. Maybe like, instead of having the time to goof off, you have to study and take research."

Paul Cheng has aligned ambitions; he is aware of what is required to become a physician and has begun to organize his life to help him reach his goal. He has selected challenging academic courses in high school, is willing to commit himself to earning high grades, and is willing to change his social circle to support his efforts to be admitted to a competitive four-year institution. Paul can describe in some detail the path to becoming a physician: what he will study in college, the number of years of medical school and residency, even the kind of physician he would like to become and what he would do. Paul believes in the efficacy of his own efforts. He also believes that luck plays a small role in whether he will be successful.

What Paul does not have is a sense of "calling" to be a physician. Intrinsic motivation to become a doctor or other professional is not part of our definition of aligned ambitions. What alignment does is to help Paul plan. It is possible that, after he is accepted into a college program, Paul will decide he no longer wants to become a doctor and that there are other professions that would give him the job security he desires. Changing occupational goals is inevitable because of changes in individual tastes and life opportunities. We try some things and find we are not good at them. Opportunities present themselves and we can choose or choose not to take advantage of them. Intrinsic motivation can help a student persevere at a life plan, but it is not a substitute for having a plan.

Rosa Lopez: An Aspiring Physician with Misaligned Ambitions

Rosa Lopez immigrated to the United States from Mexico when she was five years old and lives with her mother in an apartment building in Southern California. Her mother considers their neighborhood unsafe and doesn't allow Rosa out of the apartment building in the evenings. "When I get home my mother is already there. So she cooks, and then, when I finish dinner—I don't eat a lot—I just change clothes, do my homework, and go out for a little while. I just go downstairs. I don't go anyplace 'cause I can't go anywhere. . . . I have to just stay inside the apartment building or [on the] stairs out front, and just sit there for a while with friends."

Relations among Rosa, her stepfather, and her mother are strained. Her mother left Rosa's father when they came to the United States, and she recently separated from her second husband, a gardener. Rosa's mother and stepfather were together for about three years, but, as Rosa says, "things didn't work out." She believes her stepfather was very neglectful of her mother and rarely paid attention to her even when she was sick. Rosa's mother came from a large family with nine children, and she and a sister had to leave elementary school to work when they were very young to help the family financially. Rosa believes that these early work experiences contributed to her mother's and aunt's poor health.

For many years, Rosa's mother worked as a part-time house cleaner; she is currently employed in a packing factory. When her mother worked as a cleaning woman, Rosa had to take one Friday a month off from school to help. Whenever she missed school, she made arrangements to contact her teachers for assignments so that she was always prepared for class. Even though her mother took her out of school to help clean houses, Rosa's mother and stepfather believed she needed to obtain a good education. "They want me to study a lot so I can be somebody. My mother didn't even finish elementary school. And my [step]dad, I think he got to the same grade, or actually I think he didn't even go to school. His mother died when he was a little kid, and my [step]father had to support them. . . . That's why they want me to try hard and to be somebody. They want me to get a job, a good job, not like them."

Ever since she was nine, Rosa has wanted to become a physician. This job expectation is not shared by her mother, who thinks she should become a secretary. Rosa's mother assumes that becoming a doctor requires considerable resources that the family does not have. "My mother says to be a doctor you have to study a lot and it takes a lot of money. And, I mean, we don't have a very high income."

Rosa's interest in medicine stems from the pain and anguish her mother suffers as a result of a chronic back injury, which often leaves her immobile. "My mother's sick, and it's sad because there's nothing I can do. She's very ill, and at night she can hardly sleep. At night I see that she's like crying or something, and it makes me feel so bad. Because, I mean, she's my mother and I can't do anything. I can't find anything to tell her that makes her better because it keeps on hurting her. And that's what makes me want to be a doctor." Rosa's only reservation about becoming a doctor is her fear of "dead people." She believes, however, that she can overcome this fear.

Although Rosa has a strong desire to become a physician, she has little knowledge of the education and specialized training that are required to become one. Her knowledge of medical specialties is limited as well. She says that she would like to be a "regular doctor that takes care of patients with fevers, cancers, and other kinds of sicknesses." As for the education required, Rosa explains, "I haven't really thought about it. I have tried to ask some doctors about it, but they are busy and stuff."

School is important to Rosa, and she likes "to work hard, concentrate, and keep my grades up." In her sophomore year, her grades were mainly Bs, but she hoped by the end of the semester to receive an A in math, her favorite subject. "You have to study to be somebody," she says. Although Rosa had been on the principal's honor roll in ninth and tenth grades, her academic performance took an unfortunate turn in her junior year. "In eleventh grade, I started out pretty well. I was doing great, as far as I know. I don't know what happened to me. Because like, the second semester, I was awful. Awful, awful, awful." The slide in Rosa's performance was noticed by one of her teachers, who called her mother to find out what was happening. "I don't know, I probably got tired of it [studying]. And I started being absent a lot. I had like twenty-six absences. I just stayed home and slept. I wasn't interested at all. I mean, I thought it wasn't worth it." The school again tried to encourage Rosa to return. "Ms. Tally and my counselor, Ms. Wittleder, were calling me every single morning, telling me to come back to school, to think about my future, that school was going to be good for me. I probably got tired of them calling me every single morning telling me to come back. They asked if I was sure I wanted to drop out of school. If I did drop out I was going to lose it, you know, the education that I was getting now, and that then I was going to regret that I didn't get an education."

During this period, Rosa and her mother were having a difficult time and they rarely talked. "We'd get in fights over every single thing that happened or that I did. We would get angry with each other." Rosa believes that some of her apathy toward school was directly related to the "bad relationship" she was having with her mother. "Sometimes when my mother got home from work, she was very tired. I would try to tell her something about school or about my friends, but it was just impossible to talk to her." The situation was so bad that Rosa had considered "leaving home and dropping out of school."

In the spring of her junior year, things began to change, and Rosa's academic performance improved. Her grades went up, and she once again attended school regularly. Her counselors noticed the improvement and suggested that she learn more about how to apply for financial aid so she could attend college. At that time, Rosa was planning to attend a university after graduation, but her understanding of the differences in the types of programs offered at two-year colleges, universities, and vocational schools was limited.

As a senior in high school, Rosa remains adamant about her desire to become a doctor. She is working hard at school and expects to end up with "A's or else!" She has dropped her science class and substituted an art class: "I wanted to have a fun class for the first time in my life." Rosa expects to graduate from high school. Her confidence has been somewhat shaken, however, and earning a diploma seems less certain than in previous years: "Well, if I have the chance, I hope that I graduate."

Rosa's plans for attending college are not well defined. She is unsure where she will go to school or what the requirements are for college admission. She is expecting to return to Mexico and attend college there, although she is unable to identify where she will live or what school she will attend. Rosa is bilingual, and Spanish is spoken in her home. Her mother believes it is important for Rosa to be aware of her cultural heritage; she sent Rosa back to Mexico after her third-grade year so that she would continue to be fluent in Spanish. Rosa stayed in Mexico for two years, and when she returned she and her mother moved into her present school district. In some respects, the idea of Rosa attending college in Mexico is not unreasonable. She is fluent in Spanish, she spent two years studying in Mexico, and her mother encourages her to maintain close ties with her native country.

What seems more problematic is the scope and depth of information Rosa has concerning the education and training required for certain specialized fields of medicine. Rosa continues to want to become a "general doctor, because if you are just one speciality doctor, you are not going to know what to do, a general doctor knows everything." Rosa feels a calling to become a doctor that has persisted through her high school career, yet the knowledge to help her fulfill her ambitions is limited, and she does not have a supportive network of relatives, teachers, or friends that could provide her with the guidance and resources she needs. Her step off the academic path in her junior year had major repercussions. She was no longer taking the courses typically completed by students expecting to enter college as math or science majors. Her counselors and teachers began worrying about her dropping out of school rather than advising her about college programs. And although Rosa remained committed to her ambition, she began to take less challenging courses and started to worry about completing high school.

Rosa Lopez has a strong desire to become a physician, but unlike Paul Cheng she has no clear plan for how to achieve her goal. The absence of a coherent plan makes it difficult for her to deal with setbacks. When faced with personal adversity or lack of support, she is less able to sustain her efforts. Coherent life plans provide adolescents with strategies to cope with personal adversities. Paul resisted participating in adolescent street life even though it was common in his troubled neighborhood. Elizabeth Houghton successfully coped with her mother's death and her father's frequent business trips. Faced with personal adversities, Paul and Elizabeth were able to draw upon their coherent life plans to sustain their efforts and to recognize the consequences of their choices. However, in forming their life plans, they had much more support from their families than Rosa did.

Jordan Blazack: *An Aspiring Engineer with Aligned Ambitions*

Jordie Blazack waits outside the high school door for his three closest friends. He deeply values the friendship among the four of them and is worried about a misunderstanding that he hopes to resolve when they meet after the last school period. Jordie's relationship with two of these friends dates back to elementary school, when they were in the same Boy Scout troop. He met his other close friend during his first year in high school when they were both on the water polo team. These strong friendships of Jordie's are somewhat uncharacteristic for teenage males. Not only is the foursome a close, intimate group, but the social ties these young men have with each other also extend to their parents. "I grew up with these guys and now we are really close. We spend weekends together, we even will get our parents together." Conversation among this group of friends is fairly intense and covers every topic from schoolwork and girlfriends to an occasional focus on the future. "We talk about the future a little bit, but most of us know what the other one is going to do."

Jordie also has good relationships with his parents and his sister. His parents schedule a family day once a week; occasionally they miss a day, but for the most part they manage to get together. Jordie's parents take an active interest in his academic work and encourage him to take challenging courses. They do not let him get a job during the school year, maintaining that "my job is school."

As a senior in high school, Jordie was taking physics, calculus, humanities, computer science, and technical drawing. He
also regularly visited the math tutoring center, not for remedial
help but to put in extra time on calculus, which he was "pretty
good at" and enjoyed immensely. He believed that mastery of
mathematical skills would be important for his future, and it is
one of Jordie's strengths. He has always excelled at mathematics
and never received a grade lower than a B for any six-week grading period. He earned As in algebra, geometry, precollege algebra, trigonometry, and calculus. Jordie's expertise in math was
recognized by his family. When his mother had trouble with
household finances, she frequently asked him to help her, and
when his younger sister was having trouble in math, Jordie tu-
tored her.

Jordie sees the importance of taking steps to master specific
skills that have clear long-term benefits. Realizing that he was
having difficulty with writing, Jordie decided to take an expository writing class, which ended up being one of his favorite
classes during his senior year. In the beginning of the course, he
was unable to "put down my thoughts in a logical pattern." But
by the end of the course, there was a noticeable difference.
"When I looked at my first piece of writing at the end of the class
and then my last piece of writing there was like a day to night
difference. I was much better when I left the class."

Jordie already had a vision of what the assignments in college would be like and believed that some of his teachers were
more helpful than others in preparing him for them: "Mr. Black,
he teaches his class like a college class. I mean there are not
quizzes every day to see if you are doing the reading, there is one
paper based on the book we were supposed to have read. Judging by the paper, he knows if you read it or not. He is a really
good teacher and a strict grader so I think his class is probably
the best preparation that I had for college."

By the time he was a high school senior, Jordie had made a

definite career choice. He hoped to become a mechanical engineer, even though he realized that he might have difficulty finding a job. "I think I will probably stick with being an engineer even though everybody says it is like one of the hardest jobs to get into. I know in college a lot of people drop or switch majors but I cannot see myself switching to humanities. I like trying to figure things out. I used to play with the computer. I used to try and figure out programs and before that TVs."

Jordie had no interest in pursuing his father's occupation as a high school English teacher. He became interested in mechanical engineering during his junior year and says he chose it in part because "I think there is a certain way of thinking. Like in math you have to think in a logical step pattern. There is a definite right or wrong answer." A meeting with the dean of students also influenced his career choice. One of the first questions the dean asked was what he wanted to do in the future. Jordie replied, "I want to do something with math and I want to make a lot of money." According to Jordie, the dean then said, "I have the perfect career for you." Jordie's parents were helpful in providing him with additional information about engineering programs. When the college brochures came describing specific programs, Jordie actively set out to learn more about the field and sent back a letter requesting more information on mechanical engineering and job prospects in this field.

With information from his parents, teachers, and the brochures, Jordie began to formulate a view of what mechanical engineers do. As he explained, "What I understand, this is mostly an automotive field where they design cars and they take someone's idea of a car and they figure out how to put it into a practical application, or if they can be built, then what the modifications would be." Once he had a more developed understanding of mechanical engineering, Jordie began visiting colleges. These visits reinforced his desire to study engineering. "My interest was really a strength, and when I visited one of the leading technical institutes this winter, I found that one of the students there had a big part in designing the '96 Corvette. That sounded great, I would love to design cars. I think it would be really interesting to work for an automotive company. Actually see someone using your car on the highway and being able to say I helped design that car." It was not only the end product that was of value to Jordie but also the process of building something that held special significance. "It's just the whole, it is what you are doing is like building something and being able to look at something and actually tell how it works and the feeling that comes with knowing I helped design it. It is just like figuring out a puzzle."

For Jordie, becoming a good mechanical engineer involved mastery of academic subjects, including calculus. "Calculus is an important part of it. I think this whole mind-set of wanting to figure out things and how they work is pretty important because, I mean, what you are doing is telling them how to work and I think that has to be a pretty important part." As an engineering major, Jordie expected to do three hours of homework for every hour in the classroom. Although he did not consider himself a workaholic, he believed this was a challenge that he could master.

When asked about how much education he would need to become an engineer, Jordie said, "Well, I think one could stop at a bachelor's degree, but I really want to go for at least a master's degree. Having a master's degree will put me ahead of the others. And I will just know more about it and I'll be able to solve more difficult problems." In thinking about the future, Jordie said that he would like to stick with one job and would like to make some kind of difference. College is important to him. "I always joke about college with my parents and friends that it is just an alternative," he says, "a fallback in case I do not win the lottery. But even if I won the lottery, I would probably still go to college. I probably would not work as long and have my own hours."

After high school graduation, Jordie enrolled in a competitive midwestern public university with a nationally ranked engineering department. At first he found the experience of being away from home a bit "shocking, but toward the end of the year I really enjoyed it." He had thought about attending college in Chicago, but his parents believed that he would enjoy the experience more in a college town. Jordie's parents had both attended a large state university, and they suspected that Jordie would like attending a large school, especially one with a well-respected engineering program. They also wanted him to attend a school that offered more than just science and math, in case he changed his mind about pursuing an engineering major.

Jordie was able to transfer his advanced mathematics credits from high school, so he was a semester ahead in calculus when he started college. He has enjoyed his classes and continues to believe he will receive an undergraduate degree in mechanical engineering. His academic load in college has been rigorous: chemistry, calculus, honors English, engineering, and computer programming. In his second semester, he added physics to that mix. Jordie found his college classes "hard and they move really fast, but I don't think they are too bad. I learned more than I ever learned in high school last year." College has not changed his interest in mathematics, and his math classes continue to be his favorite. At the end of his freshman year, he had Bs in all his classes except one that he received a C in during his first semester. He is currently maintaining the academic average he needs for mechanical engineering and hopes to bring up his grades. He believes that his professors are "really good" and finds college "a lot more challenging than high school."

Receiving less than a B average was disappointing to Jordie. Not so to his parents, who thought he was doing well. "They were really surprised with how well I did on my grades, but it really upset me that I did not get over a 3.0." Jordie believes he should have gotten an A in one class, but he did not do as well as he hoped on the final and missed it by a few points. He insists that his parents never reproached him about his grades in college but rather motivated him to achieve his best.

Jordie's parents are actively involved in his college education. They were instrumental in helping him to select a college and have provided information about his career choice. But perhaps the most significant indication of Jordie's family support is that his mother's salary from her job as a nursery school teacher is being used to pay his tuition. Jordie believes that his adjustment to college has been fairly typical. Reflecting on his first year there, he says that it has been a good experience. He has had the opportunity to live somewhere else, studied in the field he is interested in, and not had the pressures and concerns of being an adult caring for a family and living independently. Jordie wishes the school were closer to a big city, but Chicago is not that far away. The most significant change that Jordie experienced during his first year of college was leaving his friends and not finding any new close friends, except for one who introduced him to mountain biking, his new avocation. He hopes to improve his grades next year and is thinking about attending graduate school. Jordie's greatest concerns are "wondering if I am going to get a job and how my life will be socially."

Brian Daniels: An Aspiring Engineer with Misaligned Ambitions

Brian Daniels's family owns and operates one of the remaining livestock farms in a small midwestern town that is quickly becoming a bedroom community for a major metropolis, even though the city is nearly two hours away by car. Work on the farm consumes much of Brian's time, and he has many responsibilities every night. "The fall is a busy season; you have planting and all of that. In the winter it slows down, but we raise a lot of an-

imals. We're probably one of the last farms around that raise a variety of animals. On a farm there are no vacation times unless you
get somebody to do the work. Most of the time we are around all
year long working with the animals." Running the farm occu-
pies much of the family's time, and dinner conversations revolve
around "the farm thing."

Brian is the youngest of four sons, two of whom have families of their own and live in a nearby county. In talking about his
family, Brian explains that his parents are considerably older than
the parents of his friends. "I don't feel that my parents are old,
but they are a lot older than everybody else. They are in their six-
ties and my friends' parents are in their forties. Mine are about
twenty years ahead. So there is a big generation gap, but for my
older brothers their age is normal." Given the age of his parents,
the whole family is involved in helping on the farm. One of his
brothers helps his father full time, and when things need to be
done, such as painting the barn, the other brothers will come
home for the weekend to help. Brian does not get paid for his
work on the farm but does receive an allowance. He also works
on other farms in the summer helping to bale hay. He takes all
his allowance and other money and places it an account to help
pay for his college expenses and perhaps his own car.

Although Brian enjoys working on the farm, he believes it
would be an unwise occupational choice. "If farming was a better occupation I would go into it. But there is no future in doing
that especially seeing how things are going right now." His parents want him to "have a better goal and a head start in life, because with farming you cannot get ahead very far." Although they
would like him to succeed and pursue a job other than farming,
Brian thinks that they are not particularly knowledgeable about
alternative careers. Everyone in his family plays an instrument,
and Brian believes that his parents are more likely to "help, and
push me into music to see what would happen, than in other careers."

Brian is "laid back," he says. "I just let everything ride. If I don't like something, I just don't do it. I do not get upset about anything." His attitude toward school in some ways reflects this disposition. He believes that all his courses are in some way connected to his future, but he does not actively strategize about what subjects to take. He expects the school to tell him what courses he needs to graduate: "They decide on what I need. The courses I take are just something that will get me passed out of high school, that will get me the credits to graduate." He views his classes as something he needs "to get to college and get a job."

As a high school senior, Brian's favorite subject was drafting and technical drawing, a course that he saw as especially important for a career in mechanical engineering. He particularly enjoyed drafting because the teacher was not very strict and the class assignments were structured so the students had considerable autonomy and could work independently. "In drafting class you can just talk about whatever you want. The teacher gives us guidelines about what we have to do and when you have to have it done. You usually have to have it done in six weeks. It is an open environment, you get to work at your own pace, there is no routine or anything like that."

Brian views design as the primary task of a mechanical engineer: "If you have a problem with something, then you redesign it." He also believes that drafting is an essential job skill and is "right in the middle" of what an engineer does. Brian considered his high school drafting class as particularly advantageous for helping him succeed in college. "If I know what is going on with drafting, then I will be way ahead when I go to college." He noted that mastering drafting would be especially valuable to him when he worked as an engineer. "As someone who knows drafting, I will be able to connect with everybody else in the field. I can connect with people higher and people lower."

Having goals and striving toward them is something that

Brian considers essential for "getting the most out of his life." "I always like striving for my goals first, and then if I have another idea come up, I can change; in that way I can get as much out of life as I possibly can." Brian considered being a mechanical engineer a "top-ranked goal because with so many jobs you have to know what you are going into before you get into it." It is not the actual job of being a mechanical engineer that he has focused on but rather the field of engineering. "Even if I do not like mechanical engineering, I can at least in the last year switch to whatever I want. I see engineering as a kind of major." From Brian's perspective, the field of engineering is very diverse and there are a number of different industries that hire engineers. If given a choice, he would like to work on projects that are farm related.

For Brian, one of the most important aspects of being an engineer is that this field would allow him considerable independence and an opportunity to create and work on his own projects. To be a good engineer, Brian believed it was necessary to master the fundamentals of mathematics and science, especially "vectors and physics." "You have to study a lot of math and physics, and there's going to be a little drafting and technical drawing but it probably will not be as prominent as computer design."

Brian assumed that his above average abilities in math and drafting were the special talents that would help him succeed in becoming an engineer. But finances might be a potential barrier to achieving his goal, he thought. "In the last couple of years, everyone has jacked up the tuition price. I can take a loan out now for junior college. But paying for a four-year college education is going to be rough."

A year after he had graduated from high school, Brian was attending junior college as a full-time student, living at home, and pursuing a major in engineering. He said that the education he is receiving at the community college is "the same education I would get at any other school but it is a cheaper way." In his first semester, he received a full scholarship from a local business; in his second semester he also received some financial assistance. His parents were not helping to pay his expenses, and he was concerned about having to cover the full cost when he transferred to a four-year school.

Brian's course load during his first year at the community college included physics, chemistry, calculus, English, and physical education. He had heard from other students that the junior college was "a lot harder than the four-year universities" and thought that might be so. His average was about a B, and "that is the lowest grades I have ever had." He attributed his performance to the different classes and teaching styles of his professors: he felt his classes were too academic and that his teachers, especially in physics, did not explain things well.

Toward the end of his first year, Brian dropped a couple of classes because of his poor performance. "In the beginning I was having pretty good grades and then at the end I started having more tests, sometimes two or three tests a week. It was hard to keep up. So I dropped some classes." The class he liked most was chemistry, both because he felt that he understood it and because many of his classmates also planned to be engineers. In reflecting on his first year, Brian said that high school had "pretty much" prepared him for college. Because he had dropped some of his courses, though, he thought he would have to attend the school for three years instead of two.

Brian spends most of his time with a country music band. The rest of the band members are in their thirties, and he is the youngest. Able to play the guitar, mandolin, and banjo, he practices for about two hours every day. On Friday nights the band plays at bars and halls, and sometimes as many as two hundred people come to hear them. At one time Brian thought he would become an engineer and music would be a hobby. "Now, I think I may work more with music and engineering would become a hobby. Right now I divide my time between the two." When asked to describe the least satisfying experiences of the past year, Brian answers "college." He just is not getting enough out of his classes, he says, and what he really wishes for is a "lucky break and being able to play in a band."

Although Brian said he felt prepared for college, his high school courses did not provide him with the skills required to succeed at the math and science he took in community college. Brian had chosen to attend community college because of limited financial resources and because he wanted to get his general requirements out of the way. Compared with Jordie, whose parents helped him find a college with a strong engineering program and to see the relationship between high school courses and college requirements, Brian did not have parental support and was not aware of how important his high school courses would be in gaining an engineering degree.

Advantages of Life Plans

Paul Cheng, Rosa Lopez, Jordie Blazack, and Brian Daniels are ambitious American teenagers. At a quick glance, these four adolescents look very similar: they have good high school academic records, and they share ambitions to attend college and to become professionals. They differ, however, in the steps they are taking to realize their ambitions. These differences stem, in part, from how they seek out challenges, create solutions, and mobilize resources.

Adolescence is a period for trying out different roles and imagining different futures.[8] It is also when students begin to accept responsibility for making decisions about how to spend time, how much effort to expend, and what steps to take. Many adolescents believe they should and can build their own life plans. This is as true of those with misaligned ambitions, like Rosa Lopez and Brian Daniels, as it is of those with aligned ambitions, like Paul Cheng and Jordie Blazack. Where adolescents with aligned and misaligned ambitions differ is in how they go about building their life plans. Two differences that reappear in the stories of these adolescents is their level of motivation and effort and their capacity to draw upon resources.

Sustaining Motivation and Effort

Perhaps no issue dominates public discussions of improving the academic performance of adolescents as much as increasing their motivation.[9] Even among ambitious adolescents, there are different levels of motivation. A characteristic of those who have aligned ambitions is that they are more likely to sustain high levels of motivation throughout their high school careers. One reason is because adolescents with aligned ambitions are more capable of identifying their own strengths and weaknesses and of creating their own internal standards of performance. When faced with problems, they are better able to diagnose the nature of the problem and to seek appropriate remedies.

Paul chose his courses in high school to prepare himself for his premedical college courses. He took three advanced-placement courses in mathematics and science and developed a project for the Westinghouse science competition. Although the Westinghouse project was not submitted in the competition, Paul described the project as a good learning experience and was able to explain how it would help with his future. Paul was well aware of the rules for college admission and studied for the college entrance examinations, collected information about various college programs, and visited schools. To learn more about the world of medicine, he took a part-time job in a hospital. Paul's ambitions to be a physician were seen as reasonable and appropriate by both his mother and his relatives.

Although Jordie planned to become an engineer rather than a doctor, he took similar steps to achieve his goals. He sought out information about the field of engineering and researched engineering schools. Like Paul, Jordie also participated in activities that would better prepare him for his career choice. He went to the math tutoring center at school for additional assistance, even though his grades in mathematics were excellent. To improve his perceived difficulties with writing, he took an expository writing course.

Both Paul and Jordie were able to describe a series of steps that they could take to reach their goals, and both had some knowledge about the educational paths that would lead to their chosen careers. Both had begun to develop life plans that were detailed and realistic. The benefits of high motivation are greatest when it produces sustained effort. Adolescents like Rosa Lopez, who display even occasional periods of low motivation, can experience significant setbacks in their efforts to reach their goals. The personal costs of some of these setbacks can be quite high.

Drawing on Resources

Adolescents with aligned ambitions are aware that to reach their goals they will need help from others. When confronted by difficult challenges, they are more likely to seek assistance than to continue to try without success or to disengage from the effort. Rosa Lopez and Brian Daniels are less knowledgeable and certain about how to reach their occupational goals than either Paul or Jordie. Rosa wants to become a physician in order to help people who are in pain, but she has little knowledge about how one becomes a physician or what kind of educational training is required. While Rosa is a conscientious student who earns high grades when she attends school, she has not taken the more difficult mathematics and science courses offered by her high school, and she has not identified small steps that she could take to prepare her for the education and training necessary to become a physician. Rosa focuses her efforts on meeting her school's standards of excellence and does not seek out additional challenges. In comparison to Paul, Rosa has less familial support and less consistent advice. Although Rosa's mother has not actively discouraged her from pursuing a degree in medicine, she has made it clear that she thinks being a secretary would be a more realistic goal.

Like Rosa, Brian has no detailed knowledge about work in his chosen field or the educational requirements for becoming a professional in it. While he is a good student in mathematics and drafting, he displays a passive orientation toward his academic work by allowing the school to choose which subjects he will study. He assumes that the school will see to it that he has the courses needed to graduate and to be admitted to college. Unlike Jordie, Brian does not attempt to enter an engineering school but rather attends the local community college with plans to transfer after completing his associate's degree. The routes to becoming a physician and an engineer are well marked, and adolescents need to know about these routes in order to decide what courses to take in high school and how to select the best postsecondary program.

As the cases presented in this chapter suggest, however, adolescents need help in developing coherent life plans. Paul has a very supportive family, particularly his mother, who strategically intervenes by urging him to study, to take college preparation courses, and to distance himself from friends who do not have similar college plans. While Paul lives in a poor neighborhood, his family offers him a protective cocoon. Rosa, on the other hand, does not have a family or a personal friend who intervenes on her behalf in a way that would help her to pursue her goals.

Jordie is like Paul in that his family was actively involved in helping him choose a college that would be right for him, given his interest in engineering. Jordie also had a mentor at school who spent time advising him on his course selections and college choices. While Brian's family was close and supportive of him, they were uninformed about his college interests. Unlike Jordie's parents, who spent considerable resources learning

about different colleges, Brian's parents did not pursue these activities.

Aligned ambitions are the core of an adolescent's life plan,
and without them it is difficult to create a meaningful plan. As
we have seen from these four cases, beyond the adolescent's talents and skills, the family and the high school play an important
part in the development of life plans. In Part II, we explore how
the family, the high school, the workplace, and the peer group
shape the formation of aligned ambitions.

The Formation of
Aligned Ambitions

II

chapter five

Channeling Ambitions in High School

n high school students begin to make choices; they decide what kind of mathematics to study, which science courses to take, whether to put forth their maximum effort or to try to "get by" with a minimum. These choices can have significant consequences for the students' lives in school as well as afterward. Their choices influence what they learn, what skills they acquire, and their qualifications for being admitted to college or hired for a job. In this chapter we examine the relationship between the organization of the curriculum and the ambitions of students.

High Schools of the 1990s

Today's American high schools are commonly referred to as "comprehensive high schools," because the curriculum covers a broad range of topics. The comprehensive curriculum is designed to provide students who plan to attend college with the necessary courses, knowledge, and skills to enter postsecondary institutions and to provide students who plan to work with the skills needed to enter the labor force. In the 1950s, the typical high school offered a college preparatory program, a general education program, a commercial program, and a vocational program. In addition to the regular high schools, there were vocational schools specifically designed to accommodate the needs of students who planned to enter the labor force and work full time directly after graduating. These vocational high schools have been in decline, and now more than 95 percent of American public high schools are comprehensive schools offering two dominant curricular strands—college preparatory and general education—that enroll 88 percent of high school students. Only 12 percent are enrolled in vocational courses.[1]

The curriculum of the comprehensive high school is organized around a wide range of subjects, including such traditional courses as English, mathematics, science, and history, as well as technical courses, remedial courses, and courses focused on health and social services. It is not unusual for a high school to offer between 200 and 350 different courses even though the number required for graduation is often 24 or less. The diversity of the high school curriculum was recently examined by Arthur Powell, David K. Cohen, and Eleanor Farr. They describe America's high schools as "shopping malls" where students can construct their own curricular plan by selecting courses from an extensive list of offerings, with little assurance that those they select constitute a meaningful education.[2]

In 1983, the National Commission on Excellence in Education issued *A Nation at Risk*, a report that set out a blueprint for reforming elementary and secondary education. An important recommendation was to increase the number of academic courses required for graduation from high school. The response to this national report was immediate and widespread. Within a few years, almost every state had increased the number of courses required. This increase in state graduation requirements, particularly in mathematics and science, had noticeable effects, including significant growth in the percentage of high school students taking four years of mathematics and science—from 13 percent in 1983 to more than 60 percent in 1997.[3]

Rather than simplifying the curriculum, however, the new state graduation requirements intensified the shopping-mall character of the American high school. Many schools added academic courses that varied in content and difficulty. Analyses of high school transcripts show a 10 percent increase in the number of different courses taken by high school students between

1980 and 1990.[4] The push for raising academic standards and preparing more students for college also blurred the boundaries separating college preparatory, general, and vocational curricular strands.

Regardless of what courses students take, high school counselors encourage them to attend college. Teachers and counselors consistently emphasize that more skills are demanded of entry-level workers. Students with vocational interests are often encouraged to attend college, and many enter community colleges to gain additional skills and credentials. Even with the increasing awareness of the skills needed for entry-level jobs, vocational programs in high schools are often viewed as undesirable by students, their parents, and school staff—including those who teach vocational courses—and many of these courses and programs are being eliminated or reorganized.[5]

In most high schools, college preparatory students and general education students are likely to study the same subjects, and students are typically grouped by course difficulty rather than course topic.[6] Nearly all high school students study chemistry, for example, but the chemistry courses differ in what is demanded of students and in the amount and type of material covered. The extensive course offerings in today's high schools are closer to a college curriculum than to the traditional 1950s high school curriculum, with its narrow academic offerings and strongly differentiated curricular tracks in vocational, business, and distributive education.

The critics of the 1950s high school desired a new model that in many ways resembles the high school of the 1990s. One of the most famous critiques of the American high school in the 1950s was written by James B. Conant, a former president of Harvard University. Conant argued that academically talented students were not being sufficiently challenged in high school and were not working hard enough. Part of the problem was that the program of academic subjects did not have sufficient range.

There were not enough advanced mathematics and science courses, and many schools did not offer a third and fourth year of foreign-language study. Conant envisioned a high school in which there would be no organized academic programs or tracks. Students would not be classified as vocational, college preparatory, or business students. Instead, classes would be organized according to their content and level of difficulty. Students would develop individualized programs that would enable them to take an advanced course in mathematics but an average-level course in social studies. Such a highly differentiated curriculum would require students to select their courses, and counselors would play a major role in helping them to make coherent and meaningful choices.[7] The high school of the 1990s offers the broad range of course offerings favored by Conant. As he predicted, this broadened curriculum has increased the importance of making informed course selections. Schools play a major role in shaping both the complexity of the curriculum and the strategies students use to make choices that are consistent with their future ambitions.

The Sloan study was specifically designed to obtain information from high schools with different socioeconomic profiles. From the thirteen high schools in the Sloan study, we have selected three—Maple Wood, Middle Brook, and Del Vista—to demonstrate how high schools can influence the formation of ambitions. Two of the three, Maple Wood and Middle Brook, are very similar in the composition of their student populations. Both schools have diverse populations, although Maple Wood has more African-Americans and Middle Brook has more recent immigrants. Thirty-three percent of Middle Brook students speak a language other than English at home. The per capita income for both school sites is over $50,000, and more than 70 percent of the parents who have adolescents in the respective schools have graduated from college. Del Vista, the third high school, also has a highly diverse population, with many Asian and Hispanic students. The per capita income is lower than at the other two schools, and 43 percent of the parents have college or advanced degrees. Regardless of their own levels of educational attainment, the parents at all three schools have very high educational expectations for their adolescents.[8]

These high schools differ in their curricular organization and in the extent to which students are encouraged to plan for their futures.[9] The curriculum at Maple Wood is college preparatory, and almost 90 percent of its graduates attend either two-year or four-year colleges. The profile of Middle Brook is nearly identical to Maple Wood with respect to dropout rates, although fewer students (80 percent) enter college directly after high school. The situation is somewhat different at Del Vista, where 20 percent of the students drop out and only 50 percent enter college directly after high school.

At Maple Wood High School, helping students plan their high school careers is central to the school's mission. The school encourages students to take responsibility for managing their high school careers through their curricular choices. To help students do this, school personnel seek to make them aware of the skills and course prerequisites they will need to gain entry into advanced-level courses in subject areas of particular interest to them. Among the schools in the Sloan study, Maple Wood High had one of the highest percentages of students with aligned ambitions.

At Middle Brook High School, helping students gain admission to the most prestigious colleges for which they are qualified is the school's primary mission. The school's strategy for fulfilling this mission can be characterized as "reaching"—that is, encouraging all students to seek admission to colleges for which the odds of their acceptance are low. This focus increases the chances that students will overestimate the importance of education for their careers. Among schools in the Sloan study, Middle Brook High had the highest percentage of students who overestimated the amount of education they would need for their desired occupations.

The third school, Del Vista High School, can be described as "forgiving"—that is, it tries to make certain that all its students graduate from high school and are prepared at least to attend the local community college. Key strategies for accomplishing this mission are to offer a fairly uniform curriculum and to provide a variety of second chances for students with academic and social problems. Students in a forgiving high school are less likely to place a great deal of importance on the amount of education they will need, and among schools in the Sloan study Del Vista had the highest percentage of students who underestimated the amount of education needed for their desired occupations.

Among the three schools, Maple Wood had the highest proportion of students with aligned ambitions, at 44 percent, followed by Middle Brook, at 41 percent, and then Del Vista, at 32 percent (fig. 5.1). In all three schools, students with misaligned ambitions were more likely to overestimate rather than underestimate the amount of education needed for the jobs they desired. This was particularly the case at Middle Brook, where almost half the students overestimated—and less than 10 percent underestimated—the amount of education they would need. In contrast, almost 25 percent of the students at Del Vista High School

Fig. 5.1 Ambitions of Students in Three High Schools

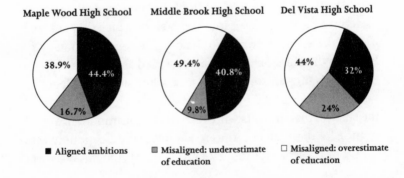

Maple Wood High School   Middle Brook High School   Del Vista High School

38.9%   44.4%   16.7%   49.4%   40.8%   9.8%   44%   32%   24%

■ Aligned ambitions   ▣ Misaligned: underestimate   ☐ Misaligned: overestimate
                            of education   of education

underestimated the amount of education they would need for their desired occupations.

Maple Wood High School: Encouraging Planfulness

Maple Wood High School celebrated its 125th anniversary in the spring of 1998. Once a small one-story building, the present school is a sprawling two-story complex that covers approximately four square city blocks. The high school is located in Maple Wood, an upper-middle-class suburb of a large midwestern city, graced with lush maple trees, picturesque single-family homes, and scattered stately apartment buildings. Maple Wood is situated along a suburban corridor running west of the city, a location that has made it an attractive living choice for its residents, many of whom hold white-collar jobs. Maple Wood is known as one of the few suburban areas of the city that is economically, racially, and ethnically diverse.[10]

The school system of Maple Wood has an exceptional reputation, and many residents cite its schools as an important reason for choosing to live here. Maple Wood High School has extensive facilities, programs, and human resources. The school has an impressive two-story library, three auditorium spaces, two swimming pools, an outdoor stadium, and a large indoor fieldhouse. The school is also the production site of a local student-run cable television show. Like most American high schools that are built in a T formation, the long green hallways are lined with row upon row of black tin student lockers that clang loudly when opened and then slammed shut. A balcony area near the main auditorium serves as a gallery for student artwork. With approximately three thousand students, Maple Wood is a large high school by American standards. The student population is 64 percent white, 28 percent African-American, 4 percent Asian, and 4 percent Hispanic. The racial and ethnic makeup of the school reflects the changing composition of the suburban community, which has attracted increasing numbers of African-Americans during the past decade. The average daily attendance rate is 96 percent, and the dropout rate is 5 percent, which is slightly lower than the national average.

A Maple Wood High School student of the 1950s would be overwhelmed by the sheer number of academic programs, clubs, and activities available in the 1990s. Maple Wood offers more than two hundred courses. Each student is required to take about twenty of them to graduate. Administrators, teachers, and counselors concur that there is a pervasive emphasis on academic subjects at Maple Wood. One counselor explained that many students take four years of English although only three are required, and "the vast majority of students take three to four years of math, even though the graduation requirement is only two." The curriculum of the school is organized into five clusters: mathematics, science, and technology; communications; historical, cultural, and global studies; fine and performing arts and applied arts; and physical education.

Courses within a given cluster are designated as regular, honors, and accelerated or advanced placement. Placement of students in courses is based on the student's preference, teachers' and counselors' recommendations, prior academic work in the subject, test results, study habits, motivation, and attendance record. Students can move among classes of different levels of difficulty with parental permission, and if recommended by a teacher or a counselor. According to the counseling staff, the final decision on course placement rests with the parent: "A student can be put into a class based on the fact that the parent wants her there. Let's say a student is in a regular-level course doing A and B work, and a parent says, 'You know, my child is really doing well, and she is barely working at it and I think she could do better, and I want her to have the opportunity.'" Although there is mobility among regular, honors, and accelerated classes within specific subjects and clusters, placement in an advanced-level course in one subject does not guarantee advanced placement in other subjects. Being in an honors mathematics and science course does not necessarily mean that a student will be placed in an honors English, history, or foreign-language class.

The curricular planning process at Maple Wood involves thinking about the long term. These plans are developed in consultation with the student, the student's parents, and the student's counselor—or, in the language of Maple Wood High School, the student's "dean." Parents are expected to participate in the course selection process, and every year a general catalog is sent home that lists all the subjects offered that year. In January, there is a major mailing that contains complete course registration information and a letter to the parents informing them of the date of registration—usually sometime in February—and inviting them to call the student's counselor for an individual appointment. Some parents who have had other children in the school are fairly familiar with the process and are knowledgeable about options. According to the counseling staff, other parents usually become actively involved in the planning process after they meet with a counselor.[11]

The emphasis placed on parents becoming actively involved in their adolescent's course selection is not merely rhetoric. We conducted several analyses concerning the frequency with which students discussed course selections and school experiences with their parents. Across the three high schools examined, Maple Wood students consistently reported spending more time with their parents discussing school course selections.[12]

Each student at Maple Wood High School is assigned to a dean at the beginning of freshman year, and the dean is responsible for that student until graduation. The longevity of this social tie increases the chances that strong bonds will form among the student, the student's parents, and the dean. Deans perceive their responsibilities to be broader than those of a traditional high school counselor. Explicit policies direct the dean to coun-

sel students and their parents about the student's educational, behavioral, and personal problems. In addition, the dean has specific responsibilities in the areas of student testing, college admission, vocational planning, and scholarships and financial aid.
Students may see the dean at any time during the school day, although they are encouraged to schedule interviews before or after school or during lunch and study hall periods.

Deans are full-time counselors and have a caseload of 225
students who are assigned alphabetically. Every dean, therefore,
has some students interested in attending four-year universities
as well as some who plan to attend two-year colleges. As one dean
explained, the school focuses on "the whole child. We have a
holistic approach and everything that happens for a student in
the course of his or her four years here happens through the
dean. We are responsible primarily, of course, for the academic
counseling, for the scheduling of the students, for maintaining
the transcript, and for making sure that kids take an appropriate
load, making sure they meet graduation requirements—that is,
making sure that the courses that kids take not only meet the minimum graduation requirements, but also meet the requirements
for admission to colleges, admission to state schools, wherever
kids and their families think that they want to go." Part of a dean's
job is learning from the students about their goals and then "getting them in the right course." "We use a four-year plan. We sit
down with freshmen and say 'let's try to think about a four-year
plan. It's not engraved in stone. It can change at a whim. But let's
try to do that.' For a lot of students it gives them some direction,
it gives them some focus."

A goal at Maple Wood is to match students' interests and
abilities with the proper individual courses. This is remarkably
similar to Conant's vision of how to reform the 1950s high
school by abolishing curricular tracks and encouraging the development of individualized programs so that students could, for
example, take a very demanding mathematics course and a so-

cial studies course of moderate difficulty. The highly differentiated curriculum at Maple Wood allows students to build a program that is tailored to their individual interests and talents.

Deans at Maple Wood encourage students early in their high school careers to consider what they would like to do after high school. This encouragement usually becomes more formalized during registration at the end of the sophomore year. By then most of the students have completed their mandatory courses. As one counselor explained, "It's at this point that we begin to talk about things like, 'Do you want another year of foreign language? Are you interested in another year of lab science? Let me tell you why another year of lab science would be good.'" Some students are unclear about why they should take certain courses, and deans consider it their responsibility to explain why taking certain courses or course sequences is important. "A student will say 'Why, I don't know, I really don't know if I want to take physics,'" and counselors typically respond, "But you know, whether or not you take physics now has to do with where you're going when you leave here." The guidance that deans give students is not prescriptive but is instead oriented toward helping them make decisions that do not lock them into specific areas of study or occupations. As one counselor noted, "We no longer talk a lot with students about what are you going to major in, because it's going to change. It's going to change a couple of times. So we instead talk about the kinds of skills that we think are going to be important."

The importance of developing a plan is linked to the sequential character of many academic progressions, which makes it necessary to take basic courses before more advanced courses. The counselors are sensitive to the sequential organization of subjects like mathematics and science and emphasize the importance of making strategic decisions about what courses to take and when to take them. Certain courses also provide better preparation for gaining admission to highly competitive colleges and universities. In a high school like Maple Wood selecting courses requires systematic planning.

Deans encourage students to take courses that will maximize their opportunities to take more advanced-level classes later. One dean explained that "students need to always be thinking about a variety of options. I don't know if a student should just kind of be going about it willy-nilly, because when you get to your junior and senior year there are certain obligations and prerequisites you have to have met to get to the next level, so students need a four-year plan." The school tries to guide students to take courses that provide them with the widest range of options, so that if they decide they would like to pursue a different path after high school graduation they can. This dean observed, "I think what they need to understand is that there are some basic kinds of choices you make that make a wide variety of options open to you."

Few students at Maple Wood are counseled to take jobs immediately after high school. But the counseling staff has begun to broaden its conceptions of postsecondary education to accommodate students who either are not "ready" for or are not interested in attending four-year colleges: "We started realizing that certain kids finish up here at Maple Wood, no matter how terrific the education has been, they're not ready to be productive adults. The community we live in just doesn't provide the kind of employment opportunities that would enable them to do that, we don't have any kind of housing stock [low-income housing] that would enable them to do that." As a result, the counseling program has adopted the philosophy of trying "to make the kids understand that this [high school] is just a stepping-stone. Now it doesn't have to be a four-year college, but it needs to be something. All of us, I think, feel very uncomfortable when we have those seniors who are sitting in front of us and they say to us, 'Well, we're just going to work' and they don't have a more specific plan. We worry that they're going to get lost, that they're going to fall through a crack somewhere and when they need assistance they're not going to know where to go." The counseling program is designed to assist all students at the end of high school to "begin to make some choices and begin to look at what their further opportunities are."

In addition to seeking individual advice from their deans, students can use the Career and College Center, which offers them the option of taking a variety of career and interest assessment tests several times during their high school careers. Video materials, career resource books, and periodicals on various careers are available to students who want information about specific occupations. Laser discs, on-line systems, college catalogs, and other college resource materials are also available to students who want information about particular colleges.

Maple Wood's goal is to help students develop a four-year plan that will allow them to take advantage of the rich curricular offerings of the school. At Maple Wood, a productive life "tends to get defined as graduation from a four-year college." It is not surprising, therefore, that the school's curriculum is almost entirely academic and that almost 90 percent of the graduates attend college, with 75 percent going to four-year colleges. These figures are above the national average, which is about 60 percent attending college and 40 percent attending four-year colleges.[13]

The complex curricular maze of Maple Wood High School can be difficult to navigate. The school uses its wide range of course offerings as a way to help students develop plans for high school and for the future. To make meaningful choices, students need to be informed about which courses to take and when to take them. It is the counselors' responsibility to help students develop a plan. This emphasis on planfulness helps to provide students with a sense of agency. It encourages them to become responsible for their high school education, their decisions, and their commitments.

While the school tries to encourage all students to develop

a four-year plan, special attention is given to two groups: those who are the first generation in their families to go to college and those who are applying to the most competitive institutions. "Here at Maple Wood, we still have an awfully large population of African-American kids who are first-generation college [goers]. We try to help them understand what college is about. I think students get this very stereotypical idea of colleges, you know, college dorms and going to the quad and football games and all of that." For the academically gifted students, the school tries to help them make reasonable college choices. "In September, most of us will make a point to see our seniors who are in the top 20 percent right off, because those are the kids who will be looking at the schools that have early admission. These are the kids who will be looking at the Ivy League, let's say, and so you need to get them started very early." The school does not wait too long before meeting with the rest of the senior class. "By the end of September every single senior will have been met with face-to-face. I do mine two at a time. I try to group it so that I get kids who are very close in terms of class rank and so on, so that when we talk about college choices, we're talking about the same ball game."

The curricular choices that are available to students in high school are a stimulus for the development of life plans. In making informed curricular choices, students begin to act upon those plans. Encouraging planfulness increases the chances that students will have aligned ambitions. No other high school in the Sloan study encouraged the kind of planning that was emphasized at Maple Wood.

Middle Brook High School: "Reaching for Something Better"

The winding road to Middle Brook High School leads to a collegelike campus, where four large buildings surround a grass quadrangle that is a focal point of student life. Students come and go and many congregate at favorite spots on the grounds of the

"quad." A school with a long academic tradition, Middle Brook
was founded almost two hundred years ago and moved to its
present location in the 1940s. The brick buildings have a classi-
cal appearance and the grounds are well maintained, giving the
school the feel of a small college campus.

With more than seventeen hundred students, Middle Brook
is about an average-sized American suburban high school.[14] The
student body, however, is ethnically and racially diverse. Almost
one in three students belongs to an ethnic or racial minority, and
over a third speak a language other than English at home; Rus-
sian is the most commonly spoken second language. Students
come from more than sixty different countries and speak over
thirty-five different languages. About a quarter of the students
receive instruction in English as a second language and 20 percent receive services for learning disabilities. While ethnically
and culturally diverse, the students of Middle Brook High School
come from relatively affluent families. The average household
income is slightly more than $60,000, and more than three-
quarters of the students' parents are college graduates. Middle
Brook High School is located in a northeastern suburban community that borders a large city. During the past five years there
has been an influx of educated immigrants, many of whom are
employed in white-collar jobs.

The primary focus of Middle Brook High School is to prepare students for admission to competitive colleges. The high
school encourages them to apply to a range of schools, including prestigious colleges for which they may not be strong applicants. This strategy of reaching for something better is part of
the counseling philosophy at Middle Brook High. The curriculum also reflects this "reach strategy." There is no vocational track
at Middle Brook. All students are in the academic program, and
the school offers a demanding and diverse college preparatory
curriculum.

Almost all colleges and universities require applicants to

take college entrance examinations in verbal and mathematics skills (ACT or SAT I). Most of the schools with highly competitive admissions criteria also strongly encourage or require students to take at least three of the SAT II or ACT subject examinations in specific academic subjects. In addition, there are advanced placement (AP) examinations for students who want to earn college credit and be placed in advanced courses in college.

This complex college entrance examination structure is reflected in the course offerings at Middle Brook High School. AP courses are offered in ten subjects: French, Spanish, Latin, biology, chemistry, physics, mathematics, American history, European history, and American and comparative government and politics. The AP courses are the most demanding academic courses and are taken by students who aspire to take the AP examinations and improve the competitiveness of their high school transcript for college admissions. Each year about 130 students from Middle Brook High School take AP examinations.[15]

The honors courses are not as demanding as the AP courses. They prepare students to take the SAT II subject examinations. Students from Middle Brook High School registered for more than 860 SAT II subject examinations in 1995. In addition to AP and honors courses, there are standard courses in mathematics, the sciences, social sciences, and foreign languages that meet high school graduation and general college admission requirements. Over 360 different courses are offered, including almost 60 mathematics and science courses and almost 50 English courses. The school offers 46 language courses in five different languages (French, German, Spanish, Chinese, and Latin). More than 40 career and vocational courses are also offered, but as individual subjects, not as an organized line of the curriculum. These courses include accounting, business practice, word processing, marketing, early childhood development, restaurant management, culinary arts, and food service. Compared with Maple Wood and the other schools in the Sloan study, Middle Brook has the most extensive and differentiated course offerings in academic subjects.[16] These courses are primarily at the advanced level, and students are encouraged to take them by their parents and teachers. Students find this emphasis on academic rigor stressful and frequently question their academic capabilities.

While AP and honors courses are more academically demanding than standard courses, Middle Brook High School does not give them extra weight in calculating grade point averages. In selecting courses, students carefully weigh the benefits and liabilities of taking these more demanding courses. In contrast to Maple Wood, the emphasis is on building a portfolio of courses for college admission rather than on selecting those that further the student's long-range goals and interests.

Counselors at Middle Brook typically provide students with strategies for applying to college. They encourage the students to apply to three types of schools: safety schools, one or two colleges where the student is certain to be admitted; competitive schools, those that seem to offer a good chance of admitting them; and reach schools, at which their chances appear to be low. The emphasis on applying to reach schools makes Middle Brook different from many other high schools. The psychological costs of applying to a reach school are minimal in the sense that the student knows that gaining admission is not likely and that the safety school is almost certain to be available if needed. However, failure to be accepted by a reach school is attributed to the shortcomings of the student; after all, if the student were a better applicant, he or she might have gotten in. Encouraging students to apply to a reach school provides the counselor with a protective buffer against parents' complaints that their child is not going to a more prestigious college.

Making themselves desirable college applicants is a preoccupation of Middle Brook students. They spend considerable time managing their academic transcripts, making decisions about what subjects to take, at which level of difficulty, and with which teachers. But some counselors believe that the emphasis on admission to four-year colleges and universities does not serve all students well. As one counselor explained, "I see kids in here that could not handle college. What is concerning some of us is the kids get into schools or get into places and then can't handle it. And maybe they were a little misled because it is such the norm of this school that they all have to go to college. So that's a bit of a concern that I have, that they don't access some of the junior colleges, community colleges, or training programs because it's such a thing about going to [a four-year] college."

The school spends extensive time and effort helping students prepare for the transition to college. The school distributes a handbook called "Choice, Not Chance" that outlines who gets into college and why, a timeline for applying to college, ways to pay for it, how to prepare for interviews, and how to solicit letters of recommendation. At the very end of this booklet is a single page on choosing an occupation. The push at Middle Brook High School to send almost all its students to college fuels their ambitions and may lead some to overestimate their abilities. As one counselor said, "I think that the kids are so into a head set that the only way to succeed is college that they're unrealistic about their own abilities. I think that they will have the hardest time. There are kids that are too unrealistic and then would fall flat without marshaling their resources to think something out."

The success of Middle Brook in placing its students in four-year institutions has led to another concern—whether the students are prepared to do well in college once they are admitted. "I spent four years not only preparing students for college but preparing for them to graduate from college, and there's a difference in the preparation. We do send almost 85 percent of our population to four-year colleges. What we found out a couple of years ago, and which I think a lot of people knew already, was that less than 50 percent were graduating within the four-year period. What does that say about Middle Brook's preparation? Ninety percent of you can get into college. It's staying there. I guess it has a lot to do with contributing to the development of young people's self-awareness and self-appreciation and self-protection as well as self-promotion."

Actually developing these self-sufficient qualities, how-ever, is seen as difficult for students in an intimate school envi-ronment that fosters not only strong ties with teachers but also some dependency. "We do a lot around here. It's a curriculum-based high school and that's a pretty hard-core experience. But the fact is, the school system K through 8 is very touchy-feely, very loving, very caring, very supportive. Pretty much doing a lot more for an individual than probably they should in terms of an individual's sense of independence, so when they come up here we want them to acquire that independence. But the fact is, if the kid's in trouble everybody's coming out to help 'em, you know. . . . But we've got to do it in a way that also teaches them how to do it for themselves. I think that is probably one of the greatest obstacles."

The high school expends considerable resources for coun-seling. There is a department of pupil support services that boasts a staff of thirty-one, including guidance counselors, school psy-chologists, social workers, substance abuse preventionists, career center advisers, tutoring center coordinators, health office nurses, and a special educational programs coordinator. The ra-tio of support staff to students is 1 to 57. Despite the tremendous resources allocated for students' personal well-being, the under-lying efforts of counselors are directed at helping students fur-ther their education. This is not done overtly, and in fact, no counselors admitted that they were directing their students to-ward college. All stated that they merely "provided the resources and the student would have to pursue" them. "I believe the choices should be the students' and theirs alone and how they arrive there is based on all the adults in their lives and their friends and family. . . . [H]opefully, they will make their own decisions. I will try to present different options, which they can choose from, but . . . I don't think it's our place to . . . discourage or encourage [students] in a certain area or profession."

The belief that students should make their own decisions is supported by the sheer volume of resources that are directed toward helping them make college choices. The course schedule devotes six pages to describing what high school classes are needed to meet college entrance requirements. There are two full-time career counselors employed strictly to guide students into the "right" colleges—that is, the most academically competitive ones. The Career Center is staffed by several parent volunteers who show students how to get information about colleges on the computers and find financial aid information, and it also distributes college handbooks. The Career Center's primary function is to provide students with college information; information on job placement following high school graduation is practically nonexistent.

Counselors provide support and guidance to students through the college application process. Individual sessions with career counselors are such a popular service that it often takes a week to get an appointment. These appointments are made during lunch and before or after school so that students' classes are not interrupted. Constant contact with college recruiters is maintained by the counselors, who keep abreast of the requirements at local four-year and two-year colleges. They also devote considerable time to writing college letters of recommendation. One counselor remarked, "That's what I do with all my free time for two months." Significant time is also given to helping students prepare their personal statements. Frequently, counselors attend conferences conducted by the local colleges and keep in close contact with their admissions counselors. Different college admission counselors are also invited to the high school twice a year and allowed to conduct interviews with interested students. Students are allowed to spend unlimited time with the admission counselors and to visit with as many as they like.

Counselors are usually not willing to put pressure on schools to accept students, in part because they have long-standing relationships with the admissions offices of many colleges and universities that are built around respecting their right to make admissions decisions. In some circumstances, counselors are willing to bring information about borderline candidates to the attention of the college admission officer. Counselors at Middle Brook were more likely to do this than those at any other school in the Sloan study.

Middle Brook and Maple Wood high schools share some characteristics. Both have highly differentiated curricula, offering students many courses to choose from, and both encourage large numbers of their students to go to college. The schools differ, however, in the preparation they offer students. Maple Wood uses its curricular offerings as a way to encourage students to develop a plan for their time in high school and to link it to their plans for afterward. Middle Brook's overriding concern is to get the students ready for college admission. Having students reach for schools that are not likely to admit them can heighten their anxiety about college admission and lower their self-esteem. This philosophy fails to get students to think beyond getting into the "right college," even though that college may not complement their interests and talents.

Del Vista High School: A Forgiving High School

Architecturally, Del Vista High School looks like the typical West Coast high school often seen on evening television shows. Built in 1955, the school is a combination of one-story and two-story buildings surrounding two quadrangles. Like many West Coast high schools, the main quadrangle contains a large oak tree sur-

rounded by benches and a lawn. The school grounds include athletic playing fields with several tennis courts and a baseball dia-
mond. Del Vista High School is located in Del Vista, a large coastal
city with a population of almost a half million. The population
is almost 60 percent Caucasian, 24 percent Hispanic, and about
15 percent African-American, with a small percentage of other
races. Like many West Coast areas, housing is expensive. The median value of a home in Del Vista is over $200,000, and rents are
also expensive. The students are drawn from many communities:
the majority of them are bused from other parts of the city and
the remainder live in the middle-class neighborhoods surrounding the school. Del Vista High is a large urban school with
about thirty-six hundred students. A third of the students are not
native speakers of English, and most of them take part in the
school's programs in English as a second language.

While some high schools, like Maple Wood and Middle
Brook, have developed a highly differentiated course curriculum, others like Del Vista have eliminated curricular tracks and
developed a uniform curriculum. At Del Vista, the emphasis is
on providing all students with the same education and not separating them on the basis of performance. A phrase commonly
used by the staff of Del Vista High School is that "every student
succeeds." This view is reflected in the mission statement of the
school: "The mission of Del Vista High School is to provide all
students with an exciting, energetic learning environment that
encourages academic excellence and the development of personal qualities and skills necessary for success in life."

This emphasis on equal access to learning for all students
limits the amount of curricular differentiation and fights against
an emphasis on certain courses being more difficult or demanding than others. Del Vista considers itself a "detracked high
school," because there is one curriculum for all students. Students are not separated into one curriculum for those who will
go to work and another for those who will go to college. The fo-

cus is on creating a high minimum standard for all students. At Del Vista this standard is preparing the students to attend community college. This is how the mission of Del Vista—that "every child succeeds"—has been interpreted.

The curriculum at Del Vista High School is not as complex or rich as those at Maple Wood or Middle Brook high schools. There are not as many courses or topics for students to choose from and there are very few distinctions made in the difficulty of the courses. Del Vista does not offer extensive honors or advanced-placement classes. All students who take chemistry take a course that is similar in the material covered and in its academic demands. The simplicity of the curriculum narrows the arena in which students can make choices and lessens the need for them to think strategically about their high school careers. Del Vista High School does not advocate the kind of planning that was evident at Maple Wood High or the reach strategy that characterized Middle Brook.

Because Del Vista High School wants everyone to succeed and has organized its curriculum to try to assure that every student reaches a minimal academic standard, we describe it as a forgiving high school. Del Vista focuses its attention on keeping school attendance high and sending large numbers of students to community college. The school spends significant resources on achieving both of these goals and has some success in its efforts.

To keep students from dropping out, Del Vista has developed several programs. One is the early identification of students who are not making satisfactory progress toward their high school degree. Counselors examine the grade transcripts of all ninth-grade students to see if any are deficient in credits needed for graduation. By identifying credit deficiencies before the tenth grade, counselors believe they can show students how to make up their missing credits so they will be more likely to stay in school and graduate. A second strategy is an academic program for pregnant students who do not wish to leave Del Vista to attend an alternative high school with a "watered-down" curriculum. These students attend regular classes and the counselors provide tutoring, special workshops in parenting skills, and substantial support and encouragement.

Even with these programs, students drop out, and Del Vista has created a series of second-chance opportunities—including a night school—to coax them back to school. Enrollment in the night school is quite large, and in recent years its graduating class has been greater than 500 (around 750 graduate from the day high school). Graduates from the night program receive a high school diploma and have a formal graduation ceremony complete with robes, tassels, and celebrity speakers.

While Del Vista High School pushes to keep students in school, its major focus is encouraging all students to attend college. The staff spends a great deal of time making certain that students have the necessary coursework to be able to attend college. They also put an extra effort into managing the expectations of parents who pressure their children to achieve good grades and to enroll in the best colleges. Some of the counselors estimate that they spend half of their time "helping parents develop parenting skills and forming realistic expectations of their children."

Managing expectations is particularly difficult in a high school with a narrow curriculum. With fewer curricular choices, students are not pushed to develop plans for what they want to study and why. Their occupational ambitions are not linked to the curricular choices they face in high school. This can foster misaligned ambitions and require greater work by school staff to manage students' ambitions. Counselors often express concern over unrealistic occupational goals. "If you know all the student's test scores and the student is getting Ds and barely scraping by and they want to be a doctor, you can subtly try to lead

them into maybe thinking about becoming a radiation techni-
cian or a licensed vocational nurse or maybe something you
think they really could be successful at." A factor that contributes
to unrealistic occupational ambitions is the caseload of counselors. There is one counselor for every 550 students—more
than twice the number at Maple Wood High School—so there is
limited time to give the personal attention needed by many students.

To help build their ties with students, the school assigns
counselors to work with a group from ninth grade through graduation. The counselors hold a college information night for parents and students in their junior year. Counselors see themselves
as having an integral role in the application process. They write
the letters of recommendation, a task they say is "extremely time
consuming." These are not form letters. One counselor noted
that in each letter he tries to show something unique about the
student that demonstrates maturity and particular strengths. The
counselors also give special instructions on how to write the college essay. More important, they feel compelled to appeal when
students do not get into the college of their choice. Counselors
admit that they are rarely successful in appealing cases within the
state system of colleges and universities, but, as one observed,
"for those few that you really are willing to fight for, I think it's
worth it."

Del Vista is successful in helping its students be admitted to
college, and the majority of its graduates go on to local community colleges. These community colleges are attractive to students
because of their low cost and their flexible class schedules. Public community colleges are one of the least expensive ways to begin college work, and their schedules are designed to fit those of
working students. In an effort to attract better-prepared students,
local community colleges are offering a "scholarship"—what
the high school counselors refer to as a "signing bonus"—to any

student from the high school with a 3.5 grade point average or higher. Students who receive these scholarships are not required to stay in college or to continue after the first semester.

The community college system is seen by students as providing valuable flexibility. Students who receive low grades or do not like the requirements of one college can simply transfer to another community college in the area. As one counselor explained, "What I've heard from my students is that they all go to Del Vista City College and if they're not successful, they'll drop. They may be on probation for a year and if they don't make it they'll drop that school and go on to the next junior college and try again, and on to another as long as their parents support them."

Because the high school values graduation and college enrollment, programmatic requirements have been developed to direct the work of counselors in these two areas. There are clear graduation requirements and the process for meeting them is routine. Transitions from high school to work, however, are not handled in any systematic way. According to counselors, a potential employer will occasionally call the high school and ask about a student's attendance record, but not grades. Unlike colleges, employers rarely ask for letters of recommendation and are not concerned about students' academic performance. Counselors talked about wanting information from employers, saying that it would be useful if they would contact the school and discuss what they are looking for in their employees.

Employers do contact the school about available job openings. The school places the job descriptions on a bulletin board and the students can copy the information and follow up on it themselves. The school does not offer "practice interviews" or other assistance with the job-hunting process. Instead it offers career classes. Students in these classes take career preference tests; instructors interpret the results and provide them with information about different career paths. The purpose of these classes, according to instructors, is to expand students' career knowledge rather than to prepare them for specific careers.

The overriding focus of counseling at Del Vista is on preparing students for the transition to college—for nearly all the students, to a two-year college. This push to attend community college is pervasive throughout the school, and even teachers in technical and vocational courses encourage their students to attend community college for additional training.

High schools can influence the ambitions of their students through their messages about what is important and what students need to do. Schools can narrow or widen the curricular choices available. They can provide extensive information about going to college and little about going to work. They can focus on the importance of selecting the right high school courses for applying to college. What schools choose to emphasize influences students' goals and the ways in which they try to realize them.

Schools, like Maple Wood, that have a rich and diverse curriculum and define their mission as helping to guide students through this curricular maze are more likely to have students with aligned ambitions. Such schools emphasize the importance of having students plan for what they want to do in the future and selecting courses that will help them acquire needed knowledge and skills. Schools that do not stress planning, regardless of the complexity of their curricular maze, are more likely to have students with misaligned ambitions.

The American high school has undergone significant changes during the past four decades. Most important, the curriculum has been transformed, with an increase in the number of academic courses and a decline in vocational training. As more and more students go to college, high schools have become college preparatory schools for almost all students. The challenge for students is to select high school courses that will prepare them for the college of their choice. The curriculum of the American high school has become more like Conant's vision of what the high school should be. What is often lacking, however, is an effort to help students chart a meaningful path through the curricular maze of high school.

chapter six

Families and the Shaping
of Aligned Ambitions

oday's parents share their adolescents' high ambitions. Most expect that their children will graduate from college and become successful as adults. National studies in the 1990s show that most parents of high school seniors expect them to earn undergraduate or advanced degrees. Similar to the dramatic rise in students' educational expectations over the past twenty years, parents' expectations for their teenagers have also risen significantly.[1] In 1972, 55 percent of high school seniors reported that their parents expected them to graduate from college or earn professional or advanced degrees. The percentage of students in 1982 who said their parents had the same expectation had barely changed. By 1992, however, 76 percent of seniors reported that their parents expected them to earn a college degree or more.[2]

Although many parents have high educational expectations for their children, they often fail to draw meaningful connections between these expectations and future work opportunities. Teenagers whose parents help them understand these connections are more likely to have aligned ambitions. By helping their teenagers strategically organize and manage their lives around educational and occupational opportunities parents also motivate them to reach their ambitions. In this chapter we describe how parents shape adolescents' ambitions.

Support and Challenge in Families

Teenagers not only share their parents' educational expectations for them, they also perceive their parents in a more positive light than the literature on adolescence suggests. The media and many researchers who study family dynamics often portray conflict between adolescents and their parents, describing teenagers as feeling emotional distance from them. Such conclusions are consistent with a description of adolescence as a period of "storm and stress" in which young people are actively seeking to develop an independent identity for themselves. In contrast, the interviews and survey responses of the Sloan adolescents point to a period of some conflict and identity formation, but one not as turbulent as others have depicted. Adolescents said there were times of "not getting along with my mother or father," often mentioning conflicts with their parents "over curfew hours," "friends I hang around with," and "doing better in school." But there were few who felt things were so bad at home that they needed to leave or seek someone to talk to about it. There were instances of parental alcohol, drug, and physical abuse in the home, but these were very limited. For the most part, adolescents describe their parents as supportive, loving, and accepting of them. Over half the Sloan adolescents view their families as cooperative and willing to help when needed.[3]

Recognizing that teenagers generally have positive feelings about their parents, and their parents reciprocate, we suspected that the formation of aligned ambitions is influenced by the daily interactions adolescents have with their parents. By studying these interactions, we expected to learn what values parents have and what actions they take that can enhance the development of aligned ambitions. The Sloan study asked adolescents a series of open-ended questions about the quality of their relationships with parents, including what types of activities they enjoy together, how they feel when they are with their parents, and which family activities they wished they did not have to do. A few activities described as enjoyable were eating together, talking about their days, and making plans for college. Some of the family activities students did not enjoy included visiting relatives and doing chores. The adolescents were also asked to measure their agreement with the values and actions of their families concerning such issues as family conflict ("in the home there are lots of arguments"), emotional attachment ("how close I feel to my parents"), expectations ("my parents expect me to do my best or my parents are disappointed in me"), and self-reliance ("my parents give me a lot of independence"). The Sloan study used these adolescent responses to create scales that measure the extent to which young people perceive their parents in two dimensions of family life: as supportive, and as creating challenges for them. These scales show how easy or difficult adolescents find it to agree with statements about the quality of their relations with their parents.[4]

Most adolescents feel that their parents love and accept them, and most describe their families as cooperative and willing to help one another (fig. 6.1). Nearly half feel appreciated for who they are and perceive their parents as emotionally supportive. While most consider their parents loving and accepting, however, only a third said that they receive special attention and help when they have a problem. For most adolescents, problem situations are seen as the times when parents are least likely to intervene and offer assistance.

Overall, high levels of parental support can help adolescents feel positive about themselves, and parents can encourage high educational expectations. Among students who report that their parents are highly supportive, more than 88 percent expect to earn a college, professional, or advanced degree. Although high parent support encourages educational ambitions, it does not appear to help adolescents form aligned ambitions.[5] We suspect that this is because our measure of support is a general indicator of adolescents' emotional attachment to their families. It

Fig. 6.1 *Adolescent Perceptions of Parental Support*

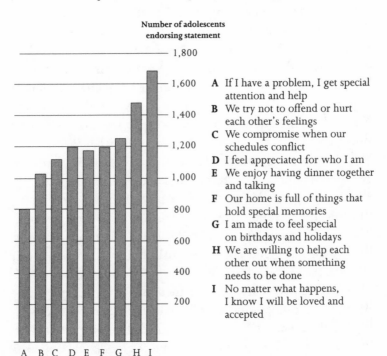

Number of adolescents endorsing statement

A If I have a problem, I get special attention and help
B We try not to offend or hurt each other's feelings
C We compromise when our schedules conflict
D I feel appreciated for who I am
E We enjoy having dinner together and talking
F Our home is full of things that hold special memories
G I am made to feel special on birthdays and holidays
H We are willing to help each other out when something needs to be done
I No matter what happens, I know I will be loved and accepted

Data from Sloan study, base-year tenth and twelfth graders (*n*=2,424)

does not isolate actions parents can take that are more likely to help form aligned ambitions.

The challenge scale describes actions that families take to help adolescents develop skills and capacities. Compared with the support items, the challenge measures are more instrumental and require specific actions by parents. They also include a set of questions that focus on parental expectations for their adolescents and others in the family. The challenge scale includes a series of items about how parents help their children prepare for adulthood, such as the parents' expectation of their child to do his or her best, to use time wisely, to work hard, and to be self-confident and independent.

Almost two-thirds of the adolescents agree that their parents expect them to do their best. Yet only a third agree that their families hold others to high expectations. In some families there is a sliding scale, and what is acceptable performance varies for different siblings. Adolescents find it a problem when they are expected to do their best but brothers and sisters are not held to the same standard. Of course, not everyone in the same family will have the same talents and skills, but holding everyone to high standards appears to characterize the most challenging families. Students who describe their parents as highly challenging, like those who report their parents high in support, are more likely to have high educational expectations. More than 89 percent of those expecting to earn at least a college degree report their parents high on the challenge scale (fig. 6.2). The challenge scale, unlike the support scale, is related to alignment: students who had aligned ambitions were more likely to consider their parents high on challenge than those who underestimated the amount of education needed for their expected job.[6]

Overall, the challenge scale describes values, attitudes, and actions that can promote self-reliance in adolescents. The various dimensions of the challenge scale describe behaviors consistent with those exhibited by young people with aligned ambitions, such as being purposeful, managing time, working hard, and pursuing their own aims. While some adolescents may perceive their parents as reinforcing skills that lead to adultlike behaviors, the parents themselves may not do all they can to help adolescents plan for the future. Some parents may believe that instilling the right "adultlike" norms and behaviors in their children is all the help they need to find a realistic path toward adulthood. Such parents thus place the major responsibility for planning for the future on the teenager or the high school.

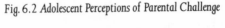

Fig. 6.2 *Adolescent Perceptions of Parental Challenge*

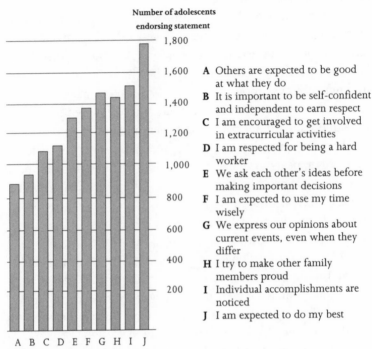

Data from Sloan study, base-year tenth and twelfth graders (*n* = 2,424)

Parents who take strategic actions regarding their adolescents' problems are more likely to influence how they organize and manage their lives. One type of strategic action parents can take is to create opportunities for adolescents to engage in life planning that can affect their views of the future. An example is Elizabeth Houghton, whose father spent considerable time with her discussing the importance of attending a college with a quality program in the fields that interest her. Close family ties and frequent communication are characteristic of families that researchers have described as rich in social capital.

Social Capital and the Formation of Aligned Ambitions

What parents consider important for an adolescent to do—
whether it is getting good grades, taking challenging courses, or
applying to a competitive college—builds an orientation toward
the future. In families where these messages are clearly and consistently communicated through family discussions and parental
actions, adolescents are more likely to share their parents' sense
of what is important—how they should spend their time alone,
at school, and with friends. Strong relationships among family
members form a source of social capital that the adolescent can
draw upon in planning for the future.

Social capital's function as a family resource was first artic-
ulated by James S. Coleman. To become successful adults, Coleman argued, adolescents need to be part of families with strong
relationship ties between parents and themselves. Critical information and values can be channeled from the parents through
these ties, and it is easier to communicate norms, standards, and
expectations. Such ties are a form of social capital in much the
same way that education is a form of human capital. Unlike human capital, however, which is a property of an individual, social capital is a property of a collectivity, such as the family. Social capital relies on collective assets, shared norms among all
family members that are linked to positive outcomes.[7]

It is not simply communication that Coleman perceives as
meaningful, but also what norms are conveyed to adolescents.
We argue that these norms and specific parental actions influence the development of an adolescent's ambitions. Parents need
to do more than communicate to their teenagers the importance
of a college education. They have to take action: accompany adolescents on college visits, arrange for financial assistance, assist
in judging the program of a college and whether it is the right
one for them.

The role of parents in helping adolescents plan for their futures now appears to be more critical. Parents who are willing to

discuss their adolescents' future and how to achieve their personal goals are perhaps more important because other institutions, such as the school, are sometimes ill equipped to do it. High schools seldom allocate sufficient resources to meet the counseling needs of every teenager. They often have too little time to provide an adolescent with more than basic information about which college to attend. As we have seen, high school counselors have a minimal role in helping students decide where to apply to college. For students who choose to work full time after graduation, high schools provide minor career placement services, as most orient their students toward college and have weak ties to the labor force. This lack of intervention by the high school about choosing a college and gaining employment shifts more responsibility to parents to take a stronger role in helping their teenagers make informed choices about their futures.

Our interest in the relation between ambitions and parent involvement flows from several factors. First, while we recognize that supportive and challenging relationships in families are important for encouraging expectations, they do not focus on actions that can be helpful to adolescents. Second, although parents' education and resources affect their children's educational attainment, it is the family's social capital, the strong social ties within the family, that can be a resource for students with aligned ambitions. Prior research on families has shown the importance of such familial ties for improving academic performance.[8]

We began by investigating the relation between alignment and social processes, examining the frequency with which parents discuss schooling and future plans with their adolescents. We looked at the number of times adolescents reported discussing topics studied in class and their grades with their parents. With respect to the future, we looked at how often adolescents reported discussing with their parents preparation for the SAT and ACT, going to college, and their career plans.

We suspected that teenagers with parents who discussed

their futures with them and took actions that would help them plan for life after high school would be more likely aspire to earn professional and advanced degrees. The routes for earning these degrees are long and highly competitive. To successfully earn such a degree requires extensive social and financial resources on the part of parents and their adolescents. We assumed that adolescents with aligned ambitions and the highest educational expectations would be more likely to have parents who engage in planning activities.

Using data from the Sloan study, we divided the sample into four groups: those who planned only to graduate from high school, those who planned to graduate from college, those who planned to earn a master's degree, and those who expected to obtain a professional or advanced degree. Among these four groups, teenagers with aligned ambitions who expected to obtain a professional or advanced degree were more likely to discuss school and future plans with their parents than misaligned students with similar educational expectations. This association is similar across all five of the questions examined, with the greatest differences between the aligned and misaligned groups occurring in the frequency with which they said they often discussed a particular topic with their parents: most adolescents with aligned ambitions report that they often discuss things studied in class with their parents. There is also a large difference between the aligned and misaligned groups in the proportion who never discuss these topics with their parents: adolescents with misaligned ambitions are only half as likely to ever discuss what they studied in class with their parents. Students with aligned ambitions are nearly 25 percent more likely to often discuss their grades with their parents than are adolescents with misaligned ambitions (fig. 6.3).[9]

The differences in the frequency of parent-student discussions regarding going to college are the smallest among the five items. This result is not unexpected, given the high levels of ed-

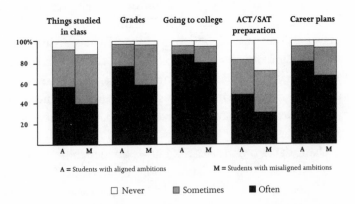

Fig. 6.3 Discussions Between Parents and Teenagers

ucational expectations. The findings on ACT and SAT preparation and career plans, however, are more marked between the two groups. Students with aligned ambitions were nearly twice as likely to often discuss SAT and ACT preparation than were those with misaligned ambitions. Similarly, the greatest difference between the two groups occurs in the "often" category on future careers: adolescents with aligned ambitions were much more likely to often discuss career preparation with their parents.

These results suggest that adolescents with aligned ambitions who aspire to professional and advanced degrees spend a significant amount of time with their parents discussing actions and strategies to help them reach their ambitions. Similar findings were also found in the open-ended interviews with students and their parents. In families where young people have aligned ambitions, there is strong interest in what happens in their courses and how well they do in school. Discussions about preparations for college entrance examinations, career plans, and the connections between schooling and work are also more likely to occur in these families.

To deepen our understanding of what occurs in families

whose young people have aligned ambitions we turned to our qualitative data. We purposely selected three cases, an adolescent with aligned ambitions and two with misaligned ambitions. In constructing these cases we used the survey data as well as the student and parent interviews. Our focus was the relationships of these three adolescents with their parents and the family processes that assist or impede the development of ambitions.[10]

Aligned for College

Nina Kruell attends a public high school with small honors classes, which she has taken since ninth grade. Nina lives with her mother, father, and brother, Peter, who is five years younger. Peter attends a special experimental program at a nearby public elementary school for gifted students, the same one that Nina attended. Describing how her family is different from those of her friends, Nina exclaims, "Well, I have two parents, and that is I guess kind of odd. And they do not yell at each other, which I guess is odd, too. We talk, and I guess a lot of people do not talk in their families." Conversations at mealtimes are often about what Nina and Peter study in school, activities they are involved in, and future tests or quizzes. Nina does very well in school. According to her mother, "Nina has her stuff done. It's done well. It's turned in. She gets As. Her teachers praise her, you know. She works very hard. On report cards we get little notes that say, 'Nina is enjoying the classroom and she shares information.' That is nice in high school to get little things like that."

Nina's mother operates a day care facility, and her father is an aerospace engineer. Both attended college, but neither graduated. Her mother went to a junior college for two years and then transferred to law school. Mrs. Kruell explains that this pattern was possible at one time: "If you had enough credits without having completed an undergraduate degree, you could transfer over." Her experiences at law school were not rewarding, and she left before obtaining her degree. Her job now, however, as the owner of a day care facility, is something she finds very emotionally satisfying.

Since Nina was a child she has been interested in becoming a veterinarian. Dogs, cats, and birds have been part of the Kruell family for some time. When she was in elementary school, Nina's parents would let her accompany them to the veterinarian and explain the work done there. In ninth grade she volunteered one day a week at a veterinary hospital. "They let me see the surgeries and everything. They explained what they were doing, how they did it, and what it meant. It was really interesting to me." In addition to her early experiences with household pets and the veterinary hospital, Nina has read many books on medicine.

Currently she is working in a veterinarian's office as a "nurse." Her responsibilities include filling out animals' history forms, "giving vaccinations, taking temperatures and weights, and writing down symptoms. I basically get the history for the doctor. I can also do suture removals. And I hold the animals, sometimes during surgery." She also works in the front office, but does not do "the tech work."

When Nina started her job, she had limited responsibilities and was basically relegated to the back of the hospital, cleaning cages. "I was the kennel girl. But after two weeks I was promoted to front desk and nurse status and they taught me how to do everything. I did not like cleaning cages." Over the next several months Nina was given additional responsibilities, and she admits that her job can be stressful. "If you have six or seven clients standing there waiting to take their dog back, waiting for a bill, waiting for a dog—that can be the worst." The only other aspect of the job that troubles Nina is making life and death decisions: "What really bothers me is putting them down, which I have done. Euthanasia, that's the other thing that I do not like about my job. We did one yesterday, an eighteen-year-old dog who would never have survived the surgery."

Nina works nineteen or twenty hours a week—two hours after school every day and nine to ten hours on Saturdays. She finds the most satisfying and enjoyable part of her job to be "learning a lot about what I want to do. I am learning all kinds of interesting diseases and common ulcers, you know, everything—stones and everything that I never knew anything about. Then I can ask myself, 'Do I really want to get into this field?'" Answering her own question, she confirms her interest, commitment, and confidence in her ability to succeed. In the future, Nina would like a practice treating large animals, like horses. She envisions that this work would be a little different, "because I will go to my patients, they will not come to me. But I probably will start out in a small-animal practice." Her early exposure to a career with work responsibilities directly tied to adult roles has helped Nina to visualize herself as a practicing veterinarian.

In addition to her job, Nina is extremely busy, taking all advanced-level classes, playing the lead in the school play, and taking a small part in her church's Christmas play. Even though she enjoys theater immensely and is taking a drama class this semester, she sees her involvement ending this year. "I do not think you can really get a master's degree in preveterinary medicine and a minor in dramatics. I have to keep in the same field." Focus and determination are very much a part of how Nina organizes and manages her time and energy. Her goal for her senior year "is to graduate with straight As" even though the classes are "much harder than in my junior year. Anatomy is a lot of memorization. AP English is a lot of critical thinking, a lot of reading outside of class. AP government, a lot of stuff outside of class, a lot of homework, a lot of research papers every week. Trigonometry, last year, I dropped that class really quickly because I was failing and now I'm doing it again and getting an A." Nina puts considerable effort into her schoolwork and sometimes considers it something like play. "I am having fun. I am really enjoying doing what I am doing, but it is definitely work and I am putting a lot of effort in it. That's what you need to do in school."

At the end of her junior year Nina had nearly enough credits to graduate. Mrs. Kruell believed that it would be in Nina's interests to graduate early: "High school bored her. She wanted to go to the university at the end of her junior year. I went over to talk to her counselors and the vice principal at the high school to see if I could get her to graduate at the end of her junior year. If she took two summer classes, she could do that. I mean that is how close she was." Despite this intervention, the school did not allow early graduation. "The school would not let her because it is policy. I was disappointed. Nina really wanted to get out and she was unable to. So we have compromised. She can start taking classes at the city college, where they have state-university-approved classes. The classes Nina is planning to take can transfer to the state university system." Mrs. Kruell feels her daughter is frustrated in high school. "She really wants to get started and does not see high school as getting her started. Nina just sees it as pushing through the mud and trying to get to her goal. Then she can get to this exciting thing she wants to do."

Nina wants most of all to attend college, and she is actively seeking one with a quality veterinary program. She has been investigating veterinary schools throughout her senior year and has contacted twenty-seven of them. She plans to apply to a highly competitive private college on the West Coast, several state schools, and one university that has an early-admission veterinary program. The university accepts only fifteen students, "so it is not likely I'll be there. But there is always a chance." Nina tries to keep her dream school "down low on my priorities because it is not for sure that it will ever happen. I really like the programs at the other smaller schools. Our state system is very expensive and much harder to start out in." She distinguishes between liberal arts colleges that offer only bachelor's degrees and research universities that grant a doctoral degree; if necessary, she plans to attend a liberal arts college and then continue in a university that awards a doctorate.

Nina expects that she will succeed in her goal of being accepted to an early-admission veterinary program "because I am taking the right classes as far as I know and getting a job in the field. I think I will be a little more appealing when I apply to colleges." She recognizes that if she is going to be accepted in the college of her choice, she needs to assemble a portfolio consisting of high grades in advanced-level courses and evidence that she has been acquiring skills and knowledge in the field she hopes to work in.

Mrs. Kruell's opinion is that her school has done a good job educating Nina, "because she is in a lot of advanced classes. I would be concerned if she were not. Nina has always been in advanced classes, she was able to get into an elite group, and she has always been taught up by her teachers. She has always had the challenges. I feel the school offers her those kinds of classes and those kinds of challenges, and I am excited about that." But not all students are enjoying the same treatment, according to Mrs. Kruell, especially those who are in the general classes. Many of these students "are not making it. The teachers are putting them down. They are teaching down to them and as a parent that concerns me."

She has not been very involved at Nina's high school, though. "Nina would not let me go," she says. "'Oh, Mom, you are going to embarrass me. I am too old for you to go into my classrooms talking to my teachers.' And I figure if she is not having a problem and she is embarrassed by my being there . . . Because it seems like a little girl thing, you know. You go and visit your elementary teacher; you do not visit your high school teacher. You have to pick your battles and that is not one I find a problem with."

The high school offers a course in career guidance, but Nina has not taken it. "Nina tells me it is stupid and a waste of time," Mrs. Kruell says, and she supports Nina's impression, as she too believes such courses are ineffective because they emphasize information about jobs rather than the skills needed to get a good education. Being interested in a topic, working hard, and obtaining good grades are, in Mrs. Kruell's assessment, what career counseling should be about. "Now if a child has some idea, even a vague idea, of what they want to do, then the school needs to provide some challenge. Like in Nina's case with the science stuff, if the school provides the challenge and she still gets good grades and she still likes it, then that may be career guidance in itself. Giving her a message that you are good in this, you like this, and maybe this is what you need to think about so you can buy new shoes and pay the rent one day."

The pathway to a successful future, she says, is obtaining good grades. "As for the future, I told Nina, that as a woman you go to school, you get good grades, and you will get a good job someday. And if you choose to be an independent person, you can, and if you choose to find somebody that is your life partner, that's much better. But I don't want you to ever be put in the situation where you feel like you can't. And your one ticket that will guarantee you that [is] good grades, and good grades pay off in a good job."

Mrs. Kruell recognizes that Nina is willing to work hard, especially "if she is having difficulty." But she worries that "grades come really easy to her. She can study two hours and she will ace a test." When faced with a major challenge, this ability to do well on tests can be a hindrance because she does not know how to work for a sustained period of time. "I always tell her that I think she is having difficulty in her advanced algebra because she did not work enough and that she did not put in enough time." Because she believed that Nina was not working to her full capability, she hired a tutor as the only way to save her from a poor grade. "If we did not get her a tutor she probably would have gotten a D in her advanced-level class. I really want to see her buckle down and work hard and get a B."

Traditionally, hiring a tutor was for giving extra help to average and below-average students struggling with their studies. These days, however, tutors—available in nearly every subject, from advanced French to geometry—are used even to cut the risks of receiving less than a B in an advanced-level course. Parents in the study discussed hiring tutors for their adolescents to help them keep up their grades in advanced-level courses and thereby increase their chances of a higher class rank. Advanced-level course grades are typically worth more points than those for regular courses; a B in an advanced-level course often translates to an A-plus in a standard course.

This type of "shadow education," delivered outside formal schooling to enhance performance, appears to be becoming more prevalent, particularly among students aspiring to highly prestigious colleges. In fact, tutoring is so common that many parents report calling the high school for the names of good tutors. Tutors advertise in local papers, and word of exceptional ones is shared at school, church, and community events.[11]

Mrs. Kruell sees herself as the one in the family "who carries the torch about school. I kind of go a little more overboard. Nina's father's attitude is 'whatever.' What grades she gets are fine and if she doesn't that's okay, too." Grades are extremely important to Nina's mother, and she believes they are valid measures of how hard her children are working. "I think grades are a really good indicator of what's going on, and if you are partying too much, your grades are going to show it, and so I pretty well kind of watch the grades. I am a grade person and I'll get upset if they are not doing well." She would like to see Nina attend a university and is assisting her in making her college choice. "We will give her some parameters. Some private universities are too expensive. I am sure there are sufficient schools out there where she can go." Being actively involved in the process is one of Mrs. Kruell's aims: "I plan to take her and actually see the campus once she is accepted, so she has something to base her decision on. But it is going to be pretty much her choice."

Affording Nina's college choice, however, is going to be difficult. "As for paying for it, we are going to have to refinance the house. If she will be able to make it on scholarships—well, we all live in our own little fantasy—I would really like to think that she can get some scholarship and student loans and we will supplement." Her parents' willingness to make financial sacrifices is a clear sign that they place a high value on education. The Kruells are not alone in their concern about financing their daughter's education. How to pay for college is a common worry among families of high school students. Even those ineligible for financial aid because of their high incomes see the necessity of tightening their budgets, especially if their son or daughter enrolls in a private university. Some parents take second jobs and others substantially cut household expenses.[12]

There are several factors in Nina's family life that contribute to helping her form aligned ambitions. First, the family functions as a unit, communicating, sharing, and helping one another. Second, Nina's early experiences in preparing for her chosen job were positive, and she knows her parents respect and understand her career choice. Third, the family has strong norms supporting academic achievement. Nina works hard in school and her parents recognize her effort. Effort is required to earn high grades, and high grades can create opportunities, such as admission to a highly competitive college. And, fourth, while the choice of which college to attend is seen as Nina's decision, her parents are actively involved in learning about different programs and working with her to determine what college would be the best choice for her.

Importance of College: Limited Guidance for Career Choice

Alexander Rujah attends a public high school that specializes in math and science. A. J. knows he is going to college, but when asked what type of career he plans to have, he responds, "darned if I know." He displayed a little more certainty when we interviewed him as a senior. He said he would study "computer science—something around there, yeah, I think so." In his senior year A. J. is taking three AP classes, serves as vice president of the school's chapter of the National Honor Society, is actively involved in a tutoring club at school, and must deal with the pressure of applying to highly prestigious private universities. Senior year has been "a lot of angst because of the college applications. Well, just because I am busy, and I am doing important things, important to me. . . . The work, this year the work is serious stuff. I have gone beyond my high school requirements and I am doing things that I wanted to take."

When discussing the future, A. J. is unsure. "I don't know, I don't know what I want to do in the future." His immediate goal is being admitted to a prestigious college. The process is so competitive that, like his classmates, he has a list of colleges he hopes to attend and a second set of safety schools. He says he has no long-term plans or goals, "not beyond college." His only desire for the future is to find a job that is interesting and financially secure. "I think it may be tricky to find something that is not too monotonous. I will have to look more into careers, then I worry about the money part. I really do not know." Being an adult to A. J. means "working for money." Schoolwork is not "real work," he says, "not something you have to do for a job or something like that. The pressure of real work will be greater."

A. J. differs from Nina, who is very interested in a specific job that she would like to have as an adult. Future work to A. J. is doing things you are obligated to and getting paid for it. Such a view does not stem from a lack of interests. He has many interests and is designing a science project involving theoretical astrophysics. But he has "no clue" about any specific career. What he is willing to focus his energies on is being accepted at a competitive college. His academic accomplishments at high school are a means to the end of being admitted to a prestigious university.

A. J. reports little career guidance at his school. "Teachers should in some way tell you what you could do with what you are learning. What career opportunities are available to you if you are interested in it." But that does not happen, and he suspects that he will have to figure it out in college. "You need college to get more of a taste of a particular field. I imagine that happens in internships or something like that." Although his high school does not focus on career guidance, it does pay particular attention to college admissions. Three times a year the school "fills up two buses and you go look at colleges—eleven in three days."

Both his parents are college graduates. His mother is a director of information systems for a genetics laboratory. "There are several laboratories across the country," she says. "My job is to manage the computer systems." A. J. is unfamiliar with his mother's work. "She's like a technical consultant type of thing," according to him. "She deals with the computer aspect of it. I'm not sure about the details." Mr. Rujah is an engineer with an advanced degree whose future looks uncertain to A. J. "Now he is an engineer. But the way the defense industry is going, my dad may be a pastry chef in a year, so I don't know." Both his parents expect that A. J. will obtain some advanced degree after graduating from college.

Mrs. Rujah believes the education A. J. is receiving is satisfactory, but that "he is the kind of student who would make up for it if it wasn't anyway." She thinks that learning is intrinsically appealing to her son: "He takes an enormous amount of satisfaction out of the pure subject matter. He always has been an excellent reader. He is extremely interested in learning for its own sake." While A. J. enjoys school and does well, his mother recognizes that part of the reason he excels is that "he also has this competitive edge about doing his own personal best in school situations."

Doing well in school is something his parents value highly, but they are not actively involved in the completion of his homework assignments or school projects. They do, however, provide resources for learning materials and discuss school activities and assignments at home. "I would take him to the bookstore, to the libraries," his mother says. "I used to do that all the time. Now he can do it on his own. I would support the things that he wanted to do. We obviously are very interested in what he does, and, you know, we talk about it at the dinner table, but I do not sit there and check it and deal with it." She thinks the pressure to do well in school comes from inside A. J. "He has always been a phenomenal student. I mean, it would boil him and he would come home looking like a total basket case because he screwed up a test. It would come from him."

As for directing him into a specific field or career, she thinks the best guidance she can give him is to impart certain values. Rather than suggest a specific set of ideas about what to do with one's life or what field to pursue, she would like A. J. to "take away a broad base of information about the world, that the world is a generous place with a lot of possibilities for you, that you are exceptionally wonderful as a person. I'm always trying to make sure that there is a broad base of interest, not just narrowing it into physics right away or whatever it is that he's going to go into, which is probably going to be physics or math." In contrast to the latitude Mrs. Rujah gives A. J. in career choice, she has definite educational expectations for him "to go through graduate school, probably almost absolutely, because that is his own personal interest. I do not see him stopping educationally for a while. I see him doing some kind of research or management type of thing. He is a natural leader." As for where he should go to school, she maintains that it is A. J.'s choice, but "I have expressed to him to go to a school where there is a core curriculum, so that he will be exposed to broad-based, humanitarian courses before he ends up deep into math or computers or physics. I have been discouraging him from those prestigious technical universities because it's too narrow too soon." She also recognizes that "there will be absolutely no way we can establish need. We will be paying for it. That's entirely why I am working now. My working is also a highly motivating factor to make sure that A. J. and his twin sisters can get to the place they want to be."

In A. J.'s family, the focus is on having him attend a college that will provide him with a liberal arts education. There is little discussion of what type of work he may want to do, and in fact A. J. does not expect that his parents would talk to him about his future work. Instead he believes that through schooling he will come to understand what he wants to do and needs to study. While he had hoped that this would happen in high school, he imagines that it will happen in college, in particular through his biology classes. But it is questionable whether he will learn in a college biology class what his career options are, although he may learn whether he likes or dislikes biology. A. J. could potentially leave college as unclear about his future as he was when he started.

A. J. has misaligned ambitions. He and his parents expect that he will attend graduate school and perhaps obtain a Ph.D., which is not required for most computer science jobs. Neither his school nor his parents provide information about the connections between further postsecondary education and a specific career. This lack of articulation between education and work can create unrealistic expectations about how colleges shape students' occupational choices. For example, A. J. talks about how his postsecondary biology course will give him information about future careers.

A. J. is entering college without a clear image of what he wants to study or what kind of work he would like to do. One reason he does not have aligned ambitions can be traced to his parents, who do not believe that students at this time should start thinking about their occupational futures. Mrs. Rujah believes that A. J. should experience his world, and that choosing to prepare for a specific future or taking a particular course of study will foreclose his opportunities to pursue other academic directions. We would argue that having a better understanding of the relationship between his education and a desired future job would give A. J. more focus in his course selection and a clearer perception of how college courses relate to future work. Figuring out which courses to take that relate to an occupation can be a difficult and complicated process. We suspect that college courses in biology will not give sufficient guidance about the requirements for future careers, especially careers in computer science. Without some occupational direction, once in college some students, even those who are academically gifted, can become drifting dreamers who take more than four years to finish college. And when they graduate they may still be unsure how to strategically plan for their futures.[13]

Importance of Career and Independence: Limited Guidance for College Choice

Kathy Rogers is a twelfth grader at a large public high school, and she, too, has misaligned ambitions: she underestimates how much education she will need for the career she wants as a physical therapist. Her academic performance is average, and she enjoys working on the school newspaper. After high school, Kathy plans to enter a local junior college. When she was younger, she wanted to become a doctor, but now she thinks this would involve "too much school." During her sophomore year in high school, Kathy was given a questionnaire that was "supposed to tell you what jobs you would be good at." In reviewing her responses with her counselor, she discussed one field that matched her current interests in health and helping people—physical therapy. The job of a physical therapist was particularly appealing because the educational requirements were not as demanding as some other jobs that interested her.

Kathy lives with her mother and three younger sisters in an apartment. Her parents divorced when she was thirteen, but she sees her father every week. Her mother is employed full time as the manager of an upholstery firm and owns a small business. Ms. Rogers believes she has been a positive influence on her daughter. "I am a single parent. I work a full-time job, and I have my own business. I do not have as much time as I would like to spend with Kathy. But I think we fare pretty well, considering the times we live in and the environment we live in." Living with a working single mother and three sisters creates considerable stresses and pressures for Kathy, especially because she is the eldest. Meals are frequently unscheduled because of her mother's long hours, and Kathy often has to cook and care for her younger sisters. The lack of consistent routines or family time when everyone can talk together leads Kathy to describe her family life as disorganized and unpredictable.

Kathy's mother requires her to do certain household chores and limits the time she spends with friends on school nights and the amount of television she watches. Despite this monitoring, she does not take an active interest in knowing Kathy's friends or their parents—knowledge that involved parents can use to create positive norms concerning school performance and educational attainment.[14] Spending time with other teens whose parents may be more lenient about drug use or devalue the importance of schooling can send teenagers like Kathy conflicting messages about what are acceptable values and appropriate behavior.

Ms. Rogers is even less attentive to Kathy's schoolwork. Kathy reports that her mother rarely checks to see if her homework is done, does not help her with homework, and does not give her special privileges for completing it. When asked about her involvement with her daughter's schoolwork, Ms. Rogers said she feels like "a parent trying to teach their child to drive. I do not have the patience that a person should have when they are trying to help a child. I run out of patience. I think my expectations might be kind of high. So when I can I try to refer her to assistance elsewhere"—that is, to the high school.

Ms. Rogers also believes the school should be a source of career information. "I think especially when they first get to high school, the role of the school should be one of information. They should let the student know what is available and what they need to do in order to attain whatever it is they think they want. The reason why students wait so long to make a decision about what they want to become is because they do not know what is out there. And when they are told what is out there—that is, the requirements they need in order to get into a certain school, the prerequisites—it is kind of late because they should have started in ninth or tenth grade." Many other parents of students whose ambitions are misaligned expressed similar sentiments—that the major responsibility for helping adolescents select a career path and take the appropriate steps to get there rests with the school. One reason parents depend on schools is that they may not know much about the field their child is considering. High school students are likely to aspire to jobs different from those of their parents, and many of these jobs did not exist a decade ago. Parents—even those with college degrees—said in our interviews that they were unfamiliar with the educational training needed for the occupations their adolescents were interested in.

Kathy's mother gives her considerable autonomy in making decisions about her education. Kathy explains that she, not her mother, decides which classes to take in school, and preparations for college, such as plans to take the ACT or SAT, are never discussed at home. Even though her mother is not actively involved in Kathy's studies, she has very high expectations for her daughter's educational future, hoping that she will obtain a mas-

ter's degree: "Without college or some type of skill, I think the
students will be lost. They do not have the same opportunities
that I had when I went out of school. And so for me college is a
must." So strongly does Kathy's mother believe that college is important that "by hook or crook" she will find a way to pay for it.

Despite the value she places on a college education, she has
taken a very minor role in directing Kathy's college and career
plans. The selection of what college to attend was unstructured,
and the considerations focused on cost, not the quality of the
program. "I told her to check into all of the schools that offer the
program that she is interested in with regard to physical therapy
and find those whose requirements are softer. You know, which
school can she get accepted into faster, the location, the cost." As
to whether physical therapy is the right choice for her daughter,
she says, "I think that there is no right choice. I think it should
be her decision, not mine." Being a successful teenager, according to her, requires that Kathy become more independent and
exercise sound judgment. Kathy's mother sees her responsibilities for Kathy being more limited once Kathy graduates from
high school. "She knows the apron strings are going to be cut
soon and she realizes that. Fortunately, she has matured enough
to determine what her goals are and what she is going to do with
her future."

Both Kathy's parents think it is important that she be independent, and they feel their responsibility for her will diminish
when she graduates from high school. "When you leave high
school," says her mother, "as far as I am concerned, you take on
the responsibility of adulthood." Kathy's father has a similar
view. "My dad says that after you are eighteen, you are an adult
and can be responsible for whatever you do." Kathy looks forward to being more independent. "My parents want me to be responsible, to make my own decisions, whatever I choose to do,
whatever it is. They cannot say, 'No, you can't do that,' because
they would be out of line." The parental push for independence

is reflected in Kathy's decisions about her career and postsecondary plans.

In the summer of her junior year, she started working part time in a physical therapy clinic. She enjoyed the work and her co-workers, and she was offered a full-time job immediately after graduating from high school. Kathy decided, however, that if she wanted to become a physical therapist she would need to attend college and the best plan for her was to begin a program at a local community college to become a physical therapist's assistant. "I figure with what I am doing now, I have to go to school after I graduate from high school, but two years is nothing." She envisions that after completing her training as an assistant she will go to a four-year school, explaining that most physical therapists begin as assistants, "and then after they get more experience, it is kind of easier when you know more, they may go back. So I might go back. I'm not sure."

Kathy realizes that beginning her education at a community college rather than a four-year school could put reaching her goals at risk. "My boss was telling me that most people who go to a two-year and become an assistant don't always make it. They plan to go to a four-year but they do not end up doing it or they end up quitting. I was thinking I'll try to get into a four-year but then I knew I could not afford it, so I just decided to become an assistant." As for what courses she will need to become a physical therapist's assistant, Kathy explains, "They say you need chemistry, like basically all the science classes and psychology. Some of the older patients I was working with were kind of stubborn. They did not want any young person who did not know what they were doing working on them, doing their treatment, so you have to know how to work with people."

Pursuing an education as a physical therapist's assistant is especially appealing to Kathy because she can continue to work at the clinic part time and her responsibilities will be similar to the ones she currently has. "I'll be doing clerical work and when they do not have enough physical therapy assistants there, sometimes the people that work in the front office take over their patients." However, most of her responsibilities with patients have been assisting with equipment rather than giving direct service.

Kathy's work experience has helped her in making a career choice, but it has not helped to inform her about what courses she will need to take in college and what college would give her the best quality of training for her chosen career. Her mother's criteria for selecting a college are based more on costs and logistics than the quality and placement opportunities of the program. Although her mother is supportive of Kathy's further education, she does not challenge her to get good grades or put forth her best effort in high school—rather, she stresses the need to become an independent adult. Unlike A. J.'s parents, who were knowledgeable about college admissions and types of college programs, Kathy's parents know very little about the process of being admitted to a collegiate program that would lead to a degree in physical therapy. Her mother does make judgments about the different programs but offers Kathy little advice other than to make a decision based on the cost of the program.

Parents and Adolescent Futures

When parents provide knowledge about career paths or ways to acquire such knowledge, teenagers can create a plan for reaching their goals. We could see this in the case of Jordie Blazack and the efforts of his parents to help him find the right engineering school. Parents can also help adolescents to strategically manage their time and efforts, as did Paul Cheng's mother in enrolling him in preparation courses for the college entrance examinations. Adolescents without strong family support are more likely to have unfocused life plans, turning to the high school, co-workers, and peers for guidance, as A. J. and Kathy did. Parents who recognize the relation between education and work are less likely to believe that schools will provide their adolescents with a meaningful orientation toward work, and therefore they encourage them to find opportunities that will help them develop a better understanding of their desired occupation and what is required to attain such a position.

From these descriptive cases we find that the family characteristics that help in the development of aligned ambitions are norms of high expectations, hard work, and persistence. However, it is not only norms that are important. Parents also need to take specific actions in helping their adolescents plan for the future. This can occur through family discussions of the connections between education and future work opportunities as well as through more directive actions such as arranging for specific work or internship opportunities. The job of parenting does not stop when children become adolescents or graduate from high school. Parents need to help their teenagers plan for their futures, especially because the transition from high school to postsecondary school and the labor force has become increasingly more complex.

chapter seven

Teenage Work and Internships

A traditional approach to understanding the effects of work on adolescents' development is to view work as providing opportunities to develop valuable traits and habits, such as the ability to follow directions, the desire to take on responsibility, the capacity to work in teams, and the development of specific task skills. Underlying this approach has been an assumption that a teenager is more likely to develop these traits and habits by working than by not working, and that one with such traits will be a more productive adult worker. What has received less attention is how the work experiences of adolescents influence their ambitions. This issue is the main topic of this chapter.[1]

Work is a common experience among today's teenagers, with more than 80 percent working during their high school years. Most spend about fifteen to twenty hours a week at their jobs. American teenagers are more likely to work and to work longer hours than their counterparts in other industrialized countries. Those who report not working provide different reasons why not: some because they and their parents do not want work to interfere with their schooling, others because they live in economically depressed areas with few employment opportunities and report being unable to find jobs.[2]

High school students in the 1990s are much more likely to work during the school year than they were in the 1970s. Adolescent work tends to be highly seasonal, with more teenagers working during the summer months than during the school year. Recently, however, there has been a reduction in this seasonal fluctuation: the percentage of teenage employment during the summer months is only slightly greater than during the school year. While the variation in the seasonal character of teenage work has declined, there is more variation in the time of day that teenagers work: those in the 1990s are more likely to work late-evening hours during the school year than was the case in the 1970s.[3]

Two broad societal trends have reinforced these changing work patterns. First is a rise in the number of part-time jobs available to adolescents. Most of these positions are in such low-wage jobs as cashiers in grocery stores, fast-food workers, clerks in retail sales, stockers in warehouses, or general laborers.[4] A second trend has been the extension of business hours. Many businesses, like grocery stores, department stores, and gas stations, have extended their operating hours—opening earlier and closing later. It is now possible to buy groceries as late as midnight, and some stores are open twenty-four hours a day. The rise in part-time employment and the extension of business hours have helped to increase teenage employment during the school year and at later hours.

Changes in the schedule of the American high school have also contributed to a new blending of work and school in the lives of adolescents. One of the schools in the Sloan study, for instance, reorganized its day into two shifts: students have the option of starting their school day at six-thirty in the morning and being finished by twelve-thirty, a change implemented partly to suit the needs of working adolescents. Some high schools have split schedules, with morning and afternoon shifts. Another school in the Sloan study offers night classes so students can work during the day and take their courses in the evening. All these scheduling alternatives make it easier for them to work longer hours because larger blocks of time are available before or after school.

These complex organizational changes suggest that American high schools have become more "organizationally accommodating." The schools now attempt to maximize opportunities for students to attend school by accommodating their outside interests, including their desire and need to work. Students who need to work because of financial circumstances can do so while attending high school. The flexibility of scheduling helps to create among them a sense of attachment to their schools. This is the case for students who are in work-related programs or in non-school-affiliated jobs as well as for those who are in accelerated academic programs. There are two broad indicators of increased student attachment to schooling over the past two decades: the rate of absenteeism has declined, and so has the high school dropout rate.[5]

Although the organizational features of high schools make it easier for students to work during the school year, this can have certain costs for schooling. We were interested in exploring how adolescents who are working and those who are not spend their time on school-related activities. Examining how students spend their time during the day is made possible by one of the instruments in the Sloan study: the experience sampling method (ESM), a self-reporting system that provides information about students' daily experiences. Over the period of a week, students are signaled by a preprogrammed watch that is set to beep at eight random intervals throughout each day. Upon being signaled, the students complete a short questionnaire that includes information about where they are, what type of activity they are engaged in, and how they feel about it.[6]

Using results from this method, we found that teenagers who worked during the school year spent less time at school than students who did not work—averaging about an hour less per day (fig. 7.1). In addition to being in school less, adolescents who worked spent more time commuting—on average an hour and a half a week. Adolescents who worked also spent about an hour less a day at home and fifteen minutes less a day doing

Fig. 7.1 *Activities of Employed and Unemployed High School Students*

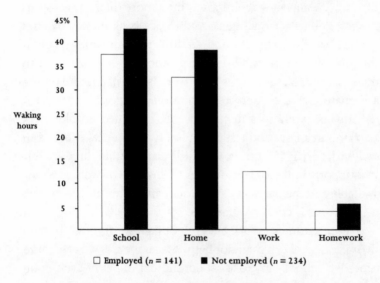

Data from Sloan study, experience sampling method, sample of tenth- and twelfth-grade focal students from the base year. The four categories are not mutually exclusive and therefore do not sum to 100. Time is also spent in transit, personal care, and leisure activities. For school, $p < .0001$; for home, $p < .01$; for homework, $p < .05$.

homework. Employment appears to change how adolescents spend their time, and the hours at the workplace appear to come at the price of time at school, at home, and doing homework.

The Nature of Teenage Work

The labor market for teenagers is considerable, but most of the jobs available require minimal skills and have little connection to high school learning experiences. These "teenage jobs" include busing tables at a restaurant, operating the cash register at a store, providing child care services, or cleaning houses. Adolescents in these jobs are often paid the minimum wage or less; they receive limited job training and typically do not receive health insurance or other benefits. These jobs tend to have few adult role models, and the tasks given to teenagers tend not to be cognitively demanding. Many view their jobs as little more than a way to earn money to buy personal items and to pay back money owed to friends, family members, and credit card companies. Many of the jobs offer no possibilities for promotion. Teenagers can remain in such jobs as long as their work is acceptable and there is a demand for their services. Additional education or formal training is rarely a requirement for continued employment. Working in a fast-food restaurant is a typical teenage job: as we saw with Calvin, it requires very little training and there are limited opportunities for advancement. This type of work is widely available and the barriers to employment are minimal—usually the only one is chronological age.[7]

Some students work but are not paid for it, often because their parents rely on them for help. Rosa Lopez, as we saw, sometimes left school early to assist her mother in her housekeeping job, and she received no compensation for her work. Rosa's experience is not an isolated one. Kesha Daniels, who lives in a very poor community on the East Coast, works as a housekeeper in a hotel with her aunt on the late-evening shift and does not get paid. Paul Cheng, the student who lives in New York and wants to become a physician, helps in his father's electronics store, and he believes his parents expect that he will work there. "I usually do not get paid, I do not expect to get paid. My parents need all the help they can get."

Most teenagers work after school, but there are some who put in thirty hours a week, mostly on weekends, when fast-food restaurants often need extra help. "I work like a dog on weekends," said one young woman with a job at one of these places. Closing the store is another task that is often assigned to teenage workers. Students and their parents describe the late hours required of young workers as a safety concern. Young people are not very committed to their work and often leave one job for another if it pays twenty-five cents more or if their paycheck will arrive sooner. How frequently one is paid is very important to teenagers. Being paid every week instead of every other week is a significant benefit for those who use their money for compact discs, concerts, gas, and clothes.

Those who supervise teenagers are often the same age or a few years older, and their teenage workers typically describe them as "fun," "nice," and "hilarious." Store managers, often referred to as the "big" or "super" managers, tend to be viewed as more responsible and more adultlike in their behaviors. However, the opportunities for teenage workers to interact with store managers are limited. Most of the training at fast-food restaurants and in sales, as Calvin described, is very short, lasting anywhere from an hour to a half day. Skills learned on the job tend to be at a low level, such as how to type in numbers or how to operate a cash register. In the teenagers' opinions, they are hired because they have "good communication skills," "are good at working with people," or "have a friendly way." These are the same skills that researchers have identified as being developed by working.[8]

Encapsulated Work Experiences

A consistent message appears from nearly all adolescents engaged in this type of teenage work: they do not view it as related to their futures. They do not describe their work as important for the job they want to have in the future; they do not believe they are developing skills that will be valuable or that their work experiences will make them more competitive for jobs in the future. For many adolescents paid work is an encapsulated experience, one that has minimal implications for who they are going to become.

Using the ESM, we examined how adolescents perceived their experiences while at work and at school. Adolescents enjoy working more than being in school. There are several differences between work and school that may help explain this finding. At work adolescents may feel more in control than at school; the tasks are more clearly defined, and it is easier to succeed. At school, where the expectations of students and their parents are high, fulfilling them is more difficult than it is at work.

When students are at work, however, they do not feel that their activities are as relevant to their futures as they do when they are at school. Since the work of adolescents seldom leads to full-time jobs, and since most adolescents aspire to attend college, the greater importance of their schooling is not surprising. Some adolescents do, however, view their paid work as having some relevance to their futures. We suspect that there are two main reasons for this. First, some students plan to use their wages for spending money in college and, therefore, there are economic benefits to working that further their college plans. Second, students and their parents often commented that working helps them organize their time more efficiently, requires them to fulfill obligations to adults other than their parents and teachers, and provides them with a sense of independence.

A typical job that a teenager is likely to hold is described by Angelina, a twelfth grader at a high school in southern Florida. The school has a special work program that allows her to leave early for her job at a chicken takeout chain where many of her friends have worked. Angelina is a cashier and has been working in the restaurant for six months, since the beginning of the school year. She works about twenty hours a week and leaves school directly for her job. There are three managers in the store—a "big" manager and two assistants—and approximately twenty employees, some of whom she knows from school. According to Angelina, a lot of time at the job is spent socializing, and "we have water fights all the time." Angelina obtained her job in a straightforward manner. She went with her mother to take her brother to a birthday party at the restaurant. When she got there, she noticed a girl she knew working at the restaurant and talking to the manager. Watching them in conversation, An-

gelina realized, "I needed to get a job here." She approached the
manager and asked, "Are you hiring any time soon?" He replied,
"Why? Do you want a job here?" This started a conversation that
ended with him handing an application to Angelina, who
promptly filled it out. He took the application, looked it over
quickly, and said, "Come in Monday and start training." For Angelina, who had never worked or volunteered before, except for
babysitting, "It was like, whoa, okay!"

Her training consisted of learning how to manage the
showroom, which included waiting on tables, participating in
the birthday shows, and selling merchandise. After a short period selling merchandise, Angelina was promoted to cashier, the
most important job one could have other than a position in the
kitchen. To be a cashier, "One has to be honest and trustworthy.
Some people do not get picked. And some people get moved
down, if money was coming up short and stuff."

Angelina believes that she is pretty good at her job, and she
uses some of the basic mathematics skills that she learned in
school to operate the cash register. She feels she knows everything about how the restaurant operates since she has had experience with merchandising and cashiering, waiting and busing
tables, overseeing the game room, and making sure that people
pay. For a while she was working long hours, "like five days out
of the week, right after school until like twelve o'clock at night.
I was getting no sleep, and I really did not have time for anything.
I was so tired the next day." She is known as very hardworking
and has received an award as employee of the month. Her mother
says it was because "any time they need someone, they call her
even when she is not scheduled." Her mother adds, "The employer has written real good reports about her. They really think
a lot of her, and she displays a lot of responsibility. She has done
real well. It has put her out there in the real world before she actually has to go."

Angelina has above-average grades and hopes to become a

physical therapist. She finds work more enjoyable than school, "because I feel like it's me in control. Instead of learning, I feel like it's me and I'm doing it for myself. And, I don't know, it is hard to explain. People look up to me. The only thing I don't like is it is a lot of work, but every job is going to be a lot of work." Angelina says she expects to keep her job through college, or "until I find a better-paying job that I enjoy. I like this job, it just depends on the financial situation." What Angelina likes about it is that it allows her to "work with people and learn what the job is about," although it is not related to the work she would like to do in the future.

Angelina's job at the chicken takeout chain is part of a cooperative work program in her high school. To be eligible for the program and to earn high school graduation credit, students have to find their own jobs and must work at least fifteen hours a week. Once the students begin working, they fill out time cards so that school officials know they are working. Employers are expected to write reports on the students' performance and verify the number of hours worked. Angelina attends school from six-thirty in the morning until twelve-thirty and then leaves for work. Her mother believes the program "is real good for the kids because it starts them off with responsibility."

The intention of the program is to give students exposure to jobs they may have an interest in, but few actually find such a job, including Angelina. Her parents tried to help her find something in her field of interest, but Angelina has continued to work at the chicken takeout. Although she is a valued employee, she is not learning skills that match her future job interests. Her primary reason for working is money. And because the restaurant has not been able to give her as many hours as she would like before college starts, Angelina is looking for another job.

Many encapsulated jobs, such as cashier and laborer, are very easy to get. During his last semester of high school, Ricky Knudsman is working two jobs, at a lumberyard and as a stock boy at a discount chain store. He is working to earn money for compact discs, clothes, and other incidentals. He plans to start at a major midwestern state university in the fall, majoring in writing. For both jobs, he heard there were openings, applied, and was accepted. When asked about why he works, he replied, "It's just the money. That's about it." He works three days after school at the store as a "peon loader." He chose this discount chain over another because it pays twenty-five cents more an hour. "The loading is pretty exhausting, carrying sixty-pound bags of concrete to someone's car who is usually parked at the far end of the parking lot." For the summer before he starts college, he plans to work at the lumberyard: "The lumber job is particularly good because you get a lot of hours." Without having to get up early for school, he can work both jobs and "stay out as late as I want." As Angelina described, many teenage jobs are for fewer hours than the students would like to work. What keeps most of them from working more hours is not the demands of schoolwork or other activities but limits imposed by their employers.

Remaining committed to the job is a problem for many young people who work at jobs that are not highly valued and where the work is routine. It is especially difficult when teenagers believe their employers are taking advantage of them. By the end of his senior year in high school, for example, Jake Roberts had worked two summer jobs and one seasonal job at Christmas. The seasonal job was at a large family-adventure park, where he helped to clean animal cages. When he first applied for the job, he recalled, "one of the things they told us was, 'You will not be working all four days, Christmas Eve, Christmas Day, New Year's Eve, and New Year's Day. You'll work three of them, but you will not work all four.' Then they had me scheduled for all four. I did not even go in on New Year's. I mean they took me away from my parents at Christmas, and that absolutely sucked."

Not only a sense of exploitation undermines the young person's commitment to work—often their treatment on the job is confusing and frustrating. Jake's first job was at a fast-food restaurant, where he says he did his best work: "I did a damn good job, but they fired me on like a bullshit excuse. I had given them my two weeks' notice, it was the end of summer and school was starting. And a week later, one week before I was supposed to get off, the boss comes up to me and says, 'Well, it is just not working out. So see ya.'" Just as some teenagers are uncommitted to their jobs, some of their employers are uncommitted to them. They have little reservation about cutting their employees' hours or firing them even when they are doing a good job.

Not all teenage work is unpleasant; adolescents can find work that is enjoyable and engaging. Britta Chang is a high school senior who works at a children's pizza parlor until nine most nights. For this job she wears the uniform of a storybook character, which she likes because it "makes work fun. The time goes by faster than in school, but it is really hot in the costume." Britta is an average student who struggles with mathematics and science. She would like to be a preschool teacher and plans to join the air force after high school. She uses the money she earns for clothes and to help her aunt, with whom she lives.

For her job as a storybook character, Britta received "special character" training. Having been through the program, she was given responsibility for training new employees, and she has already trained five people. It is not unusual for teenagers to train other teenagers—and to do it very informally—at these jobs. To qualify as a trainer Britta had to take a test, and she says, "if you pass, you get a raise and get to do the training." One of her jobs as a trainer is to help people get more into their "characters." For the daily routine, every hour there is a live show and the characters sing a song and dance. Britta really enjoys it, because "I'm not lip synching. I do the dance, and during the live show I'll be singing, and I run around the restaurant." She particularly enjoys "getting everyone to clap and getting the little kids to dance." But the best part is the children, she says. "This one kid said, 'Oh,

I know why you can't talk—you don't have batteries.' I laugh inside. . . . They can't even see my face, but I am smiling."

There is an interesting tension in adolescents' experiences
of working for pay. For most, paid work has little connection to
the work they imagine they will be doing in the future and has
little influence in shaping their ambitions. In this regard, paid
work is an encapsulated experience. Most adolescents, however,
work for pay and say they enjoy it more than school. With fewer
recreational or other organized activities available to adolescents
today, work is preferable to being alone.[9]

Family Ties and Teenage Work

Although most teenagers encapsulate their work experiences,
separating them from their educational and occupational aspirations, some jobs offer higher pay and greater opportunities for
independence and autonomy. Parents with large networks of acquaintances, some of whom may be in a hiring position, maximize their children's opportunities in seeking employment and
obtaining more desirable jobs. Most teenagers earn the minimum wage, but some earn more through sponsorship jobs that
are generally arranged by their parents. These jobs, however, still
have many of the characteristics of teenage work and do not help
to shape ambitions.

Chris Petrin lives in one of the wealthiest communities in
the United States, although he describes his family as "not even
close to the richest people around here, and my mom and dad
live in a small house." Chris is an only child. He is currently working at the community's only private country club. He does just
about everything, from "cooking to maintenance to snack bar—
all kinds of stuff." He started working at the club in the summer
of his sophomore year and continued through the next school
year, going in on weekends. "The club is pretty well closed down
during the basic school week," he says. Chris used to work at the
Bat and Tennis Club, but he quit. "One day, when I finished work-

ing, I actually figured out how much I was earning. I worked full weeks and I earned about twenty dollars. I figured out that they were totally ripping me off so I looked for another job." Finding a job in his community is particularly difficult: "It is really hard to find a job because everyone is going for them, and they get taken up real quick because it is such a small area." Chris found a job by looking through the want ads of a local college. He saw an ad for a waiter, "and I knew I had done that at Bat and Tennis so I called the guy."

Chris is an excellent student and well known among his teachers and other members of the community. In addition to working at the club, he babysits—a lot, he says. "I have a lot of people that are my friends, like adult friends. Mr. McLeland, who owns the bank, knows me and I think I am respected by him and a lot of those people, and it helps me get jobs." Chris started babysitting for the McLeland's when their son was three years old, and since then, "We've just been really good friends. I mean that's my second family, my parents and the McLelands." Chris earns money to pay for school trips and college, and he is always looking for better opportunities. He is thinking about getting a new job at the naval air base where his mother works: "The naval base has a whole listing of jobs, and because she works there I can see the list as soon as it is out. I also could go and talk to Mr. McLeland. I think he could probably help me to find a job."

Chris is a student with aligned ambitions who hopes to become a psychiatrist. He is very strategic about finding work and realizes the importance of having contacts and connections to get the jobs that pay the most. His main desire is to have enough funds for trips and spending money for college. He relies on family and friends to help him secure employment, although the jobs are not related to his interest in becoming a psychiatrist. His parents and friends place considerable emphasis on earnings, rather than encouraging him to find work that would be consistent with his occupational goals and prepare him for adulthood.

Chris's work is typical of teenage jobs obtained through family connections. Although higher paying, these jobs lack the adult-like work experiences that are often found in internships.

Internships

In contrast to teenage jobs, internships are often described by adolescents as meaningful work experiences that influence their ideas about what they would like to do and become. Internships differ from teenage work in several important ways. They provide opportunities to discover what adult jobs are like and what it takes to do one. Most are of fixed length: student interns frequently cannot stay indefinitely in a position even if they continue to do a good job. In order to continue to work at the same place, the adolescent must often return to school to develop additional skills and to gain additional knowledge and credentials.[10]

Internship experiences often help teenagers develop clearer notions about the link between schooling and work opportunities. These experiences can reinforce the importance of certain types of schooling and the mastery of specific skills and knowledge. Adolescents with internships are better able to give meaningful accounts of the work they want to do and what education and training are required to do it. In contrast, working in teenage jobs may increase adolescents' motivation to continue their education but does little to help shape their ambitions and plans. Some adolescents value internships because they signal to educators and employers that they have seen what adult work is like and know something of the demands and requirements of adult jobs. In many ways, they accrue significant advantages over other students who have never had the experience of working in a veterinarian's office or a legal aid agency.

Jorge Roderiquez's father was an accountant in Mexico, but in the United States he is a city worker. Jorge hopes to become an accountant. With the help of a friend of his mother, he has been working with a notary public during the tax season. "She was teaching me how to do taxes and the paper work," he relates, "which forms you do what with, and things like that, and I think that is important for an accountant to know how to do taxes and bookkeeping and study. In the office I learned about taxes, the accounting part. They showed me what an office environment would be like, how to work with other people, how to be professional about the things you do, when to be professional, how to dress professionally, and things like that."

Jason Ziven's parents and grandparents are medical doctors, and he has worked in his mother's pediatric office. "She sees lots of patients and kids and has a nice job, her own office, flexible hours," he says. Next, his father used "his connections to get me a job in his medical school," working with a professor three times a week. "She would show me the ropes," according to Jason. "I did some fancy little things and it eventually turned into a project. It was a great job for me. It was an introduction into the field that I probably would like to go into. The second thing is I think it helped me to sort of work independently and not rely on teachers. Instead, I worked one-on-one with the professor, someone higher up than just a regular old teacher, and being able to work with graduate students and work with professors gives you more of a higher level of learning." But even challenging work related to one's interests can be stressful. "There were times when I just wanted to quit and say, 'forget it, this is not worth anything.' You want to go out and be in the sun and on the beach and in the water and not be in this lab doing work. So I think that I'm pretty motivated and well in tune with my goals and I realize the things and obstacles you go through."

Some schools provide internships for students who have special talents or skills. Unlike other jobs, school internships tend to be competitive and often the chances for acceptance are slim. An advantage of these more formalized internship programs is that they signal to others that the student has been selected be-

cause of a special skill or talent. Most of these school-based programs are found in specialized high schools, where they are
viewed as integral to the mission of developing particular talents
and skills among the students.

Paul Cheng, who wants to be a pediatrician, provides a
good illustration of the benefits of internships. To become more
knowledgeable about the jobs of physicians, Paul was interested
in working in a medical setting. His high school has a program
that allows students to submit applications to a hospital, and in
his senior year Paul was selected for a job working there. According to him, "Basically what I'm supposed to do is, if I'm in
the emergency room, I'm just supposed to take information
from patients. Let them go see a doctor. When I'm working upstairs in the admitting office, I usually admit newborns. I take
death certificates, and help transfer patients to different hospi-
tals and you basically assign beds." The job is difficult, he says:
"Upstairs is a lot more stressful than the emergency room, 'cause
basically downstairs, what you're expected to do is one job, admit a patient and take him aside. But upstairs is basically the most
expensive part, 'cause once you're in the hospital it's like 850
bucks, and if you give a bed to someone that's not supposed to
have a bed, you can really mess up the system." Paul is obtaining
firsthand information about the setting in which doctors work.
He has been given a chance to take on responsibility in a situation that has real consequences. But at the same time, it is stressful, he says, because "there is so much responsibility."

José Secada was born in the Dominican Republic and immigrated to the United States as a young child. Eldest in a family
of six, he is fluent in English and Spanish; Spanish is the language
most frequently spoken at home. José, like Grace and Paul, attended a mathematics and science academy in the heart of a major urban area on the East Coast. The high school has an excellent academic reputation; many of the teachers hold advanced
degrees, and 85 percent of its students attend four-year colleges

after graduation. Students with high eighth-grade test scores and interest in science and mathematics compete for admission to the school, which draws applicants from diverse backgrounds.

José is an excellent student who took nearly all advanced-placement classes in his senior year, including calculus and physics. He aspires to become a lawyer, he says, "so I can help to give back to my community." He is not sure whether he wants to work in the public or the private sector, but he knows he wants "to represent the people. If they have an interest in mind, I have to represent that interest. For example, if a person is denied a loan, you know, it becomes a civil rights case. I have to represent that person until that loan is given to that person, or we can change the law." To José a law degree is a ticket to many different kinds of jobs: "You could do anything, a lot of things with a law degree—you could become a criminal lawyer, you could set up your own business, you could be a politician."

José's interest in law was partially shaped by the Legal Outreach Corporation, which operates in a public school in a Hispanic neighborhood. Legal Outreach provides academic assistance for high school students who are having difficulty in math and science, because, José says, that is "what most of them have problems in. The students are bright but do not do well in school." José tutors four days a week, two hours a day, and usually works with the same students all year. Some of his friends from other schools also tutor, and occasionally after finishing for the day they will play a pickup basketball game with students and the other tutors.

Legal Outreach, in cooperation with area schools, targets young, talented students to participate in the program. José began working with Legal Outreach as a volunteer when he was in sixth grade; he now is paid for his work. The program gave him the opportunity to participate in mock trials and also helped to arrange an internship for him in the corporation counsel's office. During the summers following his junior and senior years, he worked in a private law firm, a job that was also arranged through the program. José was accepted at a highly prestigious eastern university, where he majored in Latin American studies, and still aspires to become a lawyer. He is thinking about setting up his own legal outreach program to work with adolescents and help poor people with their legal problems.

Teenage work does not require sponsorship; there are many positions available, and hiring criteria are fairly uniform. Adolescents frequently find a job by filling out an application in a store at a local mall. Being treated as laborers, and doing laborer-type work, builds little commitment to the job and to the work setting. Students do not have many reservations about leaving a job on a day's notice to take another. These teenage work experiences become realistic previews of what a job future can be without further education. Because this is not the type of job they plan to have as adults, young people in these situations may simply escalate their educational expectations without focus and realism. Such jobs do not increase the alignment of ambitions, nor do they help generate the development of coherent life plans.

Internships, on the other hand, are more likely to help produce aligned ambitions. They can give adolescents firsthand experience with the type of work they would like to do in the future. This opportunity provides two important benefits. First, it allows them to visualize what life might be like doing this kind of work and whether it fits their interests and inclinations. Such an experience also shows them some of the difficulties and sacrifices required to be a productive worker. Second, these opportunities place them in contact with other adults performing work that is different from that of their friends and associates. The opportunity to engage in responsible work with adults allows teenagers to form a clear idea of what it is like to actually be a working adult. Being treated as a responsible worker also increases self-confidence, especially when the tasks are challenging and rely on acquired skills and knowledge. Internships can also help adolescents acquire specialized skills that will give them advantages over their peers when applying to college or for a job. Internship experiences are a kind of long-term investment. The student engages for a limited time in a desired activity with the hope and expectation that eventually the opportunity will pay off.

chapter eight

Being Alone and Being with Friends

The social world of adolescents in the 1950s was very different from that of adolescents today. Public high schools then drew their students primarily from bounded residential communities where families were likely to know their neighbors' children, as well as the children's grandparents, other relatives, and close friends. Some families lived in the same communities for several generations, and it was not uncommon for children to attend the same schools their parents had and even to have the same teachers. In these communities, parents and their children shared common understandings of what it meant to be popular and successful in adolescent society.[1]

Adolescents in the 1950s lived in a world where participation in certain activities, such as athletics and booster clubs, could give one social status in the school as well as among adults within the community. Other school organizations, such as the honor society and debate club, were for "good students," but participation in these activities did not result in popularity among teenagers at school. Academic excellence was rarely helpful in achieving peer-group popularity; only about a quarter of high school seniors would enroll in college. School dances and other social activities were important, and "dating" and "going steady" were highly valued by most teenagers. The social life of the high school was an important part of courtship, because most boys and girls married soon after high school.

The social world of today's teenagers is very different, and the markers of adolescents' social status are not as clear or as widely held by them or their parents. Being an athlete, a cheer-leader, or homecoming queen does not necessarily confer high social status. For the increasing number of young people who plan to attend college, getting good grades and participating in such organizations as academic clubs are important for college admission. And being admitted to a competitive college is an important marker of social status.

Peer groups have changed substantially since the 1950s. There are few dominant elite crowds that most students desire to become members of. There are, however, numerous smaller social groups whose composition changes from year to year. These changes in peer groups are reflected in adolescents' views of themselves. Adolescents in the 1990s are more likely to see themselves as popular. Ten percent of students in the Sloan sample considered themselves very popular, 65 percent reported that they were somewhat popular, and 25 percent said they were not popular. Considering oneself popular is probably not a misperception if one is referring to a smaller friendship group.

The creation of numerous small groups is fostered, in part, by large high schools that draw students from many different neighborhoods. Because school friends often live far apart, it can be difficult to get together outside school. Some young people have school friends whom they eat lunch with and talk with but do not see otherwise. During the past decade, many facilities like recreational parks and programs that cater to adolescents after school have closed. With fewer places to go after school other than work, adolescents can spend long periods of time alone at home.

The tight, closed peer groups so prevalent in the 1950s have been replaced by fluid friendship groups. Students often move from one group to another, and friendships change over a period of a few weeks or months. Best friends are few, and students frequently refer to peers as "acquaintances" or "associates." Building close, intimate ties with a special boyfriend or girlfriend that could lead to long-term commitment or marriage is viewed as undesirable. Few teenagers "date"; instead, they "go out" with someone, which can mean anything from spending time together to a casual relationship that is recognized by the peer group as some form of special emotional attachment. Not only has the premise of dating changed, so have the criteria for whom one can go out with. Mixed-race couples and even same-sex couples are part of the teenage social world today.[2]

In this chapter, we examine how the social life of young people helps to shape their ambitions. We begin by examining how adolescents spend their time when they are alone and when they are with friends. Then we look at the quality of adolescents' social ties with their peers by focusing on what they do with their friends, what they talk about, and the social intimacy of their relationships.

How Teenagers Spend Their Time

Students, on average, spend about 43 percent of their waking hours at school, 19 percent with their families, and 4 percent working. These social settings that we have already examined account for roughly two-thirds of their time. Adolescents also spend a significant amount of time alone—approximately 20 percent of their waking hours. They spend another 9 percent of their time with friends outside school (fig. 8.1). What is surprising is how much time teenagers spend alone, and how little they spend with friends. While researchers who study adolescents have focused on peer-group relations, few have studied how young people feel when they are alone.[3]

In the past few decades there have been several major demographic changes that directly affect the lives of teenagers. The size of the average American family has been decreasing, so adolescents are likely to have fewer siblings. As divorce rates continue to rise, more children are spending part of their childhood with a single parent. And more mothers of children under eighteen

Fig. 8.1 How High School Students Spend Time

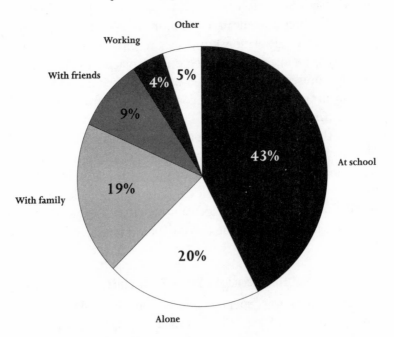

Data from Sloan study (*n* = 865)

are working, so it is less likely that there is an adult at home. In addition to these large societal changes, fewer after-school and recreational programs are available to teenagers.

The average American teenager typically spends approximately three and a half hours alone each day. Time spent alone increases as students progress from middle school through high school; twelfth graders spend close to 50 percent more time alone than sixth graders. Adolescents spend more time alone than with family or friends. When alone, they are mainly taking care of personal needs like eating, dressing, and transporting themselves from one place to another (40 percent of time alone). They also spend considerable time watching television and movies and playing video games (16 percent). Schoolwork (14 percent) and hobbies and exercise (10 percent) account for another quarter of their total time alone. About 9 percent is spent talking on the telephone. For the remainder they are thinking, doing household chores, or engaged in other activities. Although some students report drinking or using drugs when alone, these activities constitute less than one percent of the time they spend alone.[4]

How students spend their time alone differs according to the amount of time they spend alone. Adolescents who are alone more than three and a half hours a day are more likely than those who are rarely alone to watch television and to sleep and are less likely to participate in sports. On the positive side, those who spend large amounts of time alone are also more likely to use personal computers and to engage in hobbies.[5] Spending extensive time alone can be stressful. Young people report having lower self-esteem, being less happy, enjoying what they are doing less, and feeling less active when they are alone. But the ability to make productive use of time in solitude can be an important asset, especially for adolescents. Being alone can provide opportunities to develop skills and enjoy challenges. Certainly doing homework, reading, or practicing a musical instrument can be positive experiences when one is alone. In addition, being alone can help an individual turn attention inward to assess personal needs and goals. A recent study of talented teenagers found that although gifted adolescents spent more time alone than with their peers, they used their time more productively, and when they were with other people they were more likely to be with one person at a time. Even when they were with their friends, they tended to spend more time studying, thinking, and participating in structured leisure activities than average teens.[6]

Most of the adolescents in the Sloan study, however, did not engage in productive activities when they were alone. This was especially the case for students who spent a great deal of time alone. We found that adolescents with aligned ambitions were less likely than ones with misaligned ambitions to spend unusually large or small amounts of time alone. As discussed earlier, some of the characteristics of alignment, which include being engaged in organized activities, may limit the amount of time these students could be alone.

Hanging Out with Friends

Adults assume that teenagers spend most of their time outside school in the company of their friends. But in an average week most teenagers spend less than 10 percent of their waking time with friends. When they are together they tend to spend around a quarter of the time socializing—hanging out or partying; another quarter on maintaining their appearances, eating, and moving from place to place; slightly less than a quarter on homework; and about 10 percent on hobbies and exercise. The remaining 15 percent is devoted to watching television, thinking, and playing games. When they are with their friends, adolescents report having a higher sense of self-esteem and feeling happier, more powerful, and more motivated than when alone. Spending time with friends thus appears to have some psychological benefits for teenagers.[7]

On weekends, students usually spend time with their friends hanging out, going to the mall, or having parties. Jack, a tenth grader, notes that "a bunch of us get together and stay overnight. There will be about eight of us and we'll go to somebody's house and spend the night, watch movies, you know, get pizza and do stuff like that. We watch movies or go to the mall sometimes. A lot of my friends are really into computers. We do a lot with computers and stuff and that's a major weekend thing." Other weekend activities with friends include playing cards, playing Frisbee, going to a gym or sports center, playing sports, and going to church or a youth club. Young men and women participate in a wide range of sports in and out of school. Beyond the more standard ones like baseball, basketball, football, soccer, swimming, and tennis, students spoke of aerobics, bicycling, fencing, rappelling, roller-blading, sailing, skateboarding, skiing, and water polo. Students also mentioned spending extended periods with their friends camping, hunting, and taking beach and ski vacations. Without question, playing video games and watching movies and music videos are favored activities of large numbers of adolescents. But there are also aspiring actors who work in community theater, artists who paint and show their work at art fairs, dancers who prepare for recitals, and musicians who give concerts or play in bands during the week and on weekends.

Despite the wide range of activities young people engage in with their friends, the most popular are "hanging out" and talking. Teenagers enjoy talking on the phone, and some have cellular phones and beepers. Their own and others' social lives is a favored topic of conversation. While other subjects like school and sports came up, talking about each other was what students mentioned most often. The introspective character of adolescence is best reflected in the focus of their conversations—themselves.

In the following excerpt we return to Jason Ziven, who discusses his conversations with friends.

> INTERVIEWER: What kinds of things do you talk about with your friends? What kinds of subjects come up?
>
> JASON: Well, it depends on the day, or generally a lot of times we talk about school. What's happening at school, you know, different problems. Now that the year is ending it is a more social type of talking. There are lots of conversations, especially with this prom thing. A lot of people hide their mixups and their stories about trying to ask people and they were rejected, or that someone said yes and then turned them down later. And all the intricate reasons and circles of problems that just keep

compounding on themselves and things like that. And I guess rumors get spread like wildfire in this school. If you tell someone something the whole school will hear it in ten minutes. We talk about what friends are doing, what other people are doing with other people, even if we do not know them or like them. How their personalities offend us or what they did the other day or what shocks you or something like that.

The interviewer then asks what other topics come up in conversation.

> JASON: Sports, baseball. We have fun picking on our home team. And I think a lot of times people talk about—I mean this is especially what people talk about—it focuses a lot on competition. Like where you are going to college. What are you going to be doing for the summer? When are you getting a job? That is the sort of thing, you know, sort of pushing each other.
>
> INTERVIEWER: So when you talk about the future, you talk about college. What else?
>
> JASON: I don't know. People do not look too much beyond college.

Students talk very little with their friends about the future: the topic accounted for less than one percent of their time spent with friends. This is not to say that adolescents do not talk about college; where they plan to go to school is a fairly common topic, especially among high school juniors. But these conversations are about college choice, and, as Jason observes, they are primarily competitive: Where did you apply, did you get in, and do you have to attend your safety school? The path from education to work is not a topic that young people tend to discuss with each other.[8]

There are many things adolescents do not like to talk about

with their friends. While most initially say they talk about everything with their friends—boys, girls, school—they quickly
draw boundaries around certain subjects. Although "I can tell my
friends anything" is a familiar refrain, "anything" does not necessarily mean everything. Family relationships, especially arguments with a parent or disagreements with a sibling, are topics
that adolescents feel uncomfortable discussing with friends. To
friends, an adolescent may say, "My mother and I had an argument and we are not getting along," but what the argument was
about or the consequences of it are not typically shared, even
with the closest of friends. Adolescents also tend to report that
they feel hesitant talking with friends about sexual relationships.
While curiosity remains high about "how far you went sexually,"
it is not a permissible topic for conversation. In talking about his
girlfriend, Kim Lee explains that "if the friendship is really important there is nothing that we do not talk about. But I guess like
if I was with my girlfriend last night and we are doing something, I don't, I would be a little uncomfortable to talk to them
about it, whatever we did."

The Composition of Peer Groups

Nearly all teenagers can easily identify a group of people they
spend time with and know fairly intimately. In some of the Sloan
schools, these groups were very small and included only three to
five people. In other schools they were large, consisting of
twenty-five or more teenagers, all of whom a member might regard as close friends. Within these large groups there may be
smaller subgroups of best friends. Members of a group frequently talk and get together inside and outside school. We consider such groups similar to those often referred to as "cliques."[9]

Television shows and recent small-scale studies that are not
longitudinal present a traditional 1950s view of adolescent peer
groups: enduring circles of close friends with strong social ties.
These groups are seen as having strong norms that influence the

behavior of members and make them readily recognizable to outsiders. Evidence from the Sloan study suggests a strikingly different view. Adolescent friendship groups are highly fluid, changing from year to year during high school. Part of the study focused on friendships, and students were asked to identify their closest friends. High school students in tenth grade during the first year of the study named an average of eleven people as close friends. Females named slightly more close friends than males. When we asked these same students to name their closest friends two years later, the average number had declined from eleven to nine, and there was no difference between the number identified by boys and by girls.[10] Upon examining whether the close friends mentioned during tenth grade were the same as those named during twelfth grade, we found that the change in those identified as close friends was dramatic. Almost three-quarters of the closest friends named during the senior year had not been mentioned during the sophomore year.

These fluid social groups are part of the complex social landscape of most high schools. One reason young people may change their affiliations with a particular group is to avoid doing things they consider a problem, such as taking drugs. They also may change because their interests change and they want to be with the theater crowd or some other group that shares their current interests. Other students change groups because of personal conflicts. The fluidity in group memberships can make it difficult for students to recognize distinctive groups. In some of the schools students refused to identify different groups on the basis of popularity or such distinctions as "druggies," "nerds," or "jocks." They resented being asked who was in the "in crowd" or who was "really popular." "We are all friends," they would say, or, "There are not any particular groups in this school."

The absence of a strong leading crowd and the fluidity of numerous peer groups allows for a broader definition of popularity. Three-quarters of the students interviewed said they con-

sidered themselves popular. The following twelfth grader's definition of peer groups and popularity is representative of many
of the comments we heard: "I think everyone here is popular. I
mean, everyone knows about everyone else. And I do not think
there is a big, like big lines or categories of people. But they do
exist in this school. There are so many people that think they are
the most popular and everybody likes them. Those are actually
the people that are just totally fake—to everyone. Obviously, you
cannot be friends with everyone. People who say that 'I do not
hate anybody, I get along with everybody and everyone likes
me'—it is impossible. I mean there is so much competition in
this school, not only in sports but in social life—like what's cool,
what's not cool. My group of friends does not give in to all of
that." Most students refused to single out any one group as more
popular or influential than any other. Without a dominant leading crowd most students were able to feel that they were popular.

Activity-Based Groups

Although an adolescent's friends are very likely to change fairly
often, there are high school groups that are easily recognizable
and sustained over time even when their membership changes.
These groups are organized around activities: sports, theater,
student government, and social services. Similar groups for
teenagers can be found outside school, like church-sponsored
youth groups. The membership of these activity groups also
changes, but with less frequency than that of social groups. Activity groups were found across all Sloan study high schools.

Activity-based groups often play an important role in the
lives of teenagers. Adolescence is a time when young people are
trying to develop their own identities. The intense social character of the lives of adolescents reflects their exploration of different roles. Fluid peer groups are one place they try out different
roles; activity-based groups are another. Activity-based groups

are helpful to adolescents in developing social groups around common interests and in developing new skills.[11]

Activity-based groups differ from fluid peer groups in several ways. Unlike peer groups, which are organized around socializing, activity-based groups have well-defined functions, clear boundaries of membership, and established procedures for becoming a member. Membership requirements vary from a simple commitment to participate in the activities of the group, such as community service, to highly competitive tryouts for the tennis team, the school newspaper, or the orchestra. Membership in ethnic clubs or sororities is often loosely based on ascriptive characteristics such as ethnicity and social class. In talking about their friends, students often mentioned friendships based on membership in particular activity groups, including sororities, sports teams, and religious groups.

Although not as prevalent as in the 1960s and 1970s, high school sororities and fraternities still exist. Sometimes they are school sponsored and sometimes independent of the schools. Some sororities and fraternities function as service groups that raise money for the school; others are strictly social. These groups can help teens form an identity by enabling them to distinguish themselves from other groups in the school. In these tight social groups, behaviors and norms are widely shared. For example, girls in one group may wear only certain types of clothes, hang out with soccer players, and drink occasionally. The stronger the relationships within the group, the more likely the group is to exert direct pressure to behave in accordance with group norms. Kelly, a sophomore, describes her sorority.

> INTERVIEWER: Tell me a little about your friends. What are they up to? What do they do? How did you all meet and stuff?
>
> KELLY: Well, let me think. I met Holly through peer counseling. And she is also on the swim team and I am on the

swim team and we met last year. Dakota, I met her this year when I rushed with my sorority.

INTERVIEWER: A high school sorority?

KELLY: Yeah. There are about fifty to fifty-five people in it. All upper class. We are preps, we are kind of nuns.

INTERVIEWER: Nuns?

KELLY: Not that we are good or anything. We are known as the wealthy crowd. I guess you would say upper class. A clique. That is exactly why I rushed it, that is what I wanted to be in.

INTERVIEWER: Tell me about that.

KELLY: I did not want to be known as a wanderer. I wanted to be known as someone who was in a club, who was in a group, that could specify me with something.

INTERVIEWER: Why?

KELLY: Security. Gives me security knowing that I always have somewhere to go. We have fun, we go out and go mountain skiing and over spring break went to the desert. We do all that kind of stuff, which no other clubs do.

Friendships formed through religious groups were also mentioned by several students. Often these friendships were described as "very close" and as having a special personal depth and significance. One student explained, "A lot of my friends belong to my new church. My father is the assistant pastor of a new church. I really do not have a lot of friends that go to my school. . . . I can call [my church friends] true friends because I know if I was in a jam, they would help me out. None of them go to this school." When asked what kinds of things she did with friends, another student also mentioned the importance of people from church:

CONNIE: We go out to movies, go out to eat a lot. Talk on the phone quite a bit. Play putt-putt golf and we do a lot of church activities. A lot of my friends go to a Christian school. After church on Sunday nights, we will go out for hamburgers and hang out there.

INTERVIEWER: When you are with your friends what do you feel the most comfortable talking about?

CONNIE: It depends on the friends I am with. If it is my best friend, I can, I will talk about anything. I mean anything. With my church friends I will talk about things that are more personal and stuff. With my school friends normal everyday school stuff—nothing in detail.

We suspect that adolescents who have more stable peer groups are those whose friends participate in many of the same activity-based groups. In more stable peer groups it is easier to establish what is acceptable behavior than in fluid social groups. Moreover, these types of groups form a way for young people to organize their days into more productive activities. The organized structure and focus of these types of groups are likely to be helpful for the formation of life plans.

The Social Life of Adolescents

One reason friendships among teens are considered so important to study is the perceived influence of peers on a student's behaviors. As others have noted, however, most adolescents, particularly twelfth graders, do not feel pressured by peers to behave or dress in narrowly circumscribed ways.[12] We also found that students believed they were not unduly influenced by their friends; in addition, relatively few students consistently had the same best friend or a small group of friends over time. Other than best friends, some teenagers considered all others in the school to be associates or acquaintances. Instead of strong peer relationships among juniors and seniors, we found weak ties within peer groups and with others in the school. The perceived distance and level of informality in these relationships appear to have contributed to a sense of being "disconnected" from others in school.

These weak ties among groups and the relative hesitancy with which some are willing to identify a best friend or a close group of friends is partly a consequence of the social organization of the high school. Wide curricular choices in large schools make it difficult for students to be in the same classes with the same group of people, and variable schedules make it difficult for them to eat lunch with friends or even associates. As a result, many young people report feeling somewhat aimless in high school; they lack a sense of connection and have few close friends with whom they feel comfortable discussing problems or sharing ideas.

Changing friends is fairly common. From year to year we would learn about some new friendships and occasionally about ones that had remained fairly intact. New friendships can arise because of changes in class schedules, which often occur when students take more or less academically demanding courses from one year to the next. As one student notes, "I have made new friends since last year, or just gotten closer to other people that I did not know before. Most of it has to do with my class schedule. My best friend last year that I had is still my best friend." Friendships with older students also account for the frequency with which adolescents change friends. These friendships tend to occur through sports or relationships with siblings. When these friends graduate, younger students often find themselves having to form new groups of friends. Josh played baseball, and many of his older friends "are all in college right now. I am still in contact with them and I do stuff with them. I really just started getting a group of friends to hang out with this year." The fluidity of friendships is perhaps a dominant characteristic of the social life of today's adolescents.

Some students are quick to say that they do not have best or close friends, as Jason Ziven explains.

INTERVIEWER: Do you have a special group of friends?

JASON: I do not really know if I have a special group of friends because I hang out with a lot of different people. And maybe they have their groups but I sort of mix and go between groups.

INTERVIEWER: Do you have a best friend?

JASON: I don't know. I mean there are people that I would say ... I mean I have close friends but I do not know of a single best friend that I am always with or always associate with. I have girl friends and some guy friends but nobody that I like or am very close with.

In describing relationships with his friends, Tom Wilson distinguishes among those that are with school friends, family friends, and friends with whom he shares a common history.

Richard is basically a school friend. We usually talk about school, grades, you know, since we basically have most of the same teachers. Aaron was born the same day as I was. We were born in the same hospital, too, so our parents knew each other quite well. Since our parents get along really fine, we get along pretty well. Cliff, I know him since eighth grade. We went to the same junior high school and usually I talk to him during class, but sometimes during the vacations we go out, we go boating. Omar is my lab partner, so he is basically a school friend, and Neal is in my math class, and that's basically the only contact I get with him. Phillip, I have known him since eighth grade. I know his twin brother, Peter, and he is in my homeroom. So we usually play cards or go to the same gym, swim, go play basketball. Steve is also in my homeroom. We work on school projects together, and I guess that is basically it. Amy, I know her since kindergarten. We went to the same elementary and junior high school and we always had a good friendship, and I really like her.

Adolescents have complex social ties with their peers, and these ties vary in their intensity, longevity, and focus. In seeking to describe the social world of adolescents, researchers traditionally have studied peer groups. The usefulness of this idea for understanding the influence of peers on adolescent behavior may be limited, especially when the composition of these groups is frequently changing. Social ties evolve from many different sources, one of the most important of which is high school activity groups and academic classes. Adolescents consider school important to their futures, and ties formed through these school associations may have a greater effect on their ambitions than social groups do. Because teenagers spend little time talking with peers about their futures, the effect of adolescent social life in shaping ambitions is marginal.

When Sloan students were asked what they wished they could be doing, they most often mentioned being with friends—which accounted for about one-third of the responses to this question. Sleeping was the second most desired activity. Being with a special boyfriend or girlfriend was third. Guys, girls, and going out were frequent topics of conversation among many adolescents and their friends. While students frequently mentioned boyfriends or girlfriends, they typically spoke more of "going out" than dating. Talk of "dating," where a boy calls up a girl and asks her to a movie or sporting activity, was rare.

> INTERVIEWER: What do you like to talk about with your friends?
>
> MARESEA: Oh, goodness. Guys. That's the topic.

INTERVIEWER: Guys? Guys at school? Guys you are dating?

MARESEA: Yeah, that is probably the main topic that we talk about.

INTERVIEWER: Are you dating?

MARESEA [after a long pause]: No.

INTERVIEWER: No?

MARESEA: I do not know. I do not know what you call it.

Boyfriends and girlfriends typically spent more time together with groups of friends than with each other. A boy might belong to a particular group and a girl another; they would then meet up with each other at group parties. When we asked Elaine about what she did with her boyfriend, she replied, "At first we just started hanging out, and then me and him would have phone conversations that lasted for like two hours. Just talking about one thing, controversial stuff. We met at a party. Now we either hang out in our group of friends or at someone's house." Group parties, group dinners, and group activities are typical social events for many. Although certain couples are thought of as "going out," teenagers are often unsure about the current status of particular relationships. As one student remarked, "She thinks she is still going out with him, but she is wrong; he talks to me and we are going out."

Deeper romantic relationships can be found among some adolescents. These couples usually attend the same parties, but they also spend time together alone, going out to eat or driving around. At parties, boys and girls who are going out spend time together either in the group or in more secluded areas, such as in another room or outside. It appears that the only traditional forms of dating occur when a person asks someone to the junior or senior prom or when a girl asks a boy to a "turnabout dance." For many adolescents, proms or school dances may be the only conventional "dates" they have in high school.

Long-term commitments between boyfriends and girlfriends were rare. Few stayed in the same relationship for longer
than several months, but when they did, others often assumed
that the relationship was a sexual one. They rarely mentioned
planning on marrying or even dating their boyfriend or girlfriend beyond high school. Marriage was of little concern, to either boys or girls. Our evidence is consistent with results from
recent national surveys that show a decline in sexual activity
among adolescents as well as a decline in the number of teenagers
having children.

Some students reported having mixed-race romantic relationships, but these were not without problems. Often they were
worried about what their parents might think, as with one girl
who said, "They would not like that sort of thing." Another student addressed the relationship troubles that arise from cultural
and ethnic differences: "There have been a lot of problems because he is black and I am white, that was our main problem at
first. He felt that I would not be able to understand him because
I have not gone through the same experiences he goes through.
He says if I could live his life for one day, and feel the prejudice
and discrimination, then I would understand. But I think I do
understand. I am a real sensitive person."

Issues of sexual preference and sexual identity also came up
in the interviews. When asked if she was likely to marry in the
future, a twelfth grader replied, "It may be to a husband or a wife,
I am just not sure." Same-sex relationships were found among
about one percent of the high school students, which is consistent with other larger national studies.[13] In three of the high
schools there were clubs that dealt with gay and lesbian issues.
At one school an entire week was dedicated to these concerns;
invited speakers included activists who were interested in changing state legislation to offer more benefits to gay couples. Some
of the students openly discussed their sexual preferences with
interviewers but noted that they kept this information from cer-

tain friends or family members. "We talk about a lot of things. Anything from things that we like to do to what we have done. We can talk about our opinions about drugs and sex and anything. Sometimes we have real hard talks. Well, I'm gay, so with some friends I do not talk about that." A student who was struggling with "coming out" to his friends felt that it could "be a real big responsibility that could either do a lot for a lot of people or it could be very mediocre and not affect anyone."

Illegal drugs and alcohol are a part of adolescent life, and among the Sloan students most admit to drinking. Marijuana is often not considered a drug in the way that heroin and cocaine are: some students said they smoked pot but denied that they took drugs. Students were hesitant to talk about drugs, but most of them said they had friends who used drugs or knew where to buy them. Only a few admitted selling or using drugs regularly. Those who openly and repeatedly used hard drugs were rarely left untreated, and a consequence of drug use among athletes was suspension from the team. Some students spoke about entering drug-treatment centers or participating in counseling programs.[14]

Frequent drug use among friends was often given as a reason why students changed peer groups. We saw this in the case of Paul Cheng; Tom provides another example.

> TOM: Well, yeah, actually there's been a pretty big change [in my friends]. The people who I mostly hang around with now are people I met this summer, even though they had been to the school for a while. I never really hung around them until the start of last summer. And the people I used to hang with I would prefer not to be with them anymore because they have gone the wrong way, so to speak.
>
> INTERVIEWER: How so?
>
> TOM: Well, I guess you could say they were into crime. They

were taking drugs, they drink beer. I am trying to shy away. I mean I cannot, I do not hang around with them but I still try to maintain some sort of contact, like greet each other. But that's about it.

Many had concerns about being identified as drug users or being in places "where a lot of that goes on":

INTERVIEWER: Are there any sorts of things you do with your friends that you wish you didn't?

JUSTIN: Not really. We are not really that bad. There are worse people that do a lot more. There is a group of people that go and smoke and get loaded all the time. I do not find that fun at all.

INTERVIEWER: But your crowd does not really get into that?

JUSTIN: No, we stay away from that.

Drinking, however, appears to be a significant part of many adolescents' lives. As one student explained, his friends "do not do drugs. They drink every now and then, but everybody does that." Another student noted that "a lot of times after school we play handball, sometimes we play pool, and sometimes we drink a little over at my friend's house . . . once a month or so." This comment was made by a sophomore, an excellent student who was sent by his school to a space conference in Washington, D.C., and who plans to get a Ph.D. and become an aeronautical engineer. Stories of occasional drinking were shared by tenth- and twelfth-grade students in all the schools. One twelfth-grader said that students drink even when they think it is wrong: "What do I do with my friends that I do not think I should? Probably drink, that is probably the only bad thing that we do. We all know it is wrong. We know it is wrong. We just do it anyway."

Even though many students admitted to drinking occasionally, some expressed disapproval or discomfort with behaviors that were potentially risky. Threats of physical violence and the possibility of arrest were some of the concerns of adolescents who had friends who engaged in excessive drinking. "My friends, they ask me to go out and party, and I usually don't like to talk about it because it is not that I do not want to go, but it is too much. You hear too much on the news about somebody getting shot, and I do not want to be unlucky. I want to get an education. Maybe get a chance to play ball in college. It can be dangerous, especially around here. They go to parties, underground parties. My friend, he got into a fight once because he and this other guy were drunk."

In most large-scale studies of adolescents there are "worst" cases, and the Sloan study had several. A good student had a severe drinking problem: "When I was drinking a lot, when I was playing ball, I was mainly drunk on the weekends. There was a couple of times where I would go to practice and I was ripped. Then about a month ago, I was up to a case, a case and a half every night, seven days a week." Eventually this student was arrested for assault and lost a scholarship for college. A few of the females in the study became pregnant and had babies during the years we followed them. Some students stole, had serious fights, vandalized property, and shoplifted. But arrests, abuse, and sexual activity were not characteristic of most of the teens in the study. For the most part, these young people spent time hanging out with friends, going to movies, and listening to music.

The hallways of today's high schools are filled with boys and girls passing from class to class in jeans, big shirts, and boots. Only periodically can one spot striped heads of green and red, pierced eyebrows, black leather jackets, and long belt chains. While the differences in teenage dress are slight, the diversity of musical tastes is considerable. In the Coleman study in the 1950s, tastes in music were similar; nearly half the adolescents selected rock and roll as their favorite type of music, and Pat Boone was the favorite singer, easily surpassing all others, including Elvis Presley.[15] When we attempted to learn about what types of music adolescents today listen to, the list of nominations became so long that we quickly realized that variation was the norm. Students talked about many different types of music, including alternative, country, hard rock, hip-hop, light rock, jazz, reggae, rap, and rhythm and blues, and the list of favorite vocalists and bands numbered well over fifty, with few overlapping choices. The wide range in musical tastes mirrors to some extent the many choices today's young people face.

The peer groups of American teenagers today are fluid, often weakly tied together, and not very influential in the formation of future plans and aspirations. When educational and occupational aims are taken into account, the social lives of adolescents with aligned ambitions and those with misaligned ambitions differ in three basic ways. First, students with aligned ambitions were less likely to spend time alone. Second, aligned students were no more likely than others to see themselves as popular, but they were less likely to value having a special girlfriend or boyfriend. Third, their parents played a greater role in determining which friends they could associate with and were more likely to know who their friends were.[16] Friends are important to young people's lives and help to shape their sense of self, but they have a limited influence on educational goals and career plans. Peers offer little guidance about how to navigate a meaningful path through either high school or postsecondary school. The influence of peers on the life decisions of adolescents is limited. Adolescents value achievement in high school, and most plan to go on to college. But the decision about which college to attend and what occupation to pursue are based on a student's individual interests, strengths, and talents and are unlikely to be influenced by the fluid social groups to which an adolescent belongs.

Defining a Pathway

III

chapter nine

The Ambition Paradox

To realize their high ambitions, more high school graduates are attending college than ever before. In 1993, more than 2.1 million recent graduates enrolled in postsecondary institutions.[1] In deciding on college, students confront a number of complex choices: whether to attend a public or private institution, a small or large one, a traditional liberal arts college or a specialized school in a field like engineering or film. A fundamental distinction among postsecondary institutions is the type of degree offered. Four-year institutions offer primarily bachelor of arts or bachelor of science degrees. Community and junior colleges offer associate's degrees in arts or sciences earned with two years of full-time study. Proprietary institutions offer a range of certificates in such fields as cosmetology, trucking, or heating and air-conditioning repair. These certificate programs vary in length, but many can be completed in less than a year. Some community or junior colleges also offer vocational and technical certificate programs that take less than a year to complete. Over the past two decades, fewer high school graduates have been enrolling in certificate programs.[2]

While the proportion of high school graduates opting for college has increased, the distribution of students entering two-year and four-year institutions has remained fairly stable since 1972, with about one-third attending two-year institutions and two-thirds attending four-year institutions. What distinguishes recent high school seniors from those in the past, particularly those who choose to attend two-year institutions, is a change in

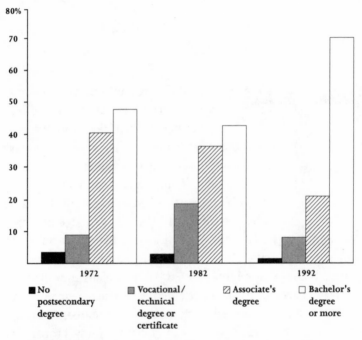

Fig. 9.1 *Educational Expectations of Students in Two-Year Institutions*

Data from senior samples of NLS-72 (weighted), HS&B 1982 (weighted),
NELS:88–94 (weighted)

their ambitions. In 1972 and 1982, less than 50 percent of students who were enrolled in two-year institutions expected to earn a bachelor's degree. Today, almost 70 percent of students who begin their college careers at two-year institutions expect to earn a bachelor's degree (fig. 9.1).[3]

High Ambitions with Low Odds

Although the ambitions of students attending two-year colleges have risen, the odds of these students transferring to a four-year college and earning a bachelor's degree are low, and the odds have declined over the past two decades. Using standard statistical methods, we estimated the likelihood of receiving a bachelor's degree for students who began their postsecondary education in two-year and four-year institutions. Our statistical model is based on a student with above-average test scores in high school who expected to obtain a bachelor's degree and whose parents had attended college and had high educational expectations for their child. To determine whether the odds of receiving a bachelor's degree had changed for students beginning in two-year institutions, we predicted the likelihood of receiving a bachelor's degree in four and five years for students who started college in 1972 and for those who started in 1982.[4]

A student who initially enrolled in a two-year institution in 1972 was 20 percent less likely to receive a bachelor's degree in four years than a comparable student who started in a four-year institution. Using 1982 data, we found that the likelihood had declined: earning a bachelor's degree after beginning at a two-year college was 28 percent less likely than for a comparable student who started in a four-year institution.

Assuming that transferring from a two-year to a four-year institution may increase the time needed to obtain a bachelor's degree, we extended our analysis to five years. But here, instead of the gap narrowing between two-year and four-year starters, the difference in completion rates actually increased: in 1982, a student beginning college in a two-year institution was 38 percent less likely to receive a bachelor's degree in five years than a comparable student who initially enrolled in a four-year institution (see Appendix B). It appears that students who begin their studies at a two-year college with the expectation of earning a bachelor's degree are choosing a long and improbable route.

The choice to attend a two-year rather than a four-year institution is often influenced by financial concerns. The primary explanation behind this decision, however, is not family income but the willingness of parents to financially support their adolescent's education. Students from families willing to provide

$5,000 or more toward their college education are six times more likely to attend four-year than two-year institutions—independent of the students' academic ability, rigor of their high school courses, family income, and parental education. African-American students are almost three times more likely than whites with similar background characteristics to attend a four-year than a two-year institution. The willingness of parents to financially support their children's education is clearly an important factor in influencing the type of postsecondary institution they attend.

The two-year college route is being chosen by more students with the ambition to attain a bachelor's degree. This creates an ambition paradox: students with high ambitions are choosing an educational route with low odds of success. How do they adapt to being caught in this ambition paradox? Do they drop out of the two-year college? Do they downsize their educational ambitions? Do they change their occupational aspirations to be more consistent with the labor market opportunities for students without bachelor's degrees? Or do they cling to their dreams and persist in their efforts to earn a bachelor's degree?

One possible response would be for students to downsize their educational ambitions to bring them more in line with their chances for success. We do not find this to be the case. Two-year college students are surprisingly consistent in their educational ambitions. Of those who began their education in a two-year college expecting to earn a bachelor's degree, two years after enrolling 87 percent still expected to earn one. Although not as common among students enrolled in two-year colleges as it is among those in four-year institutions, this sustained preference for the bachelor's degree has increased by more than 20 percent over the past ten years for students in two-year colleges.[5]

Another characteristic of students caught in this ambition paradox is that they display persistence in their efforts to earn an associate's degree: they stay enrolled and continue to work to-

ward it beyond the expected two years. The average length of
time for earning one at two-year institutions has increased over
the past twenty years, and almost a third of students who start at
one of these schools take more than two years to complete their
associate's degrees. Among 1989 seniors who earned an associate's degree, over a quarter took between four and five years to
complete it. For students who did finish within five years, the
average time it took increased from thirty-one months in 1977
to thirty-six months in 1994.[6]

It is also taking longer to earn a bachelor's degree. Since the
mid-1980s, the time it takes for college students to complete
their bachelor's degree has increased, whether they began at
two-year or four-year institutions (fig. 9.2). Among those students who started college at four-year institutions in 1989, 34
percent completed a bachelor's degree in four years, and an additional 24 percent finished it within five years. The percentage
of students earning bachelor's degrees who began at two-year
institutions has declined since 1972.[7]

Students caught in the ambition paradox also tend to stay
attached to institutions of higher education. Those who enroll in
two-year colleges are increasingly likely to still be enrolled in a
postsecondary school five years after their high school graduation. Among high school seniors who initially enrolled in two-
year institutions in 1989, almost half were still enrolled somewhere five years later.[8] Slightly more than a quarter of the
students who began their studies in a two-year institution had
transferred and were studying in a four-year college five years
later. This low transfer rate from two-year to four-year institutions has been fairly consistent over the past twenty years.[9]

The ambition paradox is a difficult trap for most students.
For some, this is because they have misaligned ambitions—their
educational expectations and occupational aspirations are inconsistent. Students who do not have well-developed life plans
and who do not have a meaningful understanding of how edu-

Fig. 9.2 Bachelor's Degree Completion Rates for Students Starting
at Two-Year and Four-Year Colleges

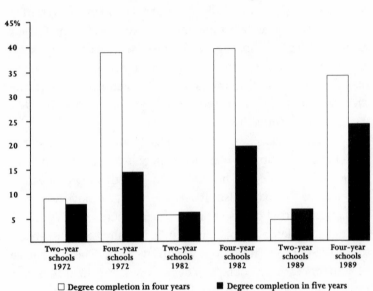

Data from senior sample NLS-72 (weighted), senior sample HS&B 1982 (weighted), senior
sample Beginning Postsecondary Student Survey (weighted)

cational routes are constructed and connected to work are not
likely to find the needed guidance in the two-year-college setting. Many expect the two-year college to serve as a platform
from which they can enter any type of program in any four-year
institution. Students like Brian Daniels (from Chapter 4), for example, frequently mentioned in interviews that they had chosen
to attend two-year institutions to get their general college requirements out of the way before transferring to a four-year college. The diversity of missions among four-year institutions and
their different admissions and credit-transfer policies makes it
extraordinarily difficult for community and junior colleges to
successfully channel students' ambitions into coherent educational plans.

Using data from our Sloan sample of beginning college students, we examined the proportion of students who had aligned ambitions in four-year and two-year institutions. Almost half the students attending four-year institutions had aligned ambitions. Students who attended two-year colleges were more likely to have their goals out of alignment: almost two-thirds of them had misaligned ambitions. Half of all students who started their postsecondary education at a two-year institution had higher educational expectations than needed for the occupations to which they aspired.[10]

The case studies for this chapter focus on young adults with high ambitions who select educational paths with low odds of reaching their goals. For the most part, these students do not attach status differences to two-year and four-year institutions: college is college, whether one attends a large university or a community college. They assume they will receive an associate's degree in two years and a bachelor's degree two years later. To explore the idea of an ambition paradox in more detail, we examine the ambitions these students had in their senior year of high school, the reasons they chose to attend particular postsecondary schools, and the match or mismatch between the academic programs they enrolled in and their occupational aspirations. We also look at the consequences of selecting a difficult path when trying to make future dreams a reality.[11]

The cases illustrate several themes about students in two-year institutions. First, there is a group of them who can be portrayed as exiting the ambition paradox by dropping out of school. Often they have financial pressures that make paying tuition bills difficult, and many have unsuccessful academic experiences in college. Although leaving the institution without their associate's degree, they are reluctant to lose their attachment to the world of postsecondary education. Many of them maintain a desire to return to college.

A second group consists of those with misaligned ambitions who frequently change their educational majors and career aims. These highly ambitious students enter two-year institutions without a coherent plan for their future. They often choose programs and courses without knowing whether the courses will transfer to four-year institutions or even whether they are required for an associate's degree. Frequently they find the courses in college more difficult than in high school because they had not taken the right high school prerequisites for the courses required in college.[12] Among this group are students recruited to play intercollegiate athletics. Athletic scholarships offered by two-year colleges can be a strong incentive for students who want to attend college but cannot play in the more competitive collegiate divisions. Their lack of appropriate high school academic preparation and a coherent life plan makes the successful transition to a four-year college difficult for these students.

A final group of students includes those with aligned ambitions who attend two-year institutions. While caught in the ambition paradox, they differ from other students in that they are more likely to persist with their academic plans even though it may take them several years to complete their associate's degree and transfer to a four-year institution. Unlike the misaligned students, these individuals have a life plan and attempt to make course selections and work decisions consistent with these plans.

Leaving Community College for Full-Time Work

In Chapter 3, we told the story of Calvin Norris, who started at a community college but left after his first semester to work full time. Cliff O'Dessa's experiences are quite similar to Calvin's. When Cliff was a senior in high school, he planned to become a mechanical engineer and assumed he would obtain a master's degree. Although Cliff had high educational expectations, he had some difficulty in mathematics and science and took less challenging courses in these subjects throughout his high school career.

When it became time to decide where to attend college, Cliff's parents gave him limited guidance about selecting a school. His father had attended a community college for two years, and his mother had a bachelor's degree. Although his parents expected him to attend college, neither of them had expressed a clear preference about where he should go. Cliff's older brother had attended the local community college for a year but had dropped out before completing his associate's degree. Cliff hoped to be able to beat his brother's record and stay in school. "I kind of wanted to be a little better than him because that's a big thing with my grandparents and parents," he recalled. But he was concerned about paying for college because his parents were unable to help.

After graduating from high school in June 1994, Cliff decided to start his college career that fall at a two-year college close to home. There were two community colleges within driving distance of his parents' house. He decided to go to the one farther away "because it is a better neighborhood. I have lived around here all my life. I got pretty sick of it. I wanted a change so I went over to this other college. It is kind of rich and classy and the facilities were real nice over there. I mean at the other school the facilities are all right but nothing in comparison."

Cliff was late in registering for his classes, so he did not have many courses to choose from. "Most of the classes were closed out and so I took anything that was available." He had no idea what he would major in despite his expressed interest in engineering in high school. Unclear about his future schooling or work plans, Cliff did not follow any particular program and just selected a series of courses: "I took an English class. It was like, writing, creative writing, stuff like that. I took algebra class, like, college algebra. U.S. history to 1877, something like that. And I believe human development. I'm not sure that's what it's called. But it was . . . it was something along those lines." Of the classes he found most satisfying Cliff said, "I like math, because, I mean, I was doing so well. The teacher was pretty nice. I wasn't that good in math before, but she made it pretty easy, so I kind of enjoyed it. I never missed anything in that class." But there were more that he disliked: "I don't like history for one. And before 1877 was kind of boring anyway. But I don't know. I don't like to write so I didn't like my English class. I'm just not too creative, you know." In general, "It was a real good college and all the teachers were all right," he said, but he just "didn't like it." Within two months, he began to have doubts about his classes and found most of them boring. "I didn't like them at all."

He ended up dropping English, history, and human development and later dropped mathematics as well. "I didn't like those classes to begin with. So, you know, it was no big deal, if I dropped them. But after a while, I did not feel like going up to college just to go to that math class." There were many demands on Cliff, and school just did not seem that attractive. The payments for his car, gasoline, and outstanding debts seemed to make his tuition and expenses too much. "I had a gas-guzzling car. I thought I could wait another, at least another year or half a semester or something until I go back because it was just taking its toll on me. I mean, I still had a job when I was in college. And then I just took it up full time after I quit. You know, it made things a little bit better, that's for sure. Less strenuous."

Cliff's parents were disappointed, but, according to him, "They know pretty much that I'm going back this fall. So they are not worrying too much." In reflecting on his two months in college and his subsequent work experiences, Cliff was not sure about his decision: "If I stayed in it, I would've been a hell of a lot better." When he was interviewed a year after graduating from high school, he said he hoped to return to college in the fall but was unsure what other classes he would take if he went back.

He was adamant that he would "definitely take that math class again. I would take some sort of English class but I'm not sure what, maybe Reading 1 because I don't mind that. History, I don't like it but I'd take it after 1877. Whatever, like early 1900s, 1940, something like that because I like the world war, both of them, and [the] Vietnam War, stuff like that."

While he was in college Cliff did not participate in any extracurricular activities. He had hoped to play soccer, but "it fell through." Working at a gas-station convenience store took up most of his time. It was his responsibility to "keep the store up, make it look nice, I kept the outside up, wiped the pumps down, cleaned a lot." This job lasted about six months. "At Quick Trip I was on my way up. I mean, it's an established company and you, if you stay in it you can make a lot of money but you have to deal with people all day every day. I am not too much of a people person. I mean I'll get along with them but, you know, dealing with them constantly every day it just, it took its toll on me."

After leaving the convenience store, Cliff began working for a car dealership, "driving parts around." But he did not like this job either: "Well, my first two days I rode in the truck with another guy, the guy who lives with me, because we work the same job. He took me around and showed me some of the places that we deliver to. It's always changing and we did not have a set path so it was kind of, 'learn on your own and you will be better off.'" Cliff's companion had been at the company for about fifteen years: "He knows everything, but there's such a turnover ratio at the place, he doesn't really get to know anybody. So he's not very likable. I did not like him, that's one reason why I quit." By June, a year after graduating from high school, Cliff began his third new job, as a roofer, a job that he learned about from his friends.

He returned to college the following fall as a first-semester freshman taking nine hours of classes and working forty-eight hours a week for the same service station as in the previous year.

Cliff needed to work full time and was not able to afford full-time tuition. Part of his college costs were covered by a loan his grandmother had given him to return to school, and he was in the process of paying her back. He had a more responsible job than when he initially began working at the service station: "The job pays really well. I've worked here for about a year and a half, roughly, and I started out as a measly part-time clerk, and now I'm up to first assistant manager, so I've jumped quite a bit. The job is to sell gasoline. It is a truck stop with diesel, and basically it's customer relations. I run the clerks, I help the manager, the main manager of the store, and I get paperwork, store merchandising, but the main thing of all is customer relations."

Cliff also changed his occupational aspirations and was now "trying to major in business." He saw himself "moving up the ladder" at the gas station, and "I could move farther in, into the corporation if I majored in business and get a higher, top executive position." To accomplish these goals, he said he hoped to earn "an associate's of business or something like that, which is transferable and then I am going to try and go to the state university and complete my bachelor's." When asked why he wanted to attend the university, Cliff said, "I heard they have a real good business program up there. A lot of my friends go up there and they have come out pretty successful. The teachers are good and it is a nice area."

Cliff stayed with the job through his second year in community college, continuing to take a reduced course load. In the fall of 1996, he was enrolled in only one course; his interests were primarily focused on his job and the relationship he had developed with his manager, whom he considered his "mentor." "I've been talking to my manager, and he knows friends of his that are in major businesses. He is kind of coaching me along the way of what major businesses expect, you know, whether it is in insurance companies or in service corporations. He has been with the company for ten years, so he has seen the odds and ends of the job and he's got a lot of friends in high places. He has helped me out considerably. He is the one who got me promoted." The strong relationship with his boss solidified Cliff's desire to advance in "the corporation." Completing a bachelor's degree, however, still remained a dream. Students like Cliff are slow to give up on their dreams and keep returning to school with the hope that somehow this time it will be different. Holding on to high occupational ambitions can be detrimental for those students whose course taking bears little reality to the education or training actually needed for the jobs they desire.

The following year Cliff did not register for school and was working full time as the manager of the truck stop where he had started three years earlier. He recently got another promotion and has a serious girlfriend. Moving in and out of a community college without obtaining a degree, as Cliff did, is a common pattern among students who begin college with high expectations but are uncertain how to accomplish their goals.

From the interview data, three major reasons appear to explain why students who enter a two-year college aiming for more than an associate's degree fail to obtain even a two-year degree. First, many have unrealistic expectations and a sketchy knowledge of what college is going to be like. They receive limited guidance in high school and college about what courses to take, and many of them take ones that do not necessarily fulfill degree requirements. Second, many are not academically strong high school students. They find themselves unprepared for the demands of college work, especially in mathematics and English courses. Third, for those whose families have few economic resources, the costs of continuing in school can be burdensome. Analyses of other data sets indicate that more of the economic burden of attending a two-year college is assumed by the students rather than the parents. Students in four-year institutions tend not to be as personally burdened by the economics of college.[13]

Downsizing Occupational Choices

Many students who enter two-year colleges with high ambitions end up downsizing their occupational aspirations. But they do not necessarily give up their desire to obtain a bachelor's or even a graduate degree. They may decide to become a social worker rather than a psychologist, a real estate broker rather than an architect, but many continue to hold on to the expectation of transferring from the community college to a four-year college or university. Most of the students in the Sloan study who attended two-year colleges ended up staying for longer than three years. They continued to have high educational expectations and to persist in the educational process, even if unsure of what they wanted to major in or the type of job they hoped to find in the future.

As a high school senior, Alison Freer wanted to become a criminal prosecutor. Her knowledge of the legal profession was quite limited. An uncle was studying to be a lawyer, but she seldom saw him. Television shows were an even less reliable source of information: "Although I know it is not like on television . . . it looks interesting." When asked how much education one needs to become a lawyer, Alison replied, "I think I need a bachelor's. I know I need a bachelor's degree, at least that's what I've been told that I need. And a lot of schooling. I think about six years maybe." College was very important to Alison, and she planned to begin her education at the local community college "for my first two years and from there I don't know where I'm going to transfer."

When asked what a lawyer does, Alison explained that she would "advise my clients of their legal rights and try to settle the cases without going to court is what you kind of really want to do. If you do go to court it's important, you have to influence other people of your opinion, you know, change their opinions on things and really tell them that your view is the right one." Alison believed she had special personal qualities that would help make her a good lawyer: "I love having the answer right away, having to be right on the ball, having to know exactly what I want to say. When it comes to something I like to get my point across and then when I'm done I like to really convince people of my opinion." According to Alison, part of being a lawyer was "knowing how to react quickly. You have to know how to talk well in front of others. Know how to use words—big ones—to make people think about what you are saying. Get people's attention." It was her ability to influence and persuade people that Alison perceived as a real strength in pursuing her career. The only barrier she envisioned to becoming a lawyer was "my conscience. My conscience would get to me if I put someone that I kinda felt was innocent, you know, if I ever put him away in jail or if I knew my client was lying but I still have to defend him."

In high school Alison lived with her mother; her father was deceased. She often worked as a babysitter for her sister's children, who lived close by. Planning eventually to get married, Alison's first priority was college. "Getting married to me is really important. But first I want all my schooling out of the way before I start having kids, because I really want to spend time with my kids and I don't want to immediately turn them over to a babysitter because I think it's important to spend time with them when they are little." Alison enjoys children, and in her senior year of high school she took a class on childhood; as part of it she assisted a teacher at a local elementary school, reading stories to the students, helping them with their numbers, and participating in their arts and crafts.

In the fall after high school, Alison enrolled in the local community college. She preferred living at home to living with friends, which she thought would be "stressful." The decision to attend community college was partly financial. Alison's mother had strongly encouraged her to enroll in a community college "to get used to college and moneywise too. It is close to home. And, you know, it is a big enough adjustment just to go to college." Her mother was also studying nursing at the same college; having both of them going to school at the same time was a financial strain, but Alison received a scholarship that covered her tuition and books, which helped substantially.

Reflecting on her choice to start out at a community college, Alison recalled, "I was scared because I did not know what I wanted to do. I knew I wasn't going to fail or do poorly in college. But I was just . . . maybe I was just scared. I was not ready to leave high school." She found college more academically difficult than high school. "In high school it is kind of like your teachers push you along and keep telling you to do your homework, you have to do this, and in college it is like they kind of don't care, you know. It's like, you either do the work or you fail, and they give you a lot more work in a shorter amount of time that you have to do. It's a lot more studying and they are a lot more strict on their grades and you cannot really talk them into giving you an A like you could in high school, at least I could, like if you're between grades. Attendance is a lot more important in college than it was in high school." Another reason college seemed more difficult was her high school preparation, which she viewed as not strong enough for the academic challenges of postsecondary school. Even though she was in several honors classes in high school, "I didn't feel they really challenged me at all."

In her first semester at the community college, Alison took psychology, history, English, and algebra. She had to take a mathematics placement test given to all entering freshmen, and on the basis of her performance she was required to take an algebra class. This course would give her credit toward her associate's degree but was not transferable to a four-year institution. Unlike her successful mathematics experiences in high school, this remedial course gave Alison considerable difficulty, and she had to take it again the second semester. Her other first semester grades were As and Bs.

After her first year, Alison began thinking about majoring in psychology and perhaps becoming a psychologist, but she still planned to earn a bachelor's or even a master's degree. As for college, "I want to get as much education as I can. The more education you have the easier it is to get a job. You make more money." The interest in psychology was sparked by the subject and her professor. "I particularly enjoyed learning about why people act the way they do. I took psychology in high school and I liked it then, but I liked it more, and probably because of the teacher I had." Her psychology professor "loved what she was doing and she said you got a real satisfaction knowing that you've helped people and everything. She was really cool, she was really open and answered any questions you had and tried to help you in any way she could to make you pass." A professor's willingness to help students succeed in college was the most important criterion Alison used to assess the quality of instruction in all her courses. Her English professor rated highly in this regard: "She is real nice. She is available any time you need help and, you know, will do anything she can to try and help you. If she knows you are doing, trying your hardest, she will pass you."

The second year after high school, Alison was still enrolled in the same community college and expected to graduate in May with an associate's degree. Her grades continued to be As and Bs, except for math, where she was earning Cs. Her GPA was 3.0, but she said she "would like to do better. I just have to dedicate myself more." She was taking general education courses with the intention of transferring to a four-year state college. No longer interested in law or psychology, Alison was not "quite sure what my major is yet, so that kind of means I'm not too sure where I'm going to transfer. That sort of depends on my major." She had not received any pressure to choose a major from staff at the community college or her family. "My mom keeps telling me I have plenty of time to figure what I want to major in, which is comforting." Despite Alison's ambivalence about her major, her educational expectations remained high. She continued to plan on transferring.

Alison was comfortable with her college choice. "I think it was a great transition from high school to college, you know, because it was a little college. You know, it is kind of like a middle-ground type thing. I had some of the same friends here, and it was just easier for me. It was close to home." She perceived herself as more organized and disciplined about her time than when she began college. She credits her organizational skills to her part-time employment at a clothing store during her second year. "It's gotten better, because I'm so much more used to college and studying and learning how to fit everything in, how to schedule everything, especially now with working. I know exactly how much time I have to study and everything, so I have to study. It's not like I can—when I first started school, I was more likely to put things off, like studying. And I'm doing better in school."

As the second assistant manager at the clothing store, she said, she was "two steps away from being manager. The job is great. I love the people I work with, which I think makes all the difference in the world. They're all girls and we all get along really well. Pretty much all of us are in college, so we have a lot in common and that makes the job go a lot better. It doesn't pay very well, but that's not why I got it. You know, I just got it to get a little extra spending money and kind of help my mom out a little bit." Her responsibilities included supervising when the manager was not in, and she was also in charge of scheduling and helping with merchandising and wall displays. She turned down a promotion because she did not want the extra responsibility to interfere with her schoolwork.

In the spring of 1996, three years after starting community college, Alison received her associate's degree in liberal arts, but she did not transfer at that time. Unsure what occupation she wanted to pursue, she started taking additional courses, one of them in criminal justice. This course changed her academic direction, and she decided to major in forensic science. After her fourth year in community college, Alison transferred to a four-year university to pursue a bachelor's degree in criminal justice. Reflecting on her educational experiences, Alison believes she was not prepared for college and blames her high school for not being more intellectually challenging. She sees two-year college as a necessary transition to a four-year college. If she could start over at community college, she would be "a little more serious about it," and now wishes she had been more focused, sought more help, and worked with the college's counseling program.

Five years after high school, Alison is a junior in a four-year public university, majoring in criminal justice and expecting to graduate in the spring of 1999. When asked her reasons for transferring to this school, she replied, "It's inexpensive because I can still live at home and it's like within walking distance, and it is pretty convenient, and it is a good school with a good reputation." Her long-range goal is to obtain her master's, but at the moment she has concentrated her energies on a bachelor of science degree. "In my junior year in high school, I wanted to be a lawyer. And then you really understand what it is all about and I felt there are too many lawyers and it's kind of a dirty job. I'm not putting anybody down for that. It's just something I couldn't feel comfortable doing. So my interests have been in the criminal justice field. So now I am interested in forensics work, dealing with homicides, fingerprinting of fabrics or clothing, trying to link who did it and the time of death, and how this person was killed."

Alison's story is similar to those of other students who begin their education at community college expecting to transfer to a four-year school. Janice Short followed a path much like Alison's: she had high educational and occupational ambitions in her senior year, hoping to earn a Ph.D. and become a psychiatrist. But she also had limited exposure to what a psychiatrist actually does and never had personal contact with anyone in this profession. Both Alison and Janice believed they were "right" for their respective jobs because of unique personality characteristics. Alison reasoned that she would make a good lawyer because she was persuasive; Janice felt that psychiatry was a good choice because she liked to help her friends solve problems. Neither had a clear sense of what these jobs actually entailed or the educational requirements needed for them.

Like Alison's mother, Janice's parents encouraged her to attend the local community college. Janice wanted to go away to school, but family finances made it impossible. She didn't achieve the grades she had hoped for in her first year of college, either, and in retrospect wished she had worked harder. After a year in college she decided to become a psychologist, lowering her aspirations as Alison did. In her second year, however, Janice once again changed her occupational aspirations to "something in biology" and consequently changed her major. "I switched to biology," she said, "so I can get a job with the state working forensics in a crime lab. The state hires chemical majors, biology majors, and physics majors with bachelor's degrees. They have a forensic scientist training program where they pay you to train for one to three years depending on which area you go into."

After finishing her associate's degree in three years, Janice transferred to a four-year state university. A junior now, she expects to graduate in two years. She finds her upper-level classes a little harder than the ones at the community college, but she does not see a difference in the quality of education. "No, I don't think there's any difference. Every school has its problems. I don't think there's much of a difference as far as classes and stuff. There's a quality of education I guess that I got at either one." At the university, however, she felt she could talk to a counselor about her goals and learn what classes to take and when to take them, whereas the counselors at the community college were "not really helpful. I think it is because you got all these students

there, and everyone wants to go to a different school, and they
cannot know what every single school wants."

Most of Janice's friends from high school went to community college, but not all of them graduated or transferred: "Some
of them did not even make it through the community college.
You know, I think a lot of them go because your parents expected
you to. You have to go to college basically to get a decent job. And
a lot of parents expect it, so I think a lot of people go, and then
once they get there they realize, 'Well, I'm not getting good
grades' and they just decide, 'Well, that's not for me.'" Her friends
who stuck it out and received an associate's degree transferred to
four-year schools—none stopped going to school. Janice places
considerable value on earning an associate's degree and then
transferring. Her sister transferred without the degree, "and she
was on academic probation the whole time. She went back to
community college and is trying to get back into the university."

With high school five years behind them, both Alison and
Janice have completed their associate's degrees and transferred
to four-year state universities. They changed their occupational
goals along the way, but they succeeded in transferring to institutions where they could continue the pursuit of a bachelor's degree. They attended community colleges thousands of miles
apart, but both are planning to major in forensic science. While
the route of transferring from community colleges to four-year
institutions is circuitous and not well traveled, it may be that
community colleges offer limited but well-marked paths for certain occupations. Even in national studies with samples of more
than ten thousand high school seniors, there may be only six
hundred who transfer from two-year colleges to four-year institutions.[14] Such small samples do not permit fine-grained analysis of the more subtle features of the transfer process, but these
stories do illustrate how some students make the transition from
two-year to four-year institutions.

The transfer process may be different for community college athletes. Athletic scholarships given by two-year colleges can be especially attractive incentives, especially for students who need the money to attend school and find that their ambition to play Division I sports is not viable, given the offers they receive. Matthew Winscott, the youngest of six, lives in a large city in the Midwest. As a freshman in high school, he made the junior varsity basketball team and continued to play JV through his sophomore year. In his junior year he became ineligible to play varsity ball after he missed too many days because of headaches—the result of an injury during his freshman season when he ran into a wall and hit his head. "So after my junior year I felt I had to get out of that situation, so I transferred schools and played varsity in my senior year for this high school and it is working out pretty well."

Transferring schools in his senior year did not turn out to be much of an adjustment problem for Matt: most of his middle school friends had gone to the new school. What he found different was the emphasis on academics. He was disappointed when his report card at the new school showed a B average. Recognizing that his grades were a result of the more difficult classes he was taking, Matt believed it was worth the extra effort: "I took harder classes than when I was at my old school because I felt that I was slacking up and I would not be prepared to go to college if I kept getting into classes I could just walk through." He wanted to become a psychiatrist, but his immediate plans were to "go to college. I want to go to college and have a successful basketball career. The start of my basketball is the start of success."

During the season a number of scouts came to see Matt play. "I got letters from big colleges and letters from small Division I schools. I got letters from all of the junior colleges around here." Disappointment struck in spring of his senior year when he tore the cartilage in his left ankle and then, after it healed, broke his right ankle. The injuries had real consequences for his scholarship opportunities. "The schools that were looking at me slowed down a lot. One or two schools were still looking but not as hard as before." At the end of the year, Matt chose to attend a community college in the state because "they paid more attention to me coming out of high school as far as scholarships go after I hurt my leg." He wanted to be able to play basketball with a scholarship, and this was the school that provided him with that opportunity.

Matt enrolled in the fall, and within weeks he sprained his back. He still had his two years of community college athletic eligibility left, so he was redshirted for his freshman year: he could practice with the team but not play in games. By the following fall his back had completely healed and he played on the college team. During his third year of community college, he received a full ride—an athletic scholarship from a university in another state that would allow him to continue to play for two more years.

His grades in the community college were mainly "Bs, with a C and an A here and there." During the summers he worked at a center with children who had been taken from their parents; he was paid and also received academic credit for the work. The experience at the center, he suggests, influenced his thoughts about the future; he now plans to become a child psychologist, "because I enjoy working with kids." Matt has downsized his ambition to be a psychiatrist but still plans on getting a master's or a Ph.D. Next year he intends to major in psychology, although he does not know much about the psychology program at the university or which of his courses he will be able to transfer.

Matt's overriding preoccupation with playing basketball influenced his college choice and the effort he was willing to put into his academic interests. "I chose to go to community college for more than one reason," he explains. "My main reason is because I love the game so much, and the other reason is I did not want to be a financial burden to my parents." His progression through the junior college took longer because of playing basketball, and his devotion to the game has exerted considerable influence on his college experience and his selection of a four-year college. It will take him longer to complete his degree than had he begun his postsecondary education at a four-year institution. Core and specialized program requirements in many university programs have lengthened the time most students need to complete a bachelor's degree, and Matt's community college courses may not all count toward his. Athletic participation can lengthen the educational process, especially with two-year schools where issues of transfer credits and personal factors like injuries can act as a deterrent to completing an associate's degree.

The Slow and Persistent Path

Some students caught in the ambition paradox, however, manage to prevail through persistence. Unlike the others in this chapter, Anne Powers has maintained the same high educational expectations and occupational aspirations she had in her senior year of high school. She has been in community college for five years and should receive her associate's degree any time now; she plans to enter a four-year college in the fall. The long road she has taken demonstrates how some students hold tightly to their ambitions and attempt to beat the odds by persevering.

When Anne was in her senior year of high school she expected to attend a competitive state university and aspired to become a child psychologist. In following this career path, she imagined that she would learn how to deal with people and work more cooperatively with them. "I do not think I am really a people person. I think I will learn how to work with people better, I think maybe learning how not to get involved, you know, personally." The decision to become a child psychologist was entirely her own; she did not know anyone who was a psychologist, nor had she ever received counseling. To become a child psychologist, Anne assumed she would need "about six years of schooling. I am not sure yet. Six years leading up to my master's."

Anne's biological father was born in Central America. Her parents are divorced, and she lives with her mother, her stepfather, and two younger sisters. Anne describes her family as "very close," and they engage in recreational activities on a regular basis and share evening meals together. She looks forward to visits with her father, whom she sees often. They typically speak in Spanish, which is not spoken in her home. Her father does not support her career plans and is "pushing me toward sales. He wants me to go into advertising because he says I have artistic skills and, you know, he thinks that is a good way to use those skills. I love my father but I am not going to do what I do not want to do."

An honors student whose favorite subject in high school was Spanish, Anne enjoyed her classes and her teachers. In her spare time she also was an elementary Sunday school teacher. She applied to two colleges and two universities. Two of the four were academically competitive, and she was accepted by all four. But she decided to attend the local community college instead. "I'm kind of like a mama's girl and I really didn't want to leave home right away," she explained. "I just wanted the security of living at home. I could have gone away but I chose not to go. I chose this school for the basics and it is close to my house and I can get a quick two-year degree and go on." Her father, however, was very disappointed that she decided to stay home instead of going away to "experience the world." Her parents pay part of her tuition, and she receives veteran's dependent benefits because of her father's time in the service. She gives her mother money every month, although her mother rarely accepts it. "I just say, 'Here Mom, you know, here is some money,' and she will say, 'No, I do not need it. You do not need to pay me, this is your house, you know.'"

In her first semester in college, Anne took general psychology, elementary algebra, humanities, English composition, and Spanish; during her second semester she took the next level of each. She also worked at a day care center in a local elementary school. Anne saw this job as "helping with my schoolwork. Sometimes I am depressed and I feel like, this is getting to me, all the studying and papers and then I go to work and the kids give me that extra boost." She enjoyed the work, and her colleagues saw her as excelling: "They say I am really good with the kids and everything, and I like doing a lot of things with them." At first all she had to do was help out another teacher, but later she was given responsibility for a group of children. Her first semester in college was very successful, and she earned all As and Bs. Overall, she considered her professors "pretty thorough." She found the difficulty level about the same as in high school; the biggest difference, she felt, was the independence.

But in her third year, Anne was still attending the community college, living at home, and planning on transferring. "I do not think they really put us in a category like freshmen or sophomores," she explained. "We're just here until we get our associate's. Most people are here four or five years." She remained convinced that community college was the right choice for her. "The classes were relatively small. I was not set with the idea of going to a big huge university where I could get lost in the crowd and all that."

Persisting in her ambitions from high school, Anne declared child psychology as her major. Her grades slipped somewhat, and during her third year she had a 2.8 average. She continued to work about twenty hours a week at the elementary school, where she had been employed for three years. She believed the job had helped greatly in affirming her career choice: "I really feel like if I had just gone through school and not been exposed to children at all and then, you know, jumped right out of school into this job I probably would have minded and would have been blown away by the things that go on."

Still Anne did not transfer to a four-year institution, even after her third year. She spent four more semesters at the community college. Now in her fifth year there, she plans to transfer to a state university in the fall, though not the competitive institution she had originally planned to attend. She now envisions it this way: "In five years I should have a job working at an elementary school because I should have my bachelor's by then and possibly my master's in five years." She has been looking into graduate programs and hopes she will be able to get the funds to apply. Through the years, Anne has taken on more financial obligations for her own schooling—she now pays for part of her tuition previously paid by her parents and her personal maintenance and other bills.

In evaluating her progress through school Anne has some regrets: "It has taken me a long enough time to get my associate's degree. I mean, I went straight out of high school straight into community college. I goofed off for like two semesters, but I have outgrown that stage and now I am more focused on what I need to do." As for immediate goals, "I'm just trying to get out of here. I am tired of looking at those walls and people." She also does not believe her studies have adequately prepared her for her career choice, "other than having a piece of paper and saying, 'Well, I went to school and I studied, you know, this and that.' I learn more in a hands-on experience, like working with the kids, than I learned in school. People are definitely much more interested in hands-on experience, you know, than sitting in class and staring at a chalkboard."

At twenty-two, Anne is still living at home. She has some financial responsibilities, but not enough to consider herself independent: "My parents are there. Within the next year, actually, I just want to be totally independent and just be self-sufficient and don't have to depend on them for anything." For her, independence will come when she moves out of her home to attend a four-year college, which she hopes to graduate from in two years. Like Alison and Janice and Matt, she has persisted through community college, and it seems likely she will succeed in making it to a four-year college. Unlike them, she has also persisted in her ambition to become a child psychologist and not downsized her career goal.

A Difficult Path

It is difficult for students to earn a bachelor's degree when they begin their postsecondary studies at two-year institutions; it is even more difficult today than it has been in the past. Despite the low odds, more students who aspire to a bachelor's degree are beginning their studies at two-year schools. Caught in the ambition paradox of trying to realize their goals by pursuing paths with low odds of success, students make adjustments. One is to gradually stop attending the two-year institution. When Cliff first started community college, he found his courses "boring" and did not do very well. He had little direction about what to take, assumed he would take the basic courses, and then "hone in on a major of some sort." With such lack of definition, Cliff could not find an educational path through community college. Twice he attempted to return and complete his associate's degree, demonstrating how reluctant he was to give up on his educational dream. He has crafted a new occupational goal of becoming a business manager, and he considers his current position as the assistant manager at a service station to be an important step up on the management ladder.

A second type of adjustment is to persist in pursuing the bachelor's degree by first completing the associate's degree and then transferring to a four-year institution. Alison and Janice display such persistence. Despite attending college full time, it took them three years to complete their associate's degrees. One reason this route is so lengthy for some students is that they have misaligned ambitions and no realistic life plan. They also receive limited information to correct their misperceptions. Many see the two-year schools as a layaway plan, investing in an associate's degree with the expectation that it will allow them to pursue a bachelor's degree. But as with most such plans, the costs are sometimes hard to assess, and paying off the loan seems to take much longer than one anticipated. One difficulty these students frequently encounter is figuring out what courses to take. Much like Alison and Janice, many of them change their major, lengthening the schooling process. Although they persist toward their goals, how they set out to achieve them often lacks direction. They only gradually develop an understanding of what steps are necessary to obtain a degree, transfer to a four-year institution, and select a major consistent with their desired occupation. Even students like Anne who are academically well-prepared and have a coherent plan of study in college can face difficulties in completing an associate's degree in two years and transferring to a four-year institution.

Students at two-year institutions can face significant obstacles in transferring to four-year schools. It can be difficult because the core curriculum in a two-year college is not necessarily consistent with the many different types of programs four-year institutions offer. Not all four-year institutions consider credits earned in two-year colleges as "college courses" and will not accept them as transfer credits. The additional costs can be considerable, both because of repeating nontransferable courses and because these schools are generally more expensive to begin with. Some community colleges have recently attempted to establish more consistent policies for transferring to four-year institutions.[15]

Students who select a two-year institution as a starting point for earning a bachelor's degree choose a slow route. Typically they are weak academically, and they do not see connections between their course work and their future occupations. These students drop courses they find difficult even though they need them to fulfill general requirements to transfer. Many become discouraged and exit. Others search for direction, but help is often not available at the institutions they attend. Their persistence is due to their ambitiousness and their understanding of the limited opportunities for workers without college degrees.

chapter ten

Supporting the Development
of Aligned Ambitions

Personal ambitions play an important role in the lives of adolescents. They shape their images of their futures, of what they are going to become and what paths they will choose to take. These dreams for the future, sometimes vivid and other times hazy, also influence daily actions. They help give additional meaning to the small accomplishments of adolescents—earning an A in an honors course, being selected for the district orchestra, receiving praise for work at an internship. As the transition from adolescence to adulthood has lengthened, ambitions play a more important role. Adolescents are seeking opportunities to develop their human capital—academic skills, work skills, and credentials. The open postsecondary education system offers teenagers many routes, and they need some knowledge of how this system works to make well-informed decisions.

A teenager's ambitions are seldom fixed; they change, often becoming more elaborate and richer in detail. Whether grand or subtle, these changes are intimately connected to adolescents' experiences as they try to realize their dreams. Such changes are apparent in the experiences of Elizabeth, Grace, and Jake. We began by examining their experiences as high school sophomores, and then followed them as they graduated from high school and went on to college. What follows is taken from interviews we conducted with them three years after they graduated from high school.

The Quest for Excellence: Elizabeth Houghton

Elizabeth is a junior at a highly competitive midwestern university where she began as a freshman. Her choice of the school was influenced primarily by its aggressive recruiting: "They put on a better show. I was on the wait list for Harvard and Stanford. But I was recruited by this school. They flew me out, took us to basketball games and the theater, and that was sort of appealing." The university offered her a four-year academic merit scholarship.

Elizabeth continues to be an excellent student and has earned straight As every quarter in college. These grades are the result of hard work and time: "It varies by quarter. I took a couple of extra courses the last two quarters and I was working on my thesis. I would spend easily forty-plus hours a week, including classes." Her major is European intellectual history with a concentration in the nineteenth century, which she chose when she started college. "I chose European history because I do not believe that history is an equal opportunity employer, so I think a Eurocentric approach is completely reasonable. I think intellectual history is more interesting than other kinds of history. It's sort of history of ideas. You get science, political science, philosophy. And I mean, total war is an intellectual concept. The date Waterloo was fought is not, but it certainly affects it." This semester Elizabeth is finishing her honor's thesis on "The French Reception of Kierkegaard," a topic she ironically acknowledges is somewhat arcane: "You know, put it on fabric and it prevents stains." She will have completed all her credits for an undergraduate degree by the end of her junior year, and next year she will take all graduate courses. After finishing four years in college, she will receive a master's degree as well as a bachelor's.

In high school Elizabeth took all advanced classes in the humanities and the sciences, but she did not study science in college—"those are not the ideas that I am good at putting together." Reflecting on whether her program was the right choice, she says, "I could have done a mediocre job in a scientific field, but I recognize that the teachers and counselors in my high school were not dedicated to my becoming a scientist. And, it was clear I was not interested; no one was going to push me in that direction. If the school recognized these talents in other students, they certainly pushed it."

School is an integral part of Elizabeth's plans for the future. "I decided kind of early on that what to do with an undergraduate degree was to get a sort of very basic introduction, or, I hope it's not an introduction at this point, but a reasonable set of ideas. That's what I eventually would like to contribute to is the history of ideas rather than anything else." In addition to history, she is interested in writing fiction. This past year, she took a course with a Pulitzer Prize–winning author and they have been corresponding. Elizabeth says that she now writes fiction "rather regularly." She is not certain about her plans after college: "I think I want to do academia possibly, I want to do fiction possibly, but I definitely don't want to do them right after school. This is preparation for those things more than anything else."

In assessing her readiness for college, she says, "I think first I was prepared by my high school and my family and all the sort of empirical data. But this college was my 'safety,' so I came here with a sense of confidence, which I did not see matched very frequently. It was a lot of the people's best shot or reach, and they were tense about how it was going to be, whereas I thought, 'Jeez, this probably is not going to be hard enough.'" The challenge was keeping her A average: "I think it is not a challenge to get an A-minus here, but the difference between an A and an A-minus is often enough to keep me well occupied," and she adds, "I think academically I work harder here than I did in high school, in part because I am doing some things that I really enjoy. I take a lot of pleasure in reading and writing." She is very focused on history, "because I think I am good at it."

The hardest intellectual challenge for Elizabeth has been

writing her thesis. "I handed in the first fifty-six pages on Thursday and, honestly, I do not think I have ever sustained anxiety for such a period. I worked all through spring break." The source materials for her thesis have been in French. "I did not know at the time that all of my sources would be in French. My French vocabulary has increased to the point where I can be anticlerical in French and almost Danish but not much else." Her estimation of the worth of her honor's thesis is good—quite good—"I think honestly that it would pass for a master's thesis if I were doing it next year. The greatest thing about it has been that it is not a story that has been told, so it is not just looking at another interpretation and making a criticism. Not negative history, it is positive history. Like I am actually figuring out the narrative and the dates myself, which has been exciting."

Elizabeth's father is paying expenses not covered by her scholarship: "The one thing my father has said is that he would rather I not work during school." He "is very interested that I get my master's degree in four years, because if I could I might as well," she says. "It is a pretty good deal. But I do not think he would have ever applied pressure in any direction. And as to whether or not I get a Ph.D., I do not think he cares. I hope to have bought some time with my master's degree, but I think there's a good chance I'll get a Ph.D." Thinking of the future, she says, "I am less certain now about what I want to do. I guess I find more that is unsavory about the academy and that makes me more nervous about coming back." Although she has immensely enjoyed her experiences at school, Elizabeth thinks that this college was probably not the best choice for her: "I would have been a better match at schools where my specialty is a serious major and there are more students in it. I am the only intellectual history major that will graduate this year."

Elizabeth considered attending law school, but now, she says, "I really do not want to practice law. For two summers I worked for the Department of Justice and I was an independent contractor and I did writing for them. It is not the kind of writing I want to do." The job involved writing congressional reports, monographs, and some correspondence and gave her considerable autonomy and responsibility. She had also thought seriously about politics, especially when she was no longer interested in journalism. Now, she feels, "I certainly will not work in a federal agency. I do not think that I still feel the same sense of obligation that I did toward citizenship. I do not think my contribution is best made there, frankly."

She sees herself in a university at thirty. "I know I can do the professorship," she claims with typical confidence, but she does have deep concerns about academic life: "I sort of eliminated options rather than choosing one. I really enjoy being in school. I cannot think of anything I would prefer to do. That is how I came up with academics. What concerns me is that faculties, I think, are sort of unpleasant organizations. The stakes are just so small." But she also dreams of becoming a writer. "Art," she pronounces, "is always a little more tenuous." "I think there is a danger of relying on fiction as a sure thing for the future. I am a little bit afraid to declare myself an artist. I think I should be. I think that once you decide that art is important it is very hard to think about anything else as important."

This summer, Elizabeth will receive a stipend from the university to go to Paris, where she will work on a small paper "on the desacralization and melodrama after the revolution. It is going to be a directed reading thing and then maybe twenty pages at the end." Next year she will return to school, take graduate courses, and work on her master's thesis: "I will write another thesis. And I will know so much more, I will find something that has two sources as opposed to thirty."

"Honestly, I am less certain about my future than I was in high school," she confesses, while remaining optimistic: "I am psyched for it. I am not concerned. Well, that is a lie. I am certainly concerned, and maybe the most, the most disconcerting feeling is not knowing exactly where you are going." But she is upbeat and feels prepared for the challenges she will face. And, "I am also starting to be very confident in creating sort of emotional tools about what to do when I am not feeling so hot. And in terms of having created the tools for success in the workplace I am confident about them too."

Charting a Future: Grace Park

A junior at a competitive university on the East Coast, Grace is pursuing a bachelor of arts in international affairs. Like Elizabeth, she decided on her major in her freshman year. Last year she declared economics as a second major so that she can earn a degree in international affairs with a concentration in international economics. Grace has always liked economics but has never been interested in any other scientific or mathematical fields: "It is just something that does not interest me and I do not think I am very good at it anyway."

College has not been a financial burden. Her expenses have been paid through federal financial aid, a university grant, and contributions from her parents, who did not have to borrow money. Despite sufficient financial support, Grace worked thirty hours a week during her freshmen and sophomore years. "Working made everything a lot harder. Right now I am just taking my classes and concentrating on my studies." Because she took extra credits in her sophomore and junior years, she expects to graduate a semester early.

Although her freshman year was difficult and her performance was not up to her standards, Grace's grades overall have been good. By her second and third years she was getting "mostly As and Bs." She spends ten to fifteen hours a week studying outside of class and seems to manage the workload pretty well. "Some of these classes are a lot of work," she reports, "but nothing really too difficult, like nothing that I cannot handle, and my biggest problem is procrastination—I just put it off and then wind up pulling an all-nighter because I have not done something I was supposed to do a week ago."

The transition from high school was difficult for Grace because of her disappointment at being rejected for the naval academy. She was not eagerly anticipating going to college: "I was not psyched about it. It was really just copping out for me. I wanted to get out of the city. I felt like I needed to kind of have my own life, getting away from the family, doing my own thing, meet different people." Despite her reservations, once she started the experience became more positive. She now ranks her college as almost a perfect choice and thinks she was well prepared for it, academically and socially. Like Elizabeth, Grace sees college as necessary preparation for adulthood. "It is like your undergraduate experience is like a background. I think whatever you study will serve you well. That is, whether or not it is exactly what you are going to be doing for the rest of your life, college is in some way related to that." But she sees limited direct connections between her classes and her long-term aims: "I am thinking about my future goals. I am looking toward business. Maybe something like, entrepreneurial, and most of my studies have been, like, economic-policy oriented. This year for the first time I am actually taking a business administration class, which I feel does apply a lot to what I will do in my future."

Grace says that working in the world of business was a desire she had all through school. "When I started high school, or even like back in elementary and junior high school, I kind of knew that I had a real business and capitalist type sense. I always thought that I would get into business. But once I got into high school and started thinking about college, I really wanted to be in the navy. So then those other thoughts kind of got buried because I was really set on being in the navy. When that did not work out and I wound up here, those ideas were back again." Her mother would like her to get a master's in business administration, but Grace is unsure: "I had been planning on getting that for the past couple of years, but recently I have been thinking that I still have plenty of time. But I have been having some other ideas that do not include the MBA, like getting into business." She would like to pursue "something entrepreneurial, like starting a business. Not just a small business. I do not feel like we are in a society where you need an MBA to do this. The thing is, I think ultimately I will have to, but it is not in my near future."

Part of Grace's ambivalence about earning an MBA has to do with her feelings about college. "I just never really thought college was for me or really did much for me. I just feel like I have been kind of going through it. I got really tired of being here." Nevertheless, she recognizes that credentials are important for being taken seriously: "I do not feel like I need to get my MBA but at the same time if I were to consider being taken seriously and accepted into this whole business world then I do have to get it. But I don't see that necessarily as part of my goal. But at the same time, five years from now and I have started this business and I am doing things and people are not going to take me seriously enough because I do not have my MBA, then I will get it because it conflicts with my goals."

Grace believes she will be successful because of her skills, abilities, and ambition. "I have this feeling and desire to do something with myself. And I feel like I have the brains for it and I have the skills and ability, so I feel like I will be successful. It runs in the family. I am very ambitious, but not as much as I used to be. I have also acquired people skills. I have always felt that my strongest point was the ability to pick up things and learn very quickly." Her current concern is finding "something I feel that I can do and something that I may enjoy. But I just don't know yet because I would like to explore my other options first." Recently she has developed an interest in marketing research. In spring quarter, she started a marketing class in which she had the opportunity to work with a famous American clothing designer: "She is really great and she said, 'If you guys are interested, if you are graduating, I would be happy to take your résumé.' I have not said anything to her yet, but I was talking to my professor about it and really considering it, but I still have some work to do at the career center."

In thinking about her future, Grace has begun to reevaluate some of her ideas about marriage and children: "At one point I was just about my career and that is all that mattered to me. Recently, I have been having these ideas, and it has become apparent to me that family is one of the most important things in anyone's life. I do not necessarily see myself as a family person, but I have been having these thoughts, if somebody asked me to marry them and move out to the boondocks, I would." Her immediate goals however, are to graduate and make "lots of money."

Drifting Dreamer: Jake Roberts

In high school, Jake had hoped to pursue a career in film. He started out in college at a large, prestigious state university but dropped out after his first semester. "I just could not do it," he says now. "I was not prepared when I went to college. My parents had just gotten divorced, and my dad had just gotten into an accident. I mean it was just a bunch of stuff at once. And when you have had relatively little to get used to, you know, other than normal high school angst, to have all of this stuff happen in such a relatively short period is just kind of overwhelming." Jake's disappointing experience in his first semester at college did not dissuade him from wanting to return. "The past two and a half years have just been real bad for me. I want to go back. This fall I am going to go to a two-year college to get my associate's, then I know I am going to graduate with honors. I am hoping to get a scholarship to go up to New York for college."

A competitive private college was recruiting Jake while he was in high school. "They were really interested in me when I did my PSATs and SATs. They sent me a lot of brochures and a lot of catalogs on their school." He believes the college has a "really good program" and thinks it would still be interested in him now, three years later. He is not sure what he is going to study, but he still wants to go into film and theater. He wants to "look into it before I jump in and say 'Yeah, I'll go!'"

Since his second year in high school, Jake has consistently stated his intention to earn a master's degree. A mathematics teacher in his sophomore year was very influential in shaping his educational expectations, and that made a lasting impression on Jake. Three years after graduation, he continues to plan on "getting at least my master's. Back when I first started high school I really just wanted to get my bachelor's because I did not even really think I needed the college education. I thought I could do everything on my own. Take on the world."

Jake has been employed full time for several months at an electronics store as a salesperson, a job he got by simply walking in and applying for it. He is responsible for retail sales and opening and closing the store. He gets along well with the manager but not with the other salespeople: "Everybody else I kind of look down on, which really is not right, but that is the way I am." He does not like the job, especially because of "the sales part, I hate business. I absolutely despise the business. The business factor of anything. It is just not what I am interested in. I like art, I like that kind of thing." He plans to quit in the fall and return to college. "I am going to devote myself to school. This is not exactly where I intended to be."

Jake has changed his occupational goal and is now exploring a career in graphic design, but he still retains his interest in film: "I want to get into film more, because now it is something I want to do rather than something that I think is going to define my place—something that is going to be, 'Oh yeah, I remember him because of that.' It is something I want to do because it is what I am interested in." Ideally, he would like to study graphic arts and film. Despite this, when he envisions his future at thirty, he says, "I probably will be a waiter somewhere. I do not know. I really stopped trying think very far. I just try to live." Although he was heavily involved with theater in high school, he has not taken part in it since. "The closest thing I had to working a job that was close to my future goals was kind of working at a movie theater. I just got to see lots of free movies and go, 'Yeah, I would really like to do this.'"

Reflecting on the past few years, Jake has many regrets: "When I was in high school I was practically a straight-A student, or at least I could have been if I had actually tried. Now, you know, after three years out of high school and realizing how little I have come to, it is just kind of, 'God, how could I let myself do this?'" His sense of frustration is particularly acute when he spends time with his friends from high school, some of whom went to college. "It gets a little frustrating sometimes when you are sitting there talking to friends that you know you are at least their intelligence equivalent. But you cannot really keep up in the conversation because you are just not as knowledgeable about everything." This, however, has become a source of motivation: "When I look at what my friends have done and then I look at what I have done, and I am like, 'Man, I could have done that.' And so I'm going to."

Elizabeth, Grace, and Jake are traveling different paths with varying degrees of success. As high school students, they all held strong images of what they were going to become. Elizabeth and Grace have developed realistic plans to achieve their goals. This planning capacity serves them well in several ways. To develop such plans requires an ability to assess their own strengths and weaknesses. It also allows them to persevere in the face of disappointments. Elizabeth was not admitted to her first-choice colleges, but she accepted the challenge of doing well at her safety school. Grace failed the medical examination for admission to the naval academy, but she constructed a new path toward her goal of working in business. Such adolescent "planners" are more likely to have a realistic flexibility that enables them to recognize real opportunities and to modify their plans to adapt to them. Elizabeth's experience doing legal assistance work helped convince her that she did not want to become a lawyer or work in government and that she was more interested in being an intellectual. Grace's chance to work with someone in marketing through her college course encouraged her to think about setting up her own firm. The strength of Elizabeth's and Grace's aligned ambitions and life plans is not that they are leading them in lockstep fashion toward a predetermined goal. Rather, their ability to formulate realistic life plans is a skill that they can draw upon to adjust and modify their course in response to their experiences.

Jake, however, is not a planner but a dreamer. His images of what he is going to accomplish in the future and how he is going to get there are unrealistic. He does not consider that a college may no longer be interested in him or that it will be difficult to earn a B.A. by first attending a two-year rather than a four-year institution. His plans are not based on knowledge of the potential pathways to reach his goals. This lack of knowledge leads Jake to construct dreamlike plans.

Helping to Shape Ambitions

While each adolescent's ambitions are personal with unique features, they are shaped by the social worlds in which teenagers live. They reflect changes in the labor market and the opportunities available for females and males. They also are shaped by the actions of adolescents and of their parents and teachers. A characteristic of adolescent ambitions on which we have focused is whether they are aligned—whether the teenager's chosen educational path matches the requirements of the occupation to which he or she aspires. Unfortunately, the majority of adolescents do not have aligned ambitions. It is possible, however, to help foster aligned ambitions through the actions of parents and school personnel concerning choices and plans for the future. Too often, however, parents, teachers, and counselors have narrowly focused their efforts on the college admission process.

Parents and Their Adolescents

During the past forty years, the relationship between parents and adolescents has undergone significant changes. Some of the changes in this relationship can be traced to changes in the American economy. The decline in real wages for high school graduates and the growing job instability among white-collar workers has helped fuel the rise in the ambitions of adolescents and their parents' ambitions for them.[1] To realize these growing ambitions, increasing numbers of adolescents are pursuing postsecondary education. This has lengthened the transition from adolescence to adulthood and extended young adults' financial dependence on their parents.

At the same time, parents are less dependent on the future earnings of their children than they were in the past. Expansion of Social Security, Medicare, and Medicaid has provided a financial safety net for older adults and dramatically reduced the number of elderly who live in poverty.[2] This independence has reduced parents' personal financial incentives to invest in their adolescent's education beyond high school. The lack of a clear reciprocity of generational obligations provides them with more latitude in making decisions about whether to support their children's postsecondary education.

It is important that parents see it as their responsibility to help their adolescents prepare for adulthood. This involves more than simply helping them get into college. Such preparation involves socializing adolescents to become trustworthy and ethically responsible. But it also involves helping them to develop skills and abilities that are similar to those displayed by students with aligned ambitions—the ability to organize their use of time, to engage in purposeful activities, to gather information and make informed decisions, to assess their own strengths and weaknesses, to seek help when needed, and to persevere in mastering specific skills and tasks.

As children grow older they tend to spend less time with their parents. But the limited time that parents spend with their adolescents can be valuable in providing them with direction. Parents can help them to be more strategic in making decisions in three ways: by becoming better informed about their adolescents, by mobilizing nonfinancial resources, and by allocating financial resources.

First, parents should know what their adolescents are studying in school. They can talk about the prerequisites for high school courses and encourage their young teenagers to take the appropriate middle school and freshman courses. In high school, parents need to continue to discuss what courses their adolescents are taking and whether these courses will prepare them for admission to an appropriate postsecondary institution. Parents also need to learn their children's social and intellectual strengths and weaknesses, and, when necessary, help them seek out appropriate assistance. Not only should parents recognize their adolescents' talents and abilities, they should also help them to see their strengths and weaknesses themselves. Parents should know the types of activities their adolescents are involved in as well as how they spend time alone. It is important to recognize that teenagers spend significant time by themselves, and that this can be psychologically stressful for most of them. Spending time alone can also be productive for teenagers, but they often need help in learning how to use it constructively.

Second, parents also can use their personal and social resources to help. If adolescents want to work, parents can help find productive jobs that will help them develop better understandings about the world of adult work. They can talk with their adolescents about what they like to do and the kind of work they might be interested in. These conversations should include discussions of what kind of education and training are necessary for particular occupations and how one gets the needed education and training. Parents can help adolescents learn about the type of work they are interested in by introducing them to people with similar jobs and pointing out internships in adult work settings or school programs. Parents should not assume that typical teenage work experiences provide adolescents with knowledge and skills that are transferable to other work settings.

Third, helping adolescents requires expending resources. We know that parents' willingness to provide financial support for their children's education affects the educational opportunities that are available. The likelihood of an adolescent starting postsecondary education at a four-year rather than a two-year institution is directly influenced by the parents' willingness to help pay for schooling. During the high school years, other forms of financial support can also have beneficial effects for adolescents' knowledge and skills development. These include academic tutors, supporting unpaid internships, and assistance with college applications—a process that is now very time consuming, burdensome, and costly.

Schools and Aligned Ambitions

Opportunities for helping adolescents develop coherent ambitions are not limited to parents: schools also have an important role to play. There are three activities schools can undertake to help adolescents form coherent ambitions: supporting more activity-based organizations, helping students to negotiate the curricular maze of high school, and offering work programs that help adolescents develop informed ambitions about the kinds of jobs and careers they would like to pursue.

Adolescence is a difficult period of development when young people are searching for an identity and defining their place in school. As we have seen, the social groups of adolescents are very fluid in their membership and, as a result, are often unstable. The fluidity of social groups weakens their ability to sustain strong norms that can influence and direct the behavior of adolescents. Activity-based groups are more stable than peer groups because their existence is tied to the activities of schools and community institutions. Such groups are useful for trying out activities and in serving as an anchor for more stable social surroundings. Schools should encourage and sustain these groups, especially those that have clear functions and clearly defined criteria for membership, even if they require little more than active participation.

Adolescents take belonging to such groups seriously and are committed to the work of the group. Participation in groups such as those in theater, music, and athletics provides opportunities for teenagers to develop their talents and abilities. Some, like Jake, may display particular talents and commitments and develop an interest in working in the theater as an adult. To help them form coherent ambitions, the adult leaders of activity groups need to be informed about how education can prepare adolescents for work in their areas of interest.

By encouraging students to think about their college choices and the kinds of courses that are needed for college admission, high schools can help them navigate through the curricular maze of high school. The shopping-mall character of the high school curriculum has probably intensified over the past ten years. High schools are offering more and more courses, particularly ones for advanced-placement credit in college. In a sense, high schools are responding to the demands of some students to be able to build an academic portfolio of interest to competitive colleges and universities.

Large comprehensive high schools provide a broad range of courses at varying levels of difficulty. Maple Wood High School is a good example of one that has used the course selection process as a way of encouraging students to think about the skills they have, the kinds of work they want to do, and how to prepare themselves for such work. At Maple Wood, the emphasis is on preparation not for work after high school but for work after postsecondary education. The program provides students with more than college counseling—it prepares them for college by helping them to make informed choices about the kind of work they want to pursue after college.

Many high schools offer students work internships, and these provide a potentially valuable experience for adolescents that can be helpful in shaping their ambitions. As we saw with Angelina, however, who works at a fast-food restaurant, many high school work programs can provide limited opportunities for students to develop their ambitions. High school work internships can expose students to "real" and responsible jobs that allow them to develop knowledge and skills that are transferable to other settings. These internships should provide opportunities to interact with adult co-workers so that students can learn about the educational and work pathways that lead to adult careers. Schools need to provide students with more internships in adult work settings instead of encouraging them to find encapsulated jobs that have limited value for helping them think about their futures.

Policies That Can Help

The American economy is changing, and the wage premium paid to college graduates is growing. The earnings and opportunities gap between those with a high school and those with a college education has increased dramatically in the past two decades. We believe that the declining labor market opportunities for high school graduates and the job instabilities for white-collar workers have helped to promote the rise in students' ambitions. More students desire access to higher education, and more are willing to undertake personal sacrifices to attend college.

In helping adolescents develop coherent ambitions, two

policy areas need to be addressed: policies that help students develop better understandings of the connections between high school and college; and policies that promote the transfer of credits from two-year to four-year institutions.

An important area of educational policy involves efforts by colleges, universities, and private foundations to introduce high school students to the college admissions process as early as their freshman year. In these programs, students begin college planning, make visits to colleges, learn about the entrance requirements of different colleges, and develop a better understanding of the connections between their work in high school and the educational opportunities available to them after high school. These programs are designed to prepare students for college, but they also should stress the importance of adolescents developing a coherent plan that incorporates their educational expectations and occupational aspirations.

Outreach programs also are being developed to encourage middle school students to learn about how to apply to college, what kinds of high school courses are needed, and how to apply for financial aid. These programs also provide students with individual tutoring in key academic subjects, such as mathematics and science. There are similar programs that encourage universities and community organizations to "adopt" middle schools in high-poverty areas and to work with students in helping them prepare for college. These types of programs have a track record in helping low-income students attend college, but the choice of an institution of higher education should be linked to the occupational orientation of the student.

There also are numerous private philanthropy efforts designed to help high school and middle school students prepare for college. Many of these programs are targeted to adolescents in high-poverty areas. High schools can learn from these programs because some of the needs of adolescents in nonpoverty neighborhoods are quite similar—learning about what is required for college, selecting courses in high school to prepare for college, understanding the educational routes to different jobs, and having personal experiences working in adult job settings.

Policies that promote the transfer of credits from two-year to four-year institutions are also needed. More and more students find themselves caught in the ambition paradox of attending a two-year institution with expectations of a bachelor's degree. They can find transferring to a four-year institution extraordinarily difficult. The case studies in Chapter 9 illustrate students' confusion about degree requirements, which courses will transfer, and admission requirements for four-year institutions. This lack of articulation, especially between public institutions, needs to be addressed if two-year institutions are going to become a meaningful pathway to four-year colleges and the bachelor's degree. There needs to be a concerted effort by state public university systems to develop policies to promote an appropriate and consistent transfer of credits from two-year to four-year institutions. It is taking longer for students to earn associate's degrees and the transfer rate from two-year to four-year institutions is modest and relatively stable. The current lack of articulation between two- and four-year institutions has in part slowed the route to obtaining a bachelor's degree.

Why Aligned Ambitions Matter

Ambitions play an important role in the lives of young people. At certain times in their school career, it is important for adolescents to have a developed sense of their ambitions and the steps needed to attain them. This is particularly the case with important school transitions, especially from high school to college. Students with aligned ambitions are more likely to be able to chart a path toward their career goals, choose a college on the basis of these goals, and make educational and work decisions that lead to the achievement of their goals.

Aligned ambitions help adolescents create coherent life

plans. They do not, however, lead teenagers in lockstep toward a specific occupation. We found that students with aligned ambitions change their occupational interests over time. This is not surprising, since adolescence is a time when young people try out different roles and discover their own talents and abilities. There are benefits, however, to having aligned ambitions even if adolescents change their occupational interests. One advantage of having aligned ambitions is that it helps adolescents to make meaningful choices.

The social world of the American adolescent is a cornucopia of choices. There is a wide range of choices regarding what social groups to join, what academic courses to take in high school, and what jobs to apply for. Adolescents make many choices, and we have seen that their choices often lack permanence: friends change, tastes change, interests change. Students with aligned ambitions are more strategic in making decisions about which courses to take, which organizations to join, and how to spend their time.

Aligned ambitions are important for the personal development of adolescents and are helpful to them in negotiating the critical transition from high school to college. During adolescence, students are gaining the knowledge and skills needed at the next stage of schooling and compiling a record of accomplishments that will lead to new opportunities for learning needed to achieve their goals. Students with high ambitions who choose an educational path with low odds for successfully reaching their goals can make decisions from which it is difficult to recover. We believe that students with aligned ambitions are more likely to successfully navigate the transition from high school to college and to make choices that increase the chances that they will realize their dreams.

The Alfred P. Sloan Study of Youth and Social Development

The Alfred P. Sloan Study of Youth and Social Development was designed to gain a holistic picture of adolescents' experiences within the social environments of their schools, families, and peer groups. This national longitudinal study with cohorts in sixth, eighth, tenth, and twelfth grades followed 1,221 students in twelve sites over a five-year period. The sample was drawn in three stages: localities, then schools within each locality, and finally students within each school. Localities were selected to satisfy the following criteria: variation in urbanicity, variation in labor-force composition and participation, and variation in race and ethnicity. Using 1990 U.S. Census information, fifteen potential sites were selected based on the degree to which their local economies were concentrated in manufacturing or services, as well as in their trend toward economic growth, stability, or decline over the past decade. To achieve a sample of adolescents whose racial and ethnic makeup would be representative of the U.S. population ages twelve to eighteen, and to ensure racial and ethnic diversity across localities, in some of the sites certain racial and ethnic groups were overrepresented in comparison to proportions in the national population. Twelve sites across the United States were selected from the original list of fifteen.

Once the sites were selected, local educational superintendents were asked to identify the high schools they considered the "most typical" of student demographic characteristics and college attendance rates in the district. Based on their recommendations, high school principals were asked to identify the elementary or middle schools that feed students into their respective high schools.

The twelve sites included thirty-three schools: twenty middle schools and thirteen high schools. To provide variation in high school programs, two specialized schools were included in the sample: a mathematics and science academy and a magnet language academy. The other eleven high schools had more traditional comprehensive curricular programs. A small honorarium for each year of participation was offered to each school.

For each elementary or middle school and each high school, two student samples were selected: focal students and cohort students. The focal students were chosen from school-prepared enrollment lists of grades six, eight, ten, and twelve. Using a stratified design at each school, student selections at each grade level were made so that they were proportionately representative of gender, race, ethnicity, and level of academic performance. Based on student records, teachers rated each of these students as academically successful, working at grade level, or having academic problems. At each school twenty-four students from each grade level were selected for the longitudinal panel.

The cohort sample was selected using the same criteria as the focal sample and was designed to provide more information about the school and peer networks for each of the focal-panel grades. Each year in the field, new cohort samples were drawn from the grade the focal students were in. If a grade enrolled no more than 150 students, the cohort sample consisted of the entire grade. Otherwise a random sample of 150 students was chosen from the grade enrollment lists.

The cohort students were administered most of the same instruments as the focal students, making it possible to aggregate information from both sample groups. The total of both the focal and cohort samples over the five years of the study is more than eight thousand students. Analyses of the focal and cohort samples revealed no differences in demographic characteristics, attitudes toward school, educational expectations, occupational aspirations, and other key variables used in this study.

Data were collected from the focal students by three methods: (1) the experience sampling method, (2) an in-depth interview (revised each year the adolescent was contacted), and (3) a battery of questionnaires. The questionnaires included the Teenage Life Survey (a modification of instruments used in the National Education Longitudinal Study of 1988–94), a Friends Sociometric Form, which provides information regarding adolescents' peer groups, and a questionnaire called the Career Orientation Survey, which measures job knowledge and occupational expectations. The cohort students completed the questionnaires but were not interviewed and did not participate in the experience sampling method.

Once the students graduated from high school only the focal sample was followed. New interview forms and brief telephone surveys were conducted with the focal sample. Questions in these instruments focused on college and work experiences. Special forms were designed for young adults in college, in college and working, working but not in college, and not working and not in college. Through the five years of the study, 84 percent of the focal sample has been retained.

Logistic Regression Models

Predicted Bachelor's Degree Completion Rates for Fall 1972 Two-Year and Four-Year Postsecondary Starters

Predictor variables	Logit coefficients for B.A. in four years	Predictor values starting at		Logit coefficients for B. A. in five years	Predictor values starting at	
		Two-year	Four-year		Two-year	Four-year
Female	.555***	0	0	.327***	0	0
Asian	–.111	0	0	.560*	0	0
Hispanic	–.285	0	0	–.580	0	0
Black	.088	0	0	–.035	0	0
Other race/ethnicity	–.040	0	0	.117	0	0
Parental education	.156***	2	2	.187***	2	2
Twelfth-grade educational expectations	.603***	2	2	.707***	2	2
Math achievement test score (standardized)	.583***	1	1	.537***	1	1
Enrolled in two-year school first fall after high school	2.303***	1	0	2.123***	1	0

	Coefficient	0	1	Coefficient	0	1
Enrolled in four-year school first fall after high school	3.370***	0	1	3.089***	0	1
Constant	-5.985***	1	1	-5.172***	1	1
-2 log likelihood	4472.01			4984.34		
Number of cases	7034			7034		
-Logit		1.582	.515		.725	-.241
Predicted probability of B.A. completion		.171	.374		.326	.560

Source: Data from National Longitudinal Study of the High School Class of 1972 (NLS-72), National Center for Education Statistics, U.S. Department of Education

Variable Key

Female: 1 = Female; 0 = Male
Asian: 1 = Asian; 0 = Other
Hispanic: 1 = Hispanic, not White; 0 = Other
Black: 1 = Black; 0 = Other
Other race/ethnicity: 1 = Native American or "other race"; 0 = Other
Parental education: 0 = H.S. or less; 1 = Some postsecondary; 2 = B.A. or B.S.; 3 = Graduate/professional
Twelfth-grade educational expectations: 0 = H.S. or less; 1 = Some postsecondary; 2 = B.A. or B.S.; 3 = Graduate/professional
Math achievement test score (standardized): NLS-72 12th-grade mathematics achievement test score in standardized metric
Enrolled in two-year school first fall after H.S.: enrolled in a two-year postsecondary institution 10/72
Enrolled in four-year school first fall after H.S.: enrolled in a four-year postsecondary institution 10/72

*p < .05; **p < .01; ***p < .001

Predicted Bachelor's Degree Completion Rates for Fall 1982 Two-Year and Four-Year Postsecondary Starters

Predictor variables	Logit coefficients for B.A. in four years	Predictor values starting at		Logit coefficients for B.A. in five years	Predictor values starting at	
		Two-year	Four-year		Two-year	Four-year
Female	.452***	0	0	.270***	0	0
Asian	−.201	0	0	−.306	0	0
Hispanic	−.225	0	0	−.437**	0	0
Black	−.485**	0	0	−.450***	0	0
Other race/ethnicity	−.909	0	0	−.877	0	0
Parental education	.158***	2	2	.237***	2	2
Twelfth-grade educational expectations	.394***	2	2	.545***	2	2
Math achievement test score (standardized)	.550***	1	1	.686***	1	1
Enrolled in two-year school first fall after high school	.738***	1	0	.734***	1	0

	b	0	1	b	0	1
Enrolled in four-year school first fall after high school	2.470***	0	1	2.448***	0	1
Constant	−4.613***	1		−4.132***	1	1
−2 log likelihood	4233.49			4665.13		
Number of cases	7314			7314		
−Logit		2.220	.488		1.148	−.566
Predicted probability of B.A. completion		.098	.380		.241	.638

Source: Data from High School and Beyond (HS&B) Sophomore Cohort, National Center for Education Statistics, U.S. Department of Education

Variable Key

Female: 1 = Female; 0 = Male
Asian: 1 = Asian; 0 = Other
Hispanic: 1 = Hispanic, not White; 0 = Other
Black: 1 = Black; 0 = Other
Other race/ethnicity: 1 = Native American or "other race"; 0 = Other
Parental education: 0 = H.S. or less; 1 = Some postsecondary; 2 = B.A. or B.S.; 3 = Graduate/professional
Twelfth-grade educational expectations: 0 = H.S. or less; 1 = Some postsecondary; 2 = B.A. or B.S.; 3 = Graduate/professional
Math achievement test score (standardized): HS&B 12th-grade mathematics achievement test score in standardized metric
Enrolled in two-year school first fall after H.S.: enrolled in a two-year postsecondary institution 10/82
Enrolled in four-year school first fall after H.S.: enrolled in a four-year postsecondary institution 10/82
*p < .05; **p < .01; ***p < .001

Matriculation at Four-Year versus Two-Year Postsecondary Institutions: October 1992

Independent variables	Model 1	Model 2	Model 3	Model 4
Female	.0858	.1425	.1256	.0777
Asian	−.1310	−.1887	−.1652	−.0708
Black	1.1527***	.9894***	.9494***	1.0284***
Hispanic	.1145	.0926	.1582	.2479
Parental education	.3534***	.3079***	.2766***	.1299**
Academic achievement	.1115***	.0529***	.0513***	.0537***
Science sequence		.2230***	.2103***	.1879***
Math sequence		.2377***	.2342***	.2210***
Income			.0575	−.1136*
Financial support				
Low support (less than $5,000) vs. Without support				−.0330
High support ($5,000 and more) vs. Without support				1.8657***
Constant	−6.2067***	−5.4585***	−5.8163***	−4.0845***

−2 log likelihood	5111.54	4040.55	3820.93	3342.86
Number of cases	5453	4731	4415	4266

Source: Data from NELS:1988–92 Second Follow-Up and NELS:1988–94 Third Follow-Up

Analyses are weighted to be representative of American students (F3F2PNWT)

Variable Key

Female: 1 = Female; 0 = Male

Asian: 1 = Asian; 0 = Other (Reference category is White, not Hispanic; Native Americans have been excluded.)

Hispanic: 1 = Hispanic, not White; 0 = Other

Black: 1 = Black; 0 = Other

Parental education: 1 = H.S. or less; 2 = Some postsecondary; 3 = B.A. or B.S.; 4 = Graduate/professional

Academic achievement: Standardized Test Composite Score (Reading, Math) from NELS:1988–92 Second Follow-Up Data

Science sequence: Score from NELS:1988–92 Second Follow-Up Transcript Component Data

Math sequence: Score from NELS:1988–92 Second Follow-Up Transcript Component Data

Income: 1 = None

    1000 = Less than $1,000   2000 = $1,000–$2,999   4000 = $3,000–$4,999

    6250 = $5,000–$7,499   8750 = $7,500–$9,999   12500 = $10,000–$14,999   17500 = $15,000–$19,999

    22500 = $20,000–$24,999   30000 = $25,000–$34,999   42500 = $35,000–$49,999   62500 = $50,000–$74,999

    87500 = $75,000–$99,999   150000 = $100,000–$199,999   200000 = $200,000 or more

Financial support: 1 [Without Support] = (1) My teenager wants to pay for his/her education without our help, and (2) None

    2 [Low Support] = (3) Less than $2,500, and (4) $2,500–$4,999

    3 [High Support] = (5) $5,000–$9,999, (6) $10,000–$14,999, (7) $15,000–$19,999 and (8) over $20,000

*p < .05; **p < .01; ***p < .001

notes

one
Ambitious Adolescents

1. Adolescence is a period of physiological and psychological development from the onset of puberty to early adulthood, or chronologically from age thirteen to nineteen. In this book, we use the terms *adolescents, youth,* and *teenagers* to refer to individuals between thirteen and nineteen who are typically in high school. With the earlier onset of puberty, some researchers have started to define the lower limit of adolescence down to remain coincident with puberty, typically occurring, especially for females, between ten and thirteen.

2. There is a comprehensive sociological literature on the status attainment process and intergenerational mobility. Within this broad tradition there have been some efforts to examine the role of ambitions; see, for example, Alan C. Kerckhoff, *Ambition and Attainment: A Study of Four Samples of American Boys,* Arnold and Caroline Rose Monograph Series of the American Sociological Association (Washington, D.C.: American Sociological Association, 1974). We see our work as continuing this line of study.

3. A detailed description of the Sloan study appears in Appendix A.

4. The story of Sarah is a composite, based on the responses of 44 misaligned high school seniors out of the 229 in the sample who enrolled in four-year colleges and remained there for three years. As a representative for this type of student, Sarah is the only composite in this book, and we constructed her using Robert Bellah's conception of a representative type (Robert N. Bellah, Richard Madsen, William M. Sullivan, Ann Swidler, and Steven M. Tipton, *Habits of the Heart: Individualism and Commitment in American Life* [Berkeley: University of California Press, 1986]). All the other cases in this book are taken from interviews, records, and survey materials of individual students in the Sloan study. We have changed the names and physical descriptions of the adolescents in an effort to protect their anonymity. The quotations are taken directly from the typed transcripts of the interviews, which record even small utterances in the tape-recorded interviews. We have made some minor grammatical changes, such as deleting repetitive uses of "you know," "uh huh," "yeah," and "like," in the quotations to make them more readable.

5. Mihaly Csikszentmihalyi and Reed Larson, *Being Adolescent: Conflict and Growth in the Teenage Years* (New York: Basic Books, 1986).

t w o
Imagining the Future

1. The cases from the 1950s are from Robert J. Havighurst, Paul Hoover Bowman, Gordon P. Liddle, Charles V. Matthews, and James V. Pierce, *Growing Up in River City* (New York: John Wiley, 1962); those from the 1990s are from the Alfred P. Sloan Study of Youth and Social Development. These two sets of cases are not directly comparable: the 1950s study was conducted in a medium-sized city and the 1990s study was nationwide. Life in River City, however, according to Robert J. Havighurst, the principal investigator in the study, was "typical" of the environment that most teenagers experienced growing up in the 1950s. The sampled student population in the Sloan study reflects the diversity in social backgrounds and race and ethnicity found in the United States today. The high schools and the communities in which they are located were also selected to reflect differences in the environments adolescents may experience in the 1990s.

"River City" is Havighurst's pseudonym for the town he studied. This study was conducted between 1951 and 1963. At the time, Havighurst was a professor of education and a member of the Committee on Human Development at the University of Chicago. We have drawn on the archives of the study, including interviews and field notes, to develop our case studies of adolescents in the 1950s, focusing specifically on the interview materials from 1958–63. These archives are in the special collection of the Regenstein Library at the University of Chicago.

2. For a critique of the historical development of a youth culture and its symbols, see James S. Coleman, ed., *Youth Transition to Adulthood: Report of the Panel on Youth of the President's Science Advisory Committee* (Chicago: University of Chicago Press, 1974). For contemporary views of life in the 1950s, see David Halberstam, *The Fifties* (New York: Fawcett Columbine, 1993); Stephanie Coontz, *The Way We Never Were: American Families and the Nostalgia Trap* (New York: Basic Books, 1992); and J. Ronald Oakley, *God's Country: America in the Fifties* (New York: Dembner Books, 1986).

3. Oakley, *God's Country*. On the mass production of suburban housing, see Kenneth Jackson, *Crabgrass Frontier: The Suburbanization of the United States* (New York: Oxford University Press, 1985).

4. Lewis Mumford, *The City in History* (New York: Harcourt, Brace and World, 1961).

5. Herbert Gans, *Levittowners: Ways of Life and Politics in a New Suburban Community* (New York: Columbia University Press, 1982).

6. Oakley, *God's Country*. It is estimated that more people watched the episode with Lucille Ball having a baby than the second inauguration of President Eisenhower the following day.

7. For a description of the importance of the car to adolescent society, see James S. Coleman, *The Adolescent Society: The Social Life of the Teenager and Its Impact on Education* (New York: Free Press of Glencoe, 1961).

8. *Digest of Education Statistics, 1996* (Washington, D.C.: U.S. Department of Education, National Center for Education Statistics, 1996), 68, 96.

9. We examined yearbooks and other curricular materials in River City to determine the number of students in the different curricular tracks. We looked for a national study from the 1950s that would verify what we observed but were unable to locate one. According to the extensive high school study that Project Talent conducted beginning in 1960, the distribution of high school seniors in different curricular programs was: college preparatory, 43 percent; general, 22 percent; commercial business, 22 percent; vocational, 8 percent; agriculture, 2 percent; and other, 3 percent. The majority of high school students in the early 1960s thus were not in the college preparatory track (our analysis of Project Talent data from 1960 high school seniors, John Flanagan, Frederick B. Davis, John T. Dailey, Marion F. Shaycoft, David B. Orr, Isadore Goldberg, and Clinton Neyman, Jr., *Project Talent: The American High School Student* [Pittsburgh: University of Pittsburgh Press, 1964]). Although many students were in curricular programs designed for making the transition from high school to work, assessments of these vocational programs at this time suggested that they did little to prepare students for viable jobs (Panel of Consultants on Vocational Education, *Education for a Changing World of Work* [Washington, D.C.: Government Printing Office, 1963]).

10. We considered several other studies of adolescents in the 1950s, most notably Coleman's *The Adolescent Society*, Wayne Gordon's *The Social System of the High School*, and Joseph Illick's *At Liberty: The Story of a Community and a Generation*. These studies proved unsuitable for our purposes: although they were extremely informative, they lacked either quantitative data or extensive qualitative interviews.

After months of organizing and reading the Havighurst study data, we became convinced that the study was rigorous and that the data were sufficiently detailed to form a sound basis for developing portraits of adolescent life in the 1950s. In the spring of 1996, we visited Havighurst's city in the hope of gaining richer insights into what he observed and heard as well as capturing a sense of how the lives of adolescents had changed. We retraced some of his steps, visited the high school and local colleges, interviewed adolescents, principals, teachers, and local officials. The richness of the 1950s interviews juxtaposed with the Sloan data helped us to develop empirically based concepts for describing changes in the experiences of adolescents in the 1950s and the 1990s.

We selected these three adolescents from the more than four hundred in the River City study because they had complete case information, including detailed interview material, school records, and an interview five years after graduation from high school. Those interviewed in 1963 form a representative sample of the original 1950s sample (Havighurst et al., *Growing Up in River City*). We decided not to include students who dropped out of high school because of our interest in making meaningful comparisons with adolescents in the 1990s. The national dropout rate has declined from about 35 percent in the 1950s to 6.5 percent in 1994 (National Center for Education Statistics, *A Comparison of High School Dropout Rates in 1982 and 1992* [Washington, D.C.: Office of Educational Research and Improvement, U.S. Department of Education, 1996]). A small percentage of today's high school students drop out, and among those who do many plan to return or take the examination for a General Education Diploma (GED).

The case materials from the 1950s included rich information on the appearance of the adolescents, the condition of their homes, and the communities in which they lived. We have extracted some of this information to create these portraits and have given the students fictitious names.

11. There are several books on the history of the real place that Havighurst called River City, and the local historical society has an extensive file of photographs dating back to the 1800s. Because Havighurst promised confidentiality to the participants in his study, it is not possible for us to cite the names of the books we consulted to verify and expand on his description of River City.

12. The median age at first marriage for females in 1957 was twenty, for males, twenty-four (Reynolds Farley, *The New American Reality: Who We Are, How We Got Here, Where We Are Going* [New York: Russell Sage Foundation, 1996]). Selected files for dropouts in the River City sample show that females who left school before graduating consistently said that their parents thought

dropping out was acceptable because they were married, or engaged to be. This finding is discussed in Havighurst et al., *Growing Up in River City*, and is elaborated by John Modell, *Into One's Own: From Youth to Adulthood in the United States, 1920–1975* (Berkeley: University of California Press, 1989).

13. *Digest of Education Statistics, 1996,* 108.

We searched for a national study conducted in the 1950s that asked high school students about their plans after high school. The Educational Testing Service (ETS) conducted a national study in 1955 of students' plans for after high school. Thirty-three thousand twelfth-grade students in 478 high schools throughout the United States in January and February 1955 were given a short aptitude test and a questionnaire requesting information relevant to their college plans. The students were asked, "What do you think you will do when you finish high school? (Suppose you do not go into military service)." In their answers, 32 percent said they expected to go to college immediately after high school, 16 percent expected to get a part-time job and go to college, 1 percent expected to get a full-time job and go to college at night, 7 percent expected to work for a year or two and then go to college, 10 percent expected to go to trade school, 27 percent expected to get a job or become an apprentice, and 7 percent listed "other" (Bruce Eckland, *Codebook, Explorations in Equality of Opportunity: A Fifteen Year Follow-Up Survey* [Chapel Hill: University of North Carolina Press, 1972]). Among ten thousand students who scored in the upper third on an aptitude test in the 1950s, nearly two-thirds expected to attend college (Glen Stice, William Mollenkopf, and Warren Torgerson, "Background Factors and College Plan Among High Aptitude Public School Seniors" [Princeton, N.J.: Educational Testing Service, 1956]).

14. Coontz, *The Way We Never Were.* As Coontz points out, these notions were idealized visions, and in many households women had to work outside the home. Our point is that females and males in the 1950s had a basic understanding of roles regarding household and employment responsibilities. When mothers began to enter the labor force in sizable numbers these role differences became less clear.

In the accounts of the home visits written by Havighurst's colleagues, there were extensive comments on the cleanliness and tidiness of homes. The importance of having a clean and well-kept home gave additional value and importance to the role of female as housekeeper.

15. Students who graduated from high school in the late 1950s were at a significant disadvantage in obtaining financial assistance for attending

college, as there were no GI benefits for this period (Carl Kaestle, "Education," in *The Encyclopedia of the United States Congress*, ed. D. C. Facon, R. H. Davidson, and M. Keller [New York: Simon and Schuster, 1996], 682–91).

16. College was often viewed in the 1950s as a way to earn a credential for certain types of jobs—teacher, lawyer, physician. The concept of going to college to obtain a liberal education not tied to some form of specific employment grew with the expansion of higher education institutions in the 1960s.

17. See Allen Sanderson, Bernard Dugoni, Kenneth Rasinski, John Taylor, and C. Dennis Carroll, *Descriptive Summary Report, with an Essay on Access and Choice in Postsecondary Education, National Education Longitudinal Study of 1988–1992* (Washington, D.C.: U.S. Department of Education, Office of Educational Research and Improvement, 1996, NCES 96-175).

18. Farley, *The New American Reality*.

19. Donald Hernandez, *America's Children: Resources from Family, Government, and the Economy* (New York: Russell Sage Foundation, 1993).

20. Frances K. Goldscheider and Linda J. Waite, *New Families, No Families? The Transformation of the American Home* (Berkeley: University of California Press, 1991).

21. According to the Sloan study data for sophomores, the median age at which students expect to work in a full-time adult job is twenty-two, and they expect to marry at twenty-four, to become a parent at twenty-six, and to retire from work at sixty-two. There are no significant differences by gender.

22. We examined the sophomore segment of the Sloan study because these students had three years of data that allowed us to study how adolescents make the transition from high school to college and to work. Another benefit was that we could compare students in the Sloan study with national statistics on high school sophomores, primarily through the National Education Longitudinal Study of 1988–94 (NELS:88–94). For an overview of the NELS:88–94 data, see *NELS:88 Base Year Through Second Follow-Up Sample Design Report* (Washington, D.C.: National Center for Education Statistics, 1996). The demographic, gender, racial, ethnic, and social class characteristics of the Sloan sophomore panel are similar to the characteristics of the sophomore panel of NELS:88–94. The one exception is that the Sloan study has a higher percentage of sophomores in two-parent households than the NELS:88–94.

In this chapter, we were interested in those Sloan sophomores who planned to graduate from college (67 percent of Sloan sophomores). From the sample of Sloan sophomores with expectations of graduating from college, we generated a list of cases separated by gender, race, ethnicity, and social class and nested by school. We selected three schools in different geographical regions of the country and read sophomore cases for each of the three schools. For each school, we chose an ambitious adolescent and selected the three cases so that they varied in their economic and familial resources. The information is taken directly from interviews, records, and survey materials of the Sloan study. We have made very minor grammatical changes in the quotations to make them more readable.

23. According to the Sloan data, of those adolescents who desired a job for which the current median level of education is less than a college degree, 56 percent expected to earn a college or graduate degree. Even among adolescents aspiring to jobs with low educational requirements over half expected to earn a college or graduate degree.

24. James S. Coleman, Barbara Schneider, Stephen Plank, Kathryn S. Schiller, Roger Shouse, and Huayin Wang, with Seh-Ahn Lee, *Redesigning American Education* (Boulder, Colo.: Westview Press, 1997).

25. Our analysis of NELS:88–94 data.

26. One of the more striking findings of studies of the new suburban communities of the 1950s was the number and speed with which voluntary associations were created (Gans, *Levittowners*).

27. "Higher Education: Students Have Increased Borrowing and Working to Help Pay Higher Tuitions" (Washington, D.C.: U.S. General Accounting Office, HEHS-98-63, February 18, 1998).

28. Our use of the concept of gender roles bears some similarity to that of "social roles" used by Robert N. Bellah, Richard Madsen, William M. Sullivan, Ann Swidler, and Steven M. Tipton in *Habits of the Heart: Individualism and Commitment in American Life* (Berkeley: University of California Press, 1986). "Social role" incorporates norms and values that individuals use to organize and give purpose and direction to their lives. At this stage in the life course, the social roles that 1950s adolescents perceived as adult roles were mainly gender specific and limited to homemaker, wage earner, and parent. Very few imagined themselves as professionals. The work of Bellah and his colleagues also includes further interpretation of social roles in the context of adult society in the 1970s.

29. See Gary Becker, *Human Capital* (New York: National Bureau of Eco-

nomic Research, 1964), and Theodore Schultz, "Investment in Human Capital," *American Economic Review* 51 (March 1961): 1–17, for further explanations of human capital.

three
Trying to Make It with a High School Diploma

1. Thomas Bailey, "Changes in the Nature of Work: Implications for Skills and Assessment," in *Workforce Readiness: Competencies and Assessment*, ed. Harold F. O'Neil, Jr. (Mahwah, N.J.: Lawrence Erlbaum Associates, 1997), 27–43; Anna Dutka, "Demographic Trends in the Labor Force," in *The Changing U.S. Labor Market*, ed. Eli Ginzberg (Boulder, Colo.: Westview Press, 1994), 18.

2. Reynolds Farley, *The New American Reality: Who We Are, How We Got Here, Where We Are Going* (New York: Russell Sage Foundation, 1996); Stephanie Coontz, *The Way We Never Were: American Families and the Nostalgia Trap* (New York: Basic Books, 1992), 149–79; Thomas Bailey, "Jobs of the Future and the Education They Will Require: Evidence from Occupational Forecasts," *Educational Researcher* 20 (1991): 11–20.

3. Lawrence Mishel, Jared Bernstein, and John Schmitt, *The State of Working America, 1996–1997* (Washington, D.C.: Economic Policy Institute, 1997); Lawrence F. Katz and Kevin M. Murphy, "Changes in Relative Wages, 1963–1987: Supply and Demand Factors," *Quarterly Journal of Economics* 107 (1992): 35–78; Marvin H. Kosters, ed., *Workers and Their Wages: Changing Patterns in the United States* (Washington, D.C.: American Enterprise Institute Press, 1991—the essays in this volume analyze broad changes in wages from the 1960s through the late 1980s, focusing on the role of education in understanding wage differentials); Frank Levy, "Incomes and Income Inequality," in *State of the Union: America in the 1990s*, vol. 1, ed. Reynolds Farley (New York: Russell Sage Foundation, 1995); Kathryn Borman, *The First Real Job* (Albany: State University of New York Press, 1991).

On the types of jobs likely to be available to high school graduates, see Ginzberg, ed., *Changing U.S. Labor Market*. On the types of knowledge and social skills likely to be required in the twenty-first century, see the Secretary's Commission on Achieving Necessary Skills, U.S. Department of Labor, *What Work Requires of Schools: A SCANS Report for America 2000* (Washington, D.C.: U.S. Department of Labor, 1991).

4. See David Stevenson, Julie Kochanek, and Barbara Schneider, "Making the Transition from High School: Recent Trends and Policies," in *The Ado-*

lescent Years: Social Influences and Educational Challenges, National Society for the Study of Education Yearbook, 1998, ed. Kathryn Borman and Barbara Schneider (Chicago: University of Chicago Press, 1998), for further description of these analyses.

5. We purposely selected a male and a female from the Havighurst data for which there were detailed work histories. For the 1990s cases, we again turned to the Sloan data for sophomores and randomly selected a male and a female who were working full time directly after high school graduation. Of the 220 sophomores in the longitudinal panel in the base year, 30 went directly to work after graduation and were not enrolled in any type of post-secondary education.

6. Our analysis of Project Talent data, 1960 seniors.

7. Mishel, Bernstein, and Schmitt, State of Working America.

8. Our analysis of data from the National Education Longitudinal Study of 1988–94 (NELS:88–94). Among the sophomore-weighted panel of NELS:88–94, the top five jobs for teenagers were fast-food worker (16.8 percent), clerk (11.3 percent), babysitter (9.7 percent), waitress (6.7 percent), and lawnworker or odd jobs (6.5 percent).

9. Our analysis of NELS:88–94 and Sloan study data. More than 95 percent of the students in both the NELS:88–94 sample and the Sloan sample believed it was "OK" to work hard for good grades. Among the 1990 NELS:88 sophomores, 50 percent stated that it was very important to their friends to get good grades, 44 percent that good grades were somewhat important to their friends, and 6 percent that good grades were not important to their friends.

10. Stevenson, Kochanek, and Schneider, "Making the Transition from High School."

11. Comparing the occupational aspirations of a national sample of sophomores in 1980 and the NELS:88–94 sophomores of 1990, one study found that in 1990 both males and females were more likely to aspire to professional occupations by age thirty (Kenneth A. Rasinski, Steven J. Ingels, Donald Rock, Judith M. Pollack, and Shi-Chang Wu, America's High School Sophomores: A Ten-Year Comparison [Washington, D.C.: U.S. Department of Education, 1993]). The occupational aspirations of females have risen and now are slightly higher in the professional categories than those of males.

The Sloan data make it possible to look more specifically at the types of jobs students aspire to. The one job among the professional category that continues to show gender differences is engineering—fewer females than males wish to become engineers. Some other jobs also continue to show gender differences.

For employed teenagers, the sophomores in the Sloan study were asked in the interviews to explain what their responsibilities were at the workplace. Context analysis of the responses to this question revealed few differences in the work responsibilities of females and males when employed at the same job. Across different job types, we found both males and females employed as babysitters, salesclerks, and fast-food servers.

12. See Robert H. Topel and Michael P. Ward, "Job Mobility and the Careers of Young Men," *Quarterly Journal of Economics* 107, no. 2 (1992): 438–79.

13. Mishel, Bernstein, and Schmitt, *State of Working America.*

14. Thomas Bailey, "Changes in the Nature of Work."

In the 1970s, the decline in the economic returns of schooling attracted considerable attention among economists (see Richard Freeman, *The Overeducated American* [New York: Academic Press, 1976]). Only recently have economists focused on explaining the dramatic rise in economic rewards for additional schooling that began in the 1980s and continues to the present (see Kosters, ed., *Workers and Their Wages*). The college premium refers to the increasing wage gap between college graduates and high school graduates (see Kevin M. Murphy and Finis Welch, "Wage Premiums for College Graduates: Recent Growth and Possible Explanations," *Educational Researcher* [May 1989]: 17–26; and Chinhui Juhn and Kevin Murphy, "Inequality in Labor Market Outcomes," *Economic Policy Review* 1 [1995]: 26–34).

15. To undertake this analysis we used the senior-weighted files from the 1955 senior sample of the Educational Testing Service, the 1960 senior sample of Project Talent, the senior sample of the National Longitudinal Study: Base Year 1972 (NLS-72), the senior sample of High School and Beyond 1980 (HS&B), and the senior sample of the National Education Longitudinal Study of 1988–94 (NELS:88–94). We used the senior sample for each of these five databases because we could derive weighted representative samples for each of the years represented in Figure 3.2. The 1955 senior sample was a nationally representative sample, as was the Project Talent sample. The High School and Beyond Study of 1980 had two cohorts, a senior cohort and a sophomore cohort. For these analyses, we use the senior cohort, which was nationally representative of high school seniors in 1980. There was only one cohort in NLS-72, and this was a nationally representative sample of seniors in 1972. The NELS:88–94 study began in 1988, when the students were in eighth grade. The eighth-grade sample was freshened in 1990

and 1992. The freshening of the sample in 1992 made it nationally representative of high school seniors in 1992.

For further information on the 1955 sample, see Bruce Eckland, *Codebook, Explorations in Equality of Opportunity: A Fifteen Year Follow-Up Survey* (Chapel Hill: University of North Carolina Press, 1972); for Project Talent, see John Flanagan, Frederick B. Davis, John T. Dailey, Marion F. Shaycoft, David B. Orr, Isadore Goldberg, and Clinton Neyman, Jr., *Project Talent: The American High School Student* (Pittsburgh: University of Pittsburgh Press, 1964); for NLS-72, see John Riccobono, Louise Henderson, Graham Burkheimer, Carol Place, and Jay Levinsohn, *National Longitudinal Study: Base Year (1972) Through Fourth Follow-Up (1979), Data File Users Manual* (Chapel Hill, N.C.: Center for Educational Research and Evaluation, Research Triangle Institute, 1981); for HS&B, see Calvin Jones, Miriam Clarke, Geraldine Mooney, Harold McWilliams, Ioanna Crawford, Bruce Stephenson, and Roger Tourangeau, *High School and Beyond Senior Cohort, Data File Users Manual* (Chicago: National Opinion Research Center, 1983); for NELS:88–94, see Steven J. Ingels, Kathryn L. Dowd, John D. Baldridge, James L. Stipe, Virginia H. Bartot, and Martin R. Frankel, *NELS:88 Second Follow-Up: Student Component Data File User's Manual* [Washington, D.C.: U.S. Department of Education, National Center for Education Statistics, 1994]).

16. Our analysis of NELS:88–94 and Sloan study data. In 1989, when we were working on *A Profile of the American Eighth Grader: NELS 88 Student Descriptive Summary*, we noticed that the educational expectations of eighth graders were very high, with most of them expecting to graduate from college. This response pattern did not differ by basic demographic factors such as gender, race, or ethnicity. We continued to analyze this variable for the NELS:88–94 sophomores. Analyses of the Sloan sophomore panel showed similar patterns. The only difference is that significantly more females expect to obtain a graduate degree. Similar findings are reported for the NELS:88–94 seniors in Patricia J. Green, Bernard L. Dugoni, Steven J. Ingels, Eric Camburn, and Peggy Quinn, *A Profile of the American High School Senior in 1992* (Washington, D.C.: U.S. Department of Education, 1995).

17. National Center for Education Statistics, *A Comparison of High School Dropout Rates in 1982 and 1992* (Washington, D.C.: Office of Educational Research, U.S. Department of Education, 1996).

18. John Bishop, "Achievement, Test Scores, and Relative Wages," in Kosters, ed., *Workers and Their Wages*, 146–86.

19. Our analysis of data from the Sloan study and projections from the Bureau of Labor Statistics, U.S. Department of Labor.

f o u r

The Importance of Aligned Ambitions

1. In major national studies, students are typically asked to name the occupation that they would like to have at age thirty. In the Sloan study we were interested in whether students had more detailed occupational ambitions. To find out, we asked students the standard survey item and then followed up with two open-ended items on a career orientation survey (COS) that was developed as part of the study. The questions asked on the COS were what job the student would like to have at thirty and what job the student thought he or she would actually have then. More than 470 actual occupations were listed, and 7,000 students answered these questions. Even students in grade six were able to envision a job they would like to have and a job that they would actually have. On national surveys students typically can choose only among ten different job categories. The extensive detail of the Sloan jobs allowed us to conduct more specific analyses of the relationship between educational expectations and occupational aspirations.

The longitudinal sample of the Sloan study is nationally representative of American high school students in 1992. We conducted detailed analyses comparing characteristics of students in the Sloan sample with students in the sample from the National Education Longitudinal Study of 1988–94 (NELS:88–94) to check on the representativeness of the Sloan sample. The Sloan study is similar to NELS:88–94, with one exception: Sloan students are slightly more likely to live in two-parent households. There are no significant differences in the two samples regarding race and ethnic distributions among the students, the highest level of education the parents have received, the educational expectations parents have for their children, or how much schooling the students expect to obtain.

We use the terms *job* and *occupation* interchangeably.

2. In sociology, investigators typically predict what a student attains—educationally and occupationally—by entering educational expectations and occupational aspirations separately in a mathematical model. This approach is described in William Sewell, Archibald O. Haller, and George W. Oblendorf, "The Educational and Early Occupational Attainment Process: Replication and Revisions," *American Sociological Review* 35 (1970): 1014–27. Given that most students are now at the high end of both educational expectations and occupational aspirations, this form of modeling may become more problematic. On this point, see Robert Hauser and Douglas Anderson, "Post–High

School Plans and Aspirations of Black and White High School Seniors: 1976–1986," *Sociology of Education* 64 (1991): 263–77. We have developed the concept of alignment to help reexamine traditional models given the dramatic changes in the ambitions of today's high school students.

3. The sample for this analysis is students in tenth and twelfth grade for the first year of the Sloan study. For every occupation listed by a student, we calculated the mean level of education of current workers in this occupation using data from the 1990 U.S. Census. We then compared each student's educational expectations with the mean education of current workers in the student's chosen occupation. Students were then categorized in three groups: those whose educational expectations matched the average level of education of workers in the adolescent's chosen occupation (aligned ambitions); those whose educational expectations were higher than the average education of workers in the adolescent's chosen occupation (misaligned ambitions); and those whose educational expectations were lower than the average education of workers in their chosen occupation (misaligned ambitions).

4. Our analyses of the parent questionnaire from the sophomore year of NELS:88–94 and the parent questionnaire from the sophomore year of the High School and Beyond 1980 study also show that the educational expectations parents have for their children have increased significantly over the past decade.

The social background findings are from a series of statistical procedures that examine the association between alignment of ambitions and student background characteristics. There are no significant differences between alignment and student background characteristics for gender and race and ethnicity at the $p < .05$ level.

5. These results are from analyses that we conducted to examine whether aligned ambitions varied among students aspiring to different types of occupations. We ran a series of descriptive statistics of alignment by occupation, using the categories of the Bureau of Labor Statistics (see Figure 3.4 for the categories). We conducted analyses of the association between alignment and the different types of occupations, controlling for students' race and gender. Of the twenty-four associations we examined, we found only a few that were significant at the $p < .05$ level. African-American students who aspire to be architects and engineers are more likely to have aligned ambitions, and Hispanic students are more likely to overestimate the amount of education needed for the jobs they aspire to. Among students

aspiring to be lawyers, females are more likely to have aligned ambitions.
A small proportion of adolescents chose occupations in the service industry, including food service, cleaning and personal services, and manual
positions, such as mechanics and farmers. Individuals employed in these occupations have the lowest average levels of education—less than college—
and high school seniors who choose these occupations are likely to have
aligned ambitions.

6. Our concept of a life plan has some similarities to that of "planful
competence" developed by John A. Clausen in *American Lives: Looking Back at the
Children of the Great Depression* (New York: Free Press, 1993). Clausen generated
his theory by analyzing the biographies of 282 individuals from the Berkeley Longitudinal Studies Project, which intensively interviewed and conducted follow-up studies on men and women over fifty years. Planful competence was defined as a trait in adolescence consisting of three dimensions:
self-confidence, dependability, and intellectual investment. Adolescents with
these qualities were more successful adults in both their family and work
lives. Clausen, a social psychologist, was primarily interested in how dimensions of personality were influenced by family social background characteristics, physical attractiveness, family and peer relationships, and occupational careers.

We view the process of life planning as an orientation that individuals have toward their educational and occupational futures. The process of
planning is not a fixed trait but rather is manifest through the actions adolescents take—such as selecting rigorous courses or seeking tutorial assistance. These actions are shaped by social relationships in the family and
school and to a lesser extent by the workplace. An adolescent who engages
in life planning takes advantage of opportunities and organizes his or her personal and social resources to overcome constraints—for example, taking an
advanced-level language course at a local community college if it is not offered in the high school.

7. In selecting the students, we tried to match them on their background characteristics, including but not limited to parental income and im-
migrant status. In a study such as this, we cannot achieve total comparabil-
ity. We recognize that many of the opportunities these students have are the
consequence of their family and community resources.

8. Erik H. Erikson, *Identity, Youth, and Crisis* (New York: Norton, 1968).

9. L. Steinberg, B. Brown, and S. Dornbusch, *Beyond the Classroom* (New
York: Simon and Schuster, 1997).

f i v e
Channeling Ambitions in High School

1. For a description of the 1950s high school curriculum, see Larry Cremin, *The Transformation of the School: Progressivism in American Education, 1876–1957* (New York: Alfred A. Knopf, 1961); and Diane Ravitch, *The Troubled Crusade: American Education, 1945–1980* (New York: Basic Books, 1983). One examination of curricular change from the late 1920s through the 1980s using a series of national surveys finds a "steady drop in the academic share of subject enrollments that begins in 1928 and continues unabated until 1961" (David Angus and Jeffrey Mirel, "The High School Curriculum," in *Learning from the Past: What History Teaches Us About School Reform*, ed. Diane Ravitch and Maris A. Vinovskis [Baltimore: Johns Hopkins University Press, 1995], 302).

2. Arthur Powell, David K. Cohen, and Eleanor Farr, *The Shopping Mall High School: Winners and Losers in the Educational Marketplace* (Boston: Houghton Mifflin, 1985). The standard measure of course time in high school is the credit or Carnegie unit. High school graduation requirements, whether state or local, are commonly expressed in such units. For a description of the organization of the curriculum and schooling in other countries, see Alan C. Kerckhoff, *Diverging Pathways: Social Structure and Career Deflections* (Cambridge: Cambridge University Press, 1993); and Harold W. Stevenson and James W. Stigler, *The Learning Gap: Why Our Schools Are Failing and What We Can Learn from Japanese and Chinese Education* (New York: Summit Books, 1992).

3. National Commission on Excellence in Education, *A Nation at Risk: The Imperative for Educational Reform* (Washington, D.C.: U.S. Department of Education, 1983). On states' responses to the commission's report, see W. Clune and P. White, "Education Reform in the Trenches: Increased Academic Course Taking in High Schools with Lower Achieving Students in States with Higher Graduation Requirements," *Educational Evaluation and Policy Analysis* 14, no. 1 (spring 1992): 2–20. On the effects of the reforms, National Center for Education Statistics, U.S. Department of Education, *The Condition of Education* (Washington, D.C.: Government Printing Office, 1995).

4. See David Stevenson, Julie Kochanek, and Barbara Schneider, "Making the Transition from High School: Recent Trends and Policies," in *The Adolescent Years: Social Influences and Educational Challenges*, National Society for the Study of Education Yearbook, 1998, ed. Kathryn Borman and Barbara Schneider (Chicago: University of Chicago Press, 1998).

5. Kevin J. Dougherty, *The Contradictory College: The Conflicting Origins, Impacts,*

and Futures of the Community College (Albany: State University of New York Press, 1994).

More than 90 percent of high school students report that their counselors encourage them to go to college. The concerns of school personnel about the work skills their students will need are reflected in the findings of Richard Murnane and Frank Levy in Teaching the New Basic Skills: Principles for Educating Children to Thrive in a Changing Economy (New York: Free Press, 1996).

During our trip to "River City," we interviewed the president of the local community college, which was undergoing extensive curricular expansion. The president noted two significant trends over the past five years: first, the increasing number of community college students who transfer to four-year institutions after completing their associate's degrees, and, second, the increasing number of technical training programs that the community college was offering in response to demand for skilled workers by local industries that did provide training. Similar national enrollment patterns are observed in Dougherty, The Contradictory College.

In our interviews, teachers and principals frequently mentioned vocational programs in high schools as problematic and said efforts were under way to either revamp the curriculum or eliminate certain technical courses. Difficulties in finding qualified teachers and highly sophisticated equipment, and low interest on the part of students and their parents, were frequently mentioned as reasons why these programs needed reorganization or elimination.

6. The issue of differentiating high school courses by level of academic difficulty is discussed in David Stevenson, Kathryn Schiller, and Barbara Schneider, "Sequences of Opportunities for Learning," Sociology of Education 67 (July 1994): 184–98. This paper builds on earlier conceptual work by A. B. Sorensen in "Organizational Differentiation of Students and Educational Opportunity," Sociology of Education 43 (1970): 355–76; and Maureen Hallinan and A. B. Sorensen, "The Formation and Stability of Instructional Groups," American Sociological Review 48 (1983): 838–51. For a review of studies on curricular differentiation, see Jeannie Oakes, Adam Gamoran, and Reba Page, "Curriculum Differentiation: Opportunities, Outcomes, and Meanings," in Handbook of Research on Curriculum: A Project of the American Educational Research Association, ed. Philip Jackson (New York: Macmillan, 1992), 570–608.

7. James B. Conant, The American High School Today (New York: McGraw-Hill, 1959).

8. The sampling frame of the Sloan study included identifying twelve communities in different regions of the country and then selecting communities that differed in the growth and decline in the service and manufacturing industries as well as their urbanicity. Special care was taken to ensure that the student populations from these twelve sites were racially and ethnically diverse and had families with a wide range of economic and social resources. After selecting the communities, the district school superintendent was asked to identify which high school best represented the racial and socioeconomic composition of the community. In four of the twelve sites, there was only one public high school in the community. A decision was made to include at least one specialized school in mathematics and science, and that school was selected for the composition of its population, its geographic location, and the labor market conditions. In another community, the superintendent suggested we study both the international baccalaureate magnet high school and another high school that was more representative of the school district; at one site, therefore, we examined two schools. Having two specialized schools allowed us to compare very academically demanding programs offered in public schools. None of the three schools described in this chapter are magnet schools. Magnet schools had the highest proportion of students with misaligned ambitions who overestimated the amount of education required for their desired occupation.

To select our three schools, we first examined the distribution of alignment and misalignment by school. The distribution of alignment for students at Maple Wood was most similar to the population as a whole. Among the twelve remaining schools, Middle Brook was among the four high schools with the highest number of misaligned students who overestimated the amount of education needed for their desired job, and Del Vista was among the four with the highest number of misaligned students who underestimated the amount of education needed for their desired job.

We conducted a series of analyses to compare the demographic characteristics of the high schools. The high schools differ significantly with respect to the highest level of parent education ($p < .0001$) and parent educational expectations for their adolescents ($p < .01$). More parents at Middle Brook expect their adolescents to earn advanced degrees.

9. Our work focuses on how public high schools today influence students' plans for the future. In the 1980s other empirical work examined how elite private schools and Catholic high schools influenced students' future

plans. For a description of how elite private high schools engaged in this process, see Peter Cookson, Jr., and Carolyn Persell, *Preparing for Power: America's Elite Boarding Schools* (New York: Basic Books, 1985); for Catholic schools, see Anthony Bryk, Valerie Lee, and Peter Holland, *Catholic Schools and the Common Good* (Cambridge: Harvard University Press, 1993).

10. Information on the racial composition and income for residents of Maple Wood was obtained from the U.S. Census for 1990.

11. The role of counselors in helping students make career and educational choices after high school has been an interest of sociologists for many years. See Aaron V. Cicourel and John I. Kitsuse, *The Educational Decision-Makers: An Advanced Study in Sociology* (Indianapolis: Bobbs-Merrill, 1963); and James E. Rosenbaum, *Making Inequality: The Hidden Curriculum of High School Tracking* (New York: John Wiley, 1976). For discussions of the changing role of high school counselors today, see Shaunti Knauth, Barbara Schneider, and Eleni Makris, "The Influence of Guidance Counselors: School Patterns," a paper presented at the American Educational Research Association, San Francisco, spring 1995; and James E. Rosenbaum, Shazia Rafiullah Miller, and Melinda Scott Krei, "Gatekeeping in an Era of More Open Gates: High School Counselors' Views of Their Influence on Students' College Plans," *American Journal of Education* 104 (August 1996): 257–79.

12. Students at Maple Wood also spent more time talking with parents about their courses than students at the other two schools. The mean level of discussion at Maple Wood was significantly higher than the other two groups at $p < .001$.

13. Of high school seniors in the spring of 1992, 62.1 percent attended a postsecondary education institution within twenty-six months of the end of their senior year (our analysis of NELS:88–94 senior cohort).

14. The average size of an American high school is approximately fifteen hundred students (*Digest of Education Statistics, 1996* [Washington, D.C.: U.S. Department of Education, National Center for Education Statistics, 1996]).

15. The rise in the number of students taking AP examinations nationally has been fairly dramatic across gender and all racial groups. In 1984, twenty-four of every thousand seniors took an AP examination; by 1995, the number had grown to sixty-six per thousand (National Center for Education Statistics, *Condition of Education*, 100).

16. Analyses show that Middle Brook offers more courses at the advanced level than Maple Wood and Del Vista ($p < .001$).

s i x
Families and the Shaping of Aligned Ambitions

1. The Sloan study included more than 340 interviews with parents, who consistently reported high educational expectations for their children. The study's Teenage Life Survey asked students how far their parents expected them to go in school. In the base-year sample of 2,241 tenth and twelfth graders, 76 percent reported that their parents expected them to graduate from college and earn advanced degrees. This percentage is similar to the twelfth-grade sample of the National Education Longitudinal Study of 1988–94 (NELS:88–94) (Jennifer Schmidt and Patrick Riley, *Alfred P. Sloan Study, Base Year Electronic Codebook* [Chicago: University of Chicago, 1998]; Steven J. Ingels, Kathryn L. Dowd, John D. Baldridge, James L. Stipe, Virginia H. Bartot, and Martin R. Frankel, *NELS:88 Second Follow-Up: Student Component Data File User's Manual* [Washington, D.C.: U.S. Department of Education, National Center for Education Statistics, 1994]).

The data from the second follow-up to NELS:88–94 parent survey show that most parents expect that their adolescents will attend college. Ninety-one percent have discussed applying to college after high school, and 74 percent would like their teenager to complete four years of college or more (Steven J. Ingels, Lisa Thalji, Paul Pulliam, Virginia H. Bartot, and Martin R. Frankel, *NELS:88 Second Follow-Up: Parent Component Data File User's Manual* [Washington, D.C.: U.S. Department of Education, National Center for Education Statistics, 1994]).

2. For information on the 1972 national survey, see John Riccobono, Louise B. Henderson, Graham J. Burkheimer, Carol Place, and Jay R. Levinson, *National Longitudinal Study: Base Year (1972) Through Fourth Follow-Up (1979), Data File Users Manual*, vol. 3 (Chapel Hill, N.C.: Center for Educational Research and Evaluation, Research Triangle Institute, 1981). For information on the 1982 survey, see Calvin Jones, Miriam Clark, Geraldine Mooney, Harold McWilliams, Ioanna Crawford, Bruce Stephenson, and Roger Tourangeau, *High School and Beyond 1980 Sophomore Cohort First Follow-Up (1982), Data File User's Manual* (Washington, D.C.: U.S. Department of Education, National Center for Education Statistics, 1983). For the 1992 national survey, see Ingels et al., *NELS:88 Second Follow-Up: Student Component*.

3. Laurence Steinberg also argues that adolescents perceive their parents more positively than is often suggested. He says that family deterioration during adolescence is less prevalent than thought, and only a small pro-

portion of families, somewhere between 5 and 10 percent, experience a dramatic deterioration in the quality of parent-adolescent relations (Laurence Steinberg, "Autonomy, Conflict, and Harmony in the Family Relationship," in *At the Threshold: The Developing Adolescent*, ed. S. Shirley Feldman and Glen R. Elliott [Cambridge: Harvard University Press, 1990], 260).

For a historical review of stress and conflict in adolescence, see Mihaly Csikszentmihalyi and Jennifer A. Schmidt, "Stress and Resilience in Adolescence: An Evolutionary Perspective," in *The Adolescent Years: Social Influences and Educational Challenges*, ed. Kathryn Borman and Barbara Schneider (Chicago: University of Chicago Press, 1998).

On the cooperativeness of families, see Charles Bidwell, Mihaly Csikszentmihalyi, Larry Hedges, and Barbara Schneider, *Images of Adolescent Work* (New York: Cambridge University Press, forthcoming), especially chapter 7, "Family Dynamics and the Occupational Formation of Children."

4. The conceptual development of the support and challenge scales grew from work on family integration and differentiation by Kevin Rathunde, "Family Context and Optimal Experience in the Development of Talent" (Ph.D. dissertation, University of Chicago, 1989), and Kevin Rathunde, "The Context of Optimal Experience: An Exploratory Model of the Family," *New Ideas in Psychology* 7 (1988): 91–97. The concept of integration and differentiation was further elaborated in Mihaly Csikszentmihalyi, Kevin Rathunde, and Samuel Whalen, *Talented Teenagers: The Roots of Success and Failure* (New York: Cambridge University Press, 1993). Rathunde further developed this line of work using the concepts of support and challenge. We have modified the Rathunde conceptualization based on the construction of new scales developed by Jennifer Schmidt, who analyzed Rathunde's items using Rasch techniques. (Rasch analysis calibrates the items according to difficulty to endorse. For a description of Rasch techniques, see Georg Rasch, *Probabilistic Models for Some Intelligence and Attainment Tests* [Copenhagen: Danmarks Paedogogiske Institute, 1960]; Benjamin Wright and Mark Stone, *Best Test Design* [Chicago: MESA Press, 1979]; and Benjamin Wright and Geoffrey H. Masters, *Rating Scale Analysis* [Chicago: MESA Press, 1983].)

In analyzing the ordering of the items, we determined that the challenge scale was a strong indicator of preparation for adulthood. Moreover, the components of the scale fit closely with many of the elements we identified as contributing to alignment. We gratefully acknowledge the important work of Csikszentmihalyi, Rathunde, Whalen, and Schmidt in this area.

5. We ran a series of descriptive statistics to determine the association

between parental support and educational expectations. Low and average levels of support are not associated with varying levels of educational expectations (less than college, college, master's, and professional or advanced degree). At high levels of parental support, however, there is a significant difference between students expecting to earn less than a college degree and those expecting to earn at least a college degree or more ($p < .0001$). We also ran a series of descriptive statistics to determine if alignment varied by family support. No significant effects were found between aligned and misaligned students and their perceptions of parental support.

6. We ran a series of descriptive statistics to determine the association between parental challenge and educational expectations. Low and average levels of challenge are not associated with varying levels of educational expectations. But there is a significant difference between students expecting to earn less than a college degree and those expecting to earn at least a college degree or higher with respect to high levels of challenge ($p < .001$). We also ran a series of descriptive statistics to determine if parental challenge was related to alignment. Students with aligned ambitions and those who overestimate the amount of education needed reported their parents higher on the challenge scale ($p < .03$) than those who underestimate their educational needs.

7. James S. Coleman, *Foundations of Social Theory* (Cambridge: Belknap Press of Harvard University Press, 1990). Other works by Coleman on social capital include "Families and Schools," *Educational Researcher* 16, no. 6 (1987): 32–38, and "Social Capital in the Creation of Human Capital," *American Journal of Sociology* 94 (1988): S95–S120, which includes an explanation of the different forms of capital. For a succinct definition of social capital, see Barbara Schneider, "The Ubiquitous Emerging Conception of Social Capital," in *Education and Sociology: An Encyclopedia*, ed. David Levinson, Peter Cookson, and Alan Sadovnik (New York: Taylor and Francis, forthcoming).

8. We have worked extensively on issues of parent involvement in children's education. Our previous work leads us to believe that to understand the process of alignment it is necessary to look more at social processes and dynamics in the family rather than more structural issues such as family composition, family income, family educational levels, and family occupational status. For some of our earlier work in this area, see David P. Baker and David L. Stevenson, "A Mother's Strategies for Children's School Achievement: Managing the Transition to High School," *Sociology of Education* 59 (1986): 156–67; David L. Stevenson and David P. Baker, "The Family-School Relation and the

Child's School Performance," *Child Development* 58 (1987): 1348–57; and Barbara Schneider and James S. Coleman, eds., *Parents, Their Children, and Schools* (Boulder, Colo.: Westview Press, 1993).

For the importance of relational ties in the family for influencing grades and cognitive performance, see Schneider and Coleman, eds., *Parents, Their Children, and Schools*. For a discussion of how relational ties in communities can influence educational attainment, see James S. Coleman and Thomas Hoffer, *Public and Private High Schools: The Impact of Communities* (New York: Basic Books, 1987).

9. The four groups were composed of the following: less than college, n = 232 (19 percent); college graduate, n = 366 (30 percent); master's degree, n = 336 (27 percent); and professional or advanced degree, n = 299 (24 percent). For the analysis of differences in aligned and misaligned students in the professional and advanced-degree category, there are 139 aligned and 160 misaligned students. Analyses of these items were conducted on all four educational expectation groups. For adolescents planning to obtain only a high school diploma, there are differences between aligned and misaligned students on discussing courses with parents: aligned students are more likely to often discuss their courses with their parents than are students who had misaligned ambitions. For those expecting to graduate from college, only discussing grades differed between aligned and misaligned students: aligned students are more likely to often discuss their grades with their parents than are misaligned students. For students expecting to obtain a master's degree, there are no differences in items between aligned and misaligned students. These differences were significant at the $p < .05$ level.

10. To select our cases we divided the sample of sophomores into three groups based on whether they were aligned, overestimated their education, or underestimated their education. We randomly selected three students, taking into account gender, high school attended, plans for the future, and completed parent interview. Because of our focus on high ambitions for this chapter we were interested in only sophomores who planned to attend college, which was 86 percent of the sophomore sample.

11. For a discussion of the concept of "shadow education," see David L. Stevenson and David P. Baker, "Shadow Education and Allocation in Formal Schooling: Transitions to University in Japan," *American Journal of Sociology* 67 (1992): 184–98.

12. In the parent interviews, it was not unusual to find parents making significant sacrifices to pay for their adolescent's college expenses. One

memorable example is the case of the Lupidas, who are both public school teachers. Elena, their daughter, has been accepted in the early-admission medical program at one of the most prestigious universities in the country. Describing how they are going to pay for their daughter's college expenses, her mother says, "Well, how we are trying to pay for it is, we started about last year in January, trying to save, a certain amount a month. We started putting the money aside at the beginning of the month in this account knowing this was going to be for Elena's college. We found out that we could do it. But by the end of the each month we ran out of money, we literally ran out of money—so we ate rice and beans. We are trying to avoid borrowing as much as we possibly can."

13. More than 45 percent of freshmen enrolled in four-year colleges do not earn a bachelor's degree within five years, according to the High School and Beyond 1980 study (see Chapter 9 of this book).

14. Coleman and Hoffer, *Public and Private High Schools.*

s e v e n
Teenage Work and Internships

1. See Jeylan Mortimer, Michael Finch, Michael Shanahan, and Seongryeol Ryu, "Work Experience, Mental Health, and Behavioral Adjustment in Adolescence," *Journal of Research on Adolescence* 2 (1992): 25–57; and Michael Finch, Michael Shanahan, Jeylan Mortimer, and Seongryeol Ryu, "Work Experience and Control Orientation in Adolescence," *American Sociological Review* 56 (1991): 597–611.

More recently, researchers have been examining the effects of adolescent employment on adult employment (Rhoda Carr, James Wright, and Charles Brody, "Effects of High School Work Experience a Decade Later: Evidence from the National Longitudinal Study," *Sociology of Education* 69 [1996]: 66–81). Findings that show negative effects of early teenage employment on adult wages appear in Joseph Hotz, Lixin Xu, Marta Tienda, and Avner Ahituv, "The Returns to Early Work Experience in Transition from School to Work for Young Men in the U.S.: An Analysis of the 1980s," unpublished manuscript, University of Chicago, 1995. Generally, researchers agree that the effects of adolescent employment on academic performance and attainment are only slightly negative (Carr, Wright, and Brody, "Effects of High School Work Experience"), or inconsequential (Jeylan T. Mortimer and Monica Johnson, "Adolescents' Part-Time Work and Educational Achievement," in

The Adolescent Years: Social Influences and Educational Challenges, ed. Kathryn Borman and Barbara Schneider [Chicago: University of Chicago Press, 1998]); for another view, see Ellen Greenberger and Laurence Steinberg, *When Teenagers Work: The Psychological and Social Costs of Adolescent Employment* (New York: Basic Books, 1986).

2. The percentage of teenagers working is from our analysis of data from the National Education Longitudinal Study of 1988–94 (NELS:88–94). The hours that adolescents work have remained relatively stable over the past twenty years (our analysis of data from the National Longitudinal Study: Base Year 1972 [NLS-72], High School and Beyond 1980 [HS&B], and NELS: 88–94). Likelihood of teenagers in other industrialized countries working is from U.S. Department of Education, National Center for Education Statistics, *Pursuing Excellence: A Study of U.S. Twelfth-Grade Mathematics and Science Achievement in International Contexts* (Washington, D.C.: Government Printing Office, 1998).

Teenagers' reasons for not working are from Mercer L. Sullivan, *Getting Paid: Youth, Crime, and Work in the Inner City* (Ithaca, N.Y.: Cornell University Press, 1989); and William Julius Wilson, *When Work Disappears: The World of the New Urban Poor* (New York: Alfred A. Knopf, 1996). Adolescents who do not work are more likely to live in families with considerable economic resources or very limited ones; they also are more likely to be racial and ethnic minorities (our analysis of NELS:88–94).

3. National Research Council, *Protecting Youth at Work* (Washington, D.C.: National Academy Press, 1998).

4. Our analysis of NELS:88–94 and Sloan data.

5. National Center for Education Statistics, *A Comparison of High School Dropout Rates in 1982 and 1992* (Washington, D.C.: Office of Educational Research and Improvement, U.S. Department of Education, 1996).

6. The experience sampling method was developed in the 1970s by Mihaly Csikszentmihalyi. For further elaboration on how the ESM is used in studies of adolescents, see Mihaly Csikszentmihalyi and Reed Larson, *Being Adolescent* (New York: Basic Books, 1986). Other sources that describe the ESM, though not as extensively, are Mihaly Csikszentmihalyi and Isabella Csikszentmihalyi, eds., *Optimal Experience: Psychological Studies of Flow in Consciousness* (Cambridge: Cambridge University Press, 1988); Mihaly Csikszentmihalyi, *Flow: The Psychology of Optimal Experience* (New York: Harper and Row, 1990); and Mihaly Csikszentmihalyi, *Finding Flow: The Psychology of Engagement with Everyday Life* (New York: Basic Books, 1997).

7. For a description of the variation in types of teenage employment see Mark Schoenhals, Marta Tienda, and Barbara Schneider, "The Educational and Personal Consequences of Adolescent Employment," *Social Forces* (forthcoming); and Charles Bidwell, Barbara Schneider, and Kathryn Borman, "Working: Perceptions and Experiences of American Teenagers," in Borman and Schneider, eds., *The Adolescent Years.*

In their interviews, adolescents frequently discussed how they got their jobs. Often, they could not apply for jobs because the restaurants and stores required them to be seventeen years old.

8. See Mortimer and Johnson, "Adolescents' Part-Time Work and Educational Achievement."

9. Adolescent participation in extracurricular activities in school has been declining (Patricia Green, Bernard Dugoni, and Steven Ingels, *Trends Among High School Seniors, 1972–1992* [Washington, D.C.: U.S. Department of Education, National Center for Education Statistics, 1995]). Similarly, there is some evidence that recreational facilities that traditionally served teenagers are now closed in some communities (personal communication from the MacArthur Foundation). Among adolescents who work, their work experiences are affectively more positive than being alone (Charles Bidwell, Mihaly Csikszentmihalyi, Larry Hedges, and Barbara Schneider, *Images of Adolescent Work* (New York: Cambridge University Press, forthcoming).

10. The characteristics of the internship experience we discuss have also been used to describe successful "apprenticeships." For a discussion of positive apprentice-type experiences, see Lynn Olsen, *The School to Work Revolution* (Lexington, Mass.: Addison-Wesley, 1997).

e i g h t
Being Alone and Being with Friends

1. See James S. Coleman, *The Adolescent Society: The Social Life of the Teenager and Its Impact on Education* (New York: Free Press of Glencoe, 1961).

2. To understand norms of adolescent friendship and romantic relationships today, in this chapter we relied heavily on the intensive interviews for the first three years of the study. The friend sections of the interviews contained several series of questions regarding what adolescents did with friends, what they talked about, whether they had a special boyfriend or girlfriend, what things they did with their friends that they wished they didn't,

and whether their best friends changed from one year to another. We use many of the phrases of the students in portraying their relationships and social life.

3. How teenagers spend their total time in an average week was calculated based on the experience sampling method responses of the base-year tenth- and twelfth-grade student longitudinal sample. Estimates for the amount of time spent alone for the high school sample in the third year of the study were nearly identical to the first-year estimates. Amount of time spent alone does not vary by gender, race and ethnicity, or parent education.

4. The difference in time spent alone by grade was significant at the $p < .0001$ level. The average time spent alone per week by sixth graders was 19.8 hours, for eighth graders 25.3, for tenth graders 25.4, and for twelfth graders 28.8.

Students were asked what they were "doing" when they were beeped. Based on their responses we developed an extensive list of different categories of activities. Collapsing categories based on frequencies, we developed a list of fifteen activities. Drug and alcohol use while spending time alone was one of the few rarely mentioned "doing" activities.

5. We divided the base-year high school sample into three groups: those who were rarely alone ($n = 124$), those who were alone for an average amount of time, ($n = 120$), and those who were alone often ($n = 131$). T-tests were employed to examine the differences between those who were rarely alone and those who were alone more than average. For television viewing, the mean for the frequently-alone group was 11.8 hours per week; for the rarely-alone group it was 7.7 and was significant at $p < .001$. For sleeping during the day, the mean for the frequently-alone group was 4.6 hours per week; for the rarely-alone group, 3.1. There is a significant difference between the two groups at the $p < .01$ level. Given that many of the students have to get up at five in the morning to attend high school, it is not unexpected that adolescents want, and perhaps need, more sleep. For playing a sport, the frequently-alone group was 1.3 (number of sport activities) whereas the rarely-alone group was 2.2. There was a significant difference between the two groups at the $p < .02$ level.

The findings on personal computers and hobbies were based on responses from the Teenage Life Survey. T-tests were employed and there was a significant difference between the rarely alone group and frequently alone group, $p < .001$.

6. T-tests were employed to examine the differences between those

who were rarely alone and those who were alone more than average. For those who were rarely alone the mean for self-esteem was 6.5 on a scale of 1–9, and for those often alone, 6.2. A significant difference was found at the $p < .05$ level. Those who were rarely alone were more likely to be happy (4.8 on a scale of 1–7) than those who were frequently alone (4.5). A significant difference was found at the $p < .001$ level. Those who were rarely alone were more likely to report enjoying what they were doing (6.7) than those who were frequently alone (6.4). A significant difference was found at the $p < .06$ level. For those who were rarely alone the mean for active was 4.7 and for those frequently alone it was 4.4. A significant difference was found at the $p < .02$ level.

For a discussion of the benefits and liabilities of solitude see Mihaly Csikszentmihalyi, *Finding Flow: The Psychology of Engagement with Everyday Life* (New York: Basic Books, 1997).

This recent study of gifted adolescents forms the basis of Mihaly Csikszentmihalyi, Kevin Rathunde, and Samuel Whalen, *Talented Teenagers: The Roots of Success and Failure* (New York: Cambridge University Press, 1993).

7. Similar to the analysis of time alone, we developed categories for what adolescents were doing when they were with their friends. These percentages are based on the ESM data for the base-year high school sample. Categories of activities do not vary by race and ethnicity or parent education. However, we found that boys tend to spend slightly more time with friends on homework than girls do.

T-tests comparing self-esteem when alone as opposed to with friends were significant at the $p < .001$ level; for feeling strong, $p < .001$; for feeling happy, $p < .001$; and for motivation, $p < .001$. This was the case for both boys and girls, for different racial and ethnic groups, and regardless of parent education.

8. This analysis used beeper data from the base-year high school sample. There were no significant differences between the time spent talking about the future with friends, family, or at school.

9. Distinctions among best friends, cliques, and crowds are made by Laurence Steinberg, B. Bradford Brown, and Sanford M. Dornbusch in *Beyond the Classroom: Why School Reform Has Failed and What Parents Need to Do* (New York: Simon and Schuster, 1996); what they refer to as cliques is the focus of our analysis of social groups.

10. The Sloan study gave all students a specially designed friend sociometric form that asked them to name their close friends whom they "hang

out" with. The analysis reported here was conducted on the base-year tenth-grade sample that was followed in the second and third years. The mean for tenth-grade girls was 11.1 close friends, and for tenth-grade boys, 10 close friends.

11. Erik H. Erikson, *Identity, Youth, and Crisis* (New York: Norton, 1968).

12. This point is also made by Steinberg, Brown, and Dornbusch in *Beyond the Classroom*, where it is found that the influence of the peer group begins to decline after tenth grade. Reviewing our interview data we also found the influence of the peer group to be strongest in middle school and beginning to decline in high school.

13. See Gary Remafedi, Michael Resnick, Robert Blum, and Linda Harris, "Demography of Sexual Orientation in Adolescents," *Pediatrics* 89, no. 4 (April 1992): 714–21.

14. For the Sloan student surveys, the elementary and high schools asked us to omit questions that directly asked the students how often they used drugs or drank alcohol. Instead we asked students about things they did with friends and things they wished they did not do. About a third of the high school students in the base year, second year, and third year of the study mentioned drug and alcohol use by themselves or their friends and acquaintances. These numbers appear consistent with national studies; according to *Trends in the Well Being of America's Children and Youth* (Washington, D.C.: U.S. Department of Health and Human Services, 1996), about 31 percent of twelfth graders in 1995 reported regular drinking and 25 percent reported illicit drug use.

15. Coleman, *Adolescent Society*, 22–23.

16. We employed t-tests among the base-year high school students with aligned and misaligned ambitions to determine if these groups were different from one another. For boyfriends and girlfriends the difference was significant at the $p < .04$ level; for the parent items the differences were significant at $p < .02$.

n i n e
The Ambition Paradox

1. *Digest of Education Statistics, 1997* (Washington, D.C.: U.S. Department of Education, National Center for Education Statistics, 1997). Total students enrolled in two-year and four-year institutions in the fall after high school were 49 percent of high school seniors in 1972, 52 percent in 1982, and 59

percent in 1992, according to our analysis on weighted samples of the National Longitudinal Study of 1972 (NLS-72), High School and Beyond 1980 (HS&B), and the National Education Longitudinal Study of 1988–94 (NELS:88–94).

2. More than 3,600 colleges and universities grant degrees and are accredited by an agency recognized by the U.S. Department of Education. In the 1970s, the Carnegie Foundation for the Advancement of Teaching developed a classification system to distinguish among these different types of postsecondary institutions on the basis of academic mission (*A Classification of Institutions of Higher Education: A Technical Report Sponsored by the Carnegie Commission on Higher Education* [Berkeley, Calif.: Carnegie Foundation for the Advancement of Teaching, 1973]). This classification system has been modified over the past two decades; the most recent modification appears in the *Directory of Postsecondary Institutions, 1997*, vol. 2 (Washington, D.C.: U.S. Department of Education, National Center for Education Statistics, 1997).

For comprehensive discussions of the community college see Kevin J. Dougherty, *The Contradictory College: The Conflicting Origins, Impacts, and Futures of the Community College* (Albany: State University of New York Press, 1994); and Steven Brint and Jerome Karabel, *The Diverted Dream: Community Colleges and the Promise of Educational Opportunity in America, 1900–1985* (New York: Oxford University Press, 1989).

For definitions of proprietary programs, see American Council on Education, *American Universities and Colleges*, 14th ed. (New York: Walter de Gruyter, 1992). Lists of such institutions can be found in the *Directory of Postsecondary Institutions, 1997*, vol. 2. In 1972, 5.3 percent of high school graduates chose to pursue such certificates; in 1982, 5.0 percent; and in 1992, 2.9 percent (our analysis of NLS-72, HS&B, and NELS:88–94).

Community colleges are two-year public institutions and junior colleges are two-year private institutions (*American Universities and Colleges*). We use the term two-year institutions (or colleges) to refer to both types, except when students specifically refer to a particular type of institution in their quotations.

3. In 1972, 31.8 percent of high school graduates enrolled in four-year institutions and 16.9 percent enrolled in two-year institutions; in 1982, 31.9 percent enrolled in four-year institutions and 19.8 percent in two-year institutions; and, in 1992, 40.1 percent enrolled in four-year institutions and 19.3 percent in two-year institutions (our analysis of NLS-72, HS&B, and NELS:88–94).

The educational expectations of students in two-year institutions are moving toward the expectations of students in four-year institutions. In 1992, almost 96 percent of college freshmen enrolled in four-year institutions expected to earn a bachelor's degree (our analysis of NELS:88–94).

4. To conduct this analysis, we used data from NLS-72 and HS&B. We used these data sets so that our models could contain high school information on expectations and test scores, which are related to college choice. We conducted this analysis from a base model of a white male, whose parents had more than a high school education, who expected some college and had average test scores. The student the model is based on is the type most likely to complete a bachelor's degree. Unfortunately for our purposes, longitudinal studies of postsecondary students in the 1990s either were not conducted long enough to undertake the analysis or did not contain the high school information needed to estimate our models. We would have predicted the likelihood of receiving a bachelor's degree for students who started college in 1992 using the NELS:88–94 data, but data on these students have not been collected since 1994.

5. Among second-year students in two-year colleges, educational expectations for a bachelor's degree were 73 percent in spring 1974; 67 percent in spring 1984; and 87 percent in spring 1994 (our analysis of NLS-72, HS&B, and NELS:88–94).

6. Our analysis of NLS-72 and the Beginning Postsecondary Student Longitudinal Study (BPS) conducted by the National Center for Education Statistics from 1989 to 1994.

7. To conduct this analysis we used data from NLS-72, HS&B, and BPS. NELS:88–94 was not carried out long enough to examine associate's and bachelor's completion rates for all the students in the sample. For this analysis we used the BPS sample of high school seniors who enrolled in postsecondary education for the first time in 1989. This is considered a nationally representative sample of high school seniors who started postsecondary school. These students constitute approximately 70 percent of the sample.

8. Our analysis of BPS.

9. Clifford Adelman, "Transfer Rates and the Going Mythologies," *Change* (January-February 1988): 38–41. See also Alexander C. McCormick, *Transfer Behavior Among Beginning Postsecondary Students, 1989–1994* (Washington, D.C.: U.S. Department of Education, National Center for Education Statistics, 1997).

10. A descriptive analysis (t-test) found a significant difference be-

tween the aligned and misaligned students in two- and four-year institutions at the p .02 level.

11. Among the Sloan base-year high school senior sample of 229, there were 46 students who attended two-year institutions in the fall of 1993. By the spring of 1997, three-quarters of the students remained enrolled in two-year schools.

The number of students in the Sloan study who received an associate's degree and decided not to transfer to a four-year institution was less than 5 percent. Having obtained the associate's degree, nearly all the students expected to receive more education, although in some cases not immediately.

12. Other analyses of students who transferred from two-year colleges to four-year institutions in the 1980s have found that high school academic course taking and high school achievement were significant factors in predicting whether a student transferred to a four-year institution (Valerie E. Lee and Kenneth A. Frank, "Students' Characteristics That Facilitate the Transfer from Two-Year to Four-Year Colleges," *Sociology of Education* 63 [July 1990]: 178–93; and William Velez and R. G. Javalgi, "Two-Year College to Four-Year College: The Likelihood of Transfer," *American Journal of Education* 96, no. 1 [1987]: 81–94).

13. The NELS:88–94 data show that, compared with parents of students in four-year colleges, parents of students in two-year institutions were less willing to provide financial assistance for their children's postsecondary education.

14. For example, the unweighted two-year transfer sample in BPS is 348.

15. David Lurie, *Survey of the Transferability of Associate's Degree to Four-Year Institutions* (U.S. Department of Education, ERIC Document No. ED369449, May 1994).

t e n
Supporting the Development of Aligned Ambitions

1. Richard Sennett, *Corrosion of Character* (New York: Norton, 1998).

2. U.S. Census Bureau, Historical Poverty Tables, September 29, 1997.

index

Academic performance: and college financing, 34; and educational expectations, 35; and college admissions, 40, 49–51, 54, 158, 160, 190; and adolescent ambitions, 46–47, 67; and adolescents of the 1950s, 52–53, 61; and peer-group popularity, 53, 189; and teachers, 66, 93, 97; adolescent attitudes toward, 67, 100–101, 285n9; and labor market, 70; improvements in, 75; and life plans, 85; and aligned ambitions, 89, 100–101, 156; and friendships, 89–90; and misaligned ambitions, 93–94, 105, 108, 163; and motivation, 93, 107; and parents, 96, 97, 161; and community colleges, 105, 137–38, 230; and vocational programs, 115; and uniform curriculum, 118; emphasis on, 129; and employment, 138; and social capital, 148, 297–98n8; and adolescent-parent relationships, 149, 156–57; and norms, 158, 164; and two-year institutions, 221, 227; and Sloan study, 266; and transfers from two-year to four-year institutions, 307n12

ACT: and college choice, 1, 2; and high school curriculum, 128;

and adolescent-parent relationships, 148, 150, 165

Activity-based groups, 199–202, 205, 259–60

Adolescence: data sources on, 9–11, 15; social transformation of, 51–55; and social life, 52, 191–94, 202–11; function of, 106; and teenage work, 170; definition of, 277n1. *See also* Adolescent-parent relationships

Adolescent ambitions: and college choice, 1–3, 215, 248; and dreams, 1, 4, 15, 245; and educational expectations, 3–4, 5, 6–9, 257, 261; and occupational aspirations, 3, 5, 6, 75–78, 251–52; and life plans, 4, 7, 12, 43–44; and employment, 5, 6, 11; and families, 5, 43, 45–46, 252; and wages, 5, 33, 70–76, 231; and parents, 7–8, 141, 256; and strategic choices, 7, 116; and peer groups, 8, 191, 211; and teenage work, 8, 170, 181; changes in, 11, 31–32, 289n2; and academic performance, 46–47, 67; and gender, 55; and labor market, 57; and high school curriculum, 113–19; and norms, 147; high ambitions with low odds, 216–22; and two-year institutions, 216–22, 307n11; role of, 245; case studies of, 246–56;

Adolescent ambitions (continued)
shaping of, 256–63; and intergenerational mobility, 277n2. *See
also* Aligned ambitions; Ambition
paradox; Misaligned ambitions
Adolescent-parent relationships:
and marriage, 21; and misaligned ambitions, 94, 149–50,
159–68, 298n9; and aligned ambitions, 96, 142–46, 148, 149–
58, 298n9; popular conceptions
of, 142, 295–96n3; and Sloan
study, 142–46; and adulthood
transition, 144, 166; and ACT,
148, 150, 165; and life plans,
148–49; and academic performance, 149, 156–57; and educational expectations, 149–50,
160–61, 165–66, 298n9; and
wages, 257
Adolescents of the 1950s: and
adulthood transition, 5, 18, 19,
52–53; and marriage, 5, 16, 21,
22–24, 25, 29–30, 52, 53, 61,
280–81n12; and employment,
6, 16, 27, 56, 61; studies of, 10,
19–20, 278n1; as transitional
generation, 15–16; and suburbanization, 16–17, 19, 29, 53;
and birth rate, 17–18; case studies, 18–19, 20–30, 280n10; and
high school curriculum, 18,
115, 120, 279n9; and labor market, 18, 56–62; and gender roles,
22–24, 49, 53, 54, 71; and occupational aspirations, 22–23, 25–
27, 58, 281n14; and college financing, 25, 28, 54; and finan-

cial aid, 28, 54, 281–82n15; and
high school diploma, 43, 51–52,
58–62, 71–72; and college
preparatory programs, 113,
279n9; and peer groups, 189,
197–98
Adolescents of the 1990s: and
adulthood transition, 5–6, 51;
and marriage, 5, 31, 37, 48–49,
70, 191, 207; studies of, 9–11,
278n1; case studies, 32–51; and
labor market, 33, 44, 48, 57, 62–
70; and employment stability,
35, 40–43, 58; and high school
diploma, 58, 62–70
Adulthood transition: and adolescents of the 1950s, 5, 18, 19,
52–53; and adolescents of the
1990s, 5–6, 51; and life plans,
44; and aligned ambitions, 86,
153, 264; and adolescent-parent
relationships, 144, 166; and parents, 144–45, 257, 296n4; and
adolescent ambitions, 245, 257
Advanced-placement courses: and
college admissions, 51, 54, 128;
and aligned ambitions, 85, 89,
153, 154, 155; and high school
curriculum, 120–21, 128, 129,
135, 260; tutors for, 157; rise in
use of, 294n15
Alcohol use, 90, 131, 142, 193,
208–10, 304n14
Alfred P. Sloan Study of Youth and
Social Development. *See* Sloan
study
Aligned ambitions: nature of, 6–7,
79; and families, 7, 107, 108–9,

158, 169; and high schools, 7,
117, 118, 259–61; and educational expectations, 79–81, 99–
100, 289n3; and motivation, 79,
90, 91, 107; and strategic effort,
79, 86–87; and adolescent characteristics, 82–85, 289n4; and
gender, 82, 83, 289n4, 289–
90n5; and life plans, 83–84, 86–
87, 106–7, 110, 263–64; and
advanced-placement courses, 85,
89, 153, 154, 155; and career
choices, 85, 98, 151–58, 263;
and adulthood transition, 86,
153, 264; resources for, 86,
108–10; case studies of, 87–91,
96–101, 151–58, 293n8; and
academic performance, 89, 100–
101, 156; and teenage work, 90,
96, 107, 152–53; and adolescent-parent relationships, 96,
142–46, 148, 149–58, 298n9;
and college admissions, 107,
154–55, 257, 262; and educational requirements, 109; and
high school curriculum, 139;
and parents, 141, 143, 145,
256–59, 297nn5–6; and social
capital, 147–51; and internships, 187–88, 261; and time
alone, 193–94, 211; and peer
groups, 197–98, 211; and four-
year institutions, 221; and two-
year institutions, 221, 222; and
ambition paradox, 222; fostering
of, 256–57, 264; and occupational aspirations, 264, 289–
90n5

Ambition paradox: and college
choice, 8–9, 237–38; high ambitions with low odds, 216–22;
and two-year institutions, 218–
19, 221, 222, 244, 263; and life
plans, 219–20, 222; case studies
of, 222–42; and employment,
222–27; and career choices,
228–38; and persistence, 238–
42, 244

Athletics: and adolescents of the
1950s, 52–53, 189; and scholarships, 63–64, 222, 236–37; and
occupational aspirations, 77–78;
and educational credentials, 83;
and time alone, 193; and friendships, 194–95, 196; and drug
use, 208; and college choice,
237–38

Boyfriends: and time alone, 8; and
peer groups, 190–91; and
friendships, 197; nature of, 205–
7; and aligned ambitions, 211

Career choices: and adolescent ambitions, 4; and adolescents of the
1950s, 23; and adolescents of the
1990s, 31; and marriage, 31,
253; and strategic plans, 41–42;
and parents, 45, 88–89, 92–93,
98, 102, 168, 258–59; and educational attainment, 80; and
aligned ambitions, 85, 98, 151–
58, 263; and misaligned ambitions, 103–4, 159–63, 222,
228–38; and adolescent-parent
relationships, 150; and high

Career choices (continued)
schools, 156, 160, 165. *See also*
Occupational aspirations
Career orientation survey (COS),
267, 288n1
Cohen, David K., 114
Coleman, James S., 10, 52, 147,
210
College admissions: and academic
performance, 40, 49–51, 54,
158, 160, 190; and college entrance examinations, 40, 49, 51,
89, 128; and advanced-placement courses, 51, 54, 128; and
misaligned ambitions, 94; and
aligned ambitions, 107, 154–55,
257, 262; and high schools, 117,
126–33, 260; and counselors,
122, 129–33, 137, 257; and
high school curriculum, 123–
24, 129–30; and parents, 168
College choice: and adolescent ambitions, 1–3, 215, 248; and
counselors, 1, 43, 127, 148; and
parents, 1–2, 89, 101, 109–10,
129, 157–58, 161–62, 223; and
SAT, 1, 2, 253; and ambition paradox, 8–9, 237–38; and two-year
institutions, 8, 11, 215, 305n2;
and educational attainment, 11;
and occupational aspirations, 36–
38, 42; and race or ethnicity, 126;
and college financing, 158, 168;
and misaligned ambitions, 159,
163–68; and high schools, 160,
260; and friendships, 196; and
athletics, 237–38; and aligned
ambition, 263
College entrance examinations: and
college choice, 1, 2; and college
admissions, 40, 49, 51, 89, 128;
and high school curriculum,
128; and adolescent-parent relationships, 150. *See also* ACT; SAT
College financing: and four-year
institutions, 2–3, 227, 250, 259;
and adolescents of the 1950s,
25, 28, 54; and employment, 28,
43; and educational expectations, 33–34, 54; and strategic
plans, 42; and college admissions, 49–50; and parents, 101,
149, 158, 166, 217–18, 223,
227, 248, 257, 259, 298–99n12,
307n13; and misaligned ambitions, 104–6; and transfers from
two-year to four-year institutions, 105, 241; and community
colleges, 137; and college
choice, 158, 168; and two-year
institutions, 217, 221, 223, 224,
226, 227, 229–30, 237, 243,
259. *See also* Financial aid
College preparation: and college
choice, 1–2; and high school
curriculum, 11, 54, 85, 132,
139, 222, 227, 247; and high
schools, 53–54, 106; and
aligned ambitions, 97, 100; and
teachers, 97, 115; and misaligned ambitions, 105, 106; and
counselors, 130–31; and teenage
work, 176; and educational expectations, 222–23; and two-
year institutions, 230, 233; outreach programs for, 262–63

College preparatory programs: and adolescents of the 1950s, 113, 279n9; and high school curriculum, 113–15, 127; enrollment of, 114

Commercial programs, 113

Community colleges: and higher education growth, 28, 54; and labor market, 64, 65; and misaligned ambitions, 104–6; and academic performance, 105, 137–38, 230; and vocational programs, 115, 215; and educational expectations, 130; and high school curriculum, 135, 137–39; and transfers to four-year institutions, 167, 228, 292n5; degree types, 215; and employment, 222–27, 240, 242; and athletics, 237; and families, 239. *See also* Transfers from two-year to four-year institutions; Two-year institutions

Conant, James B., 115–16, 122, 140

Counselors: and college choice, 1, 43, 127, 148; and educational expectations, 35; and life plans, 86, 123–26; and college attendance, 115, 292n5; and high school curriculum, 116, 120–26; deans as, 121–24; and college admissions, 122, 129–33, 137, 257; and graduation requirements, 122; and college preparation, 130–31; and dropout rate, 135–36; and community colleges, 138–39; role of, 148, 294n11; and two-year

institutions, 233, 234–35; and four-year institutions, 234; and aligned ambitions, 257

Course sequences, 123–24

Csikzentmihalyi, Mihaly, 10

Divorce rate, 31, 191

Dreams: and adolescent ambitions, 1, 4, 15, 245; and educational expectations, 6; and life plans, 7, 83; and aligned ambitions, 87; and ambition paradox, 221, 227

Drifting dreamers, 7, 163, 253–56

Dropout rate: and adolescents of the 1950s, 20, 21; decline in, 74–75, 172; and case studies, 93–95, 117, 120; and high school curriculum, 135–36

Drug use: and adolescent ambitions, 3–4; and friendships, 90, 164, 198, 208–9, 304n14; and counseling programs, 131; and adolescent-parent relationships, 142; and time alone, 193

Economic returns of schooling, 5, 74, 286n14

Educational attainment: and social mobility, 4, 5; and college choice, 11; of parents, 21, 32, 39, 82, 83, 117, 148, 293n8; and wages, 72–74; and career choices, 80; and norms, 164

Educational credentials: and labor market, 4, 5, 6, 7, 21–22, 33; value of, 82–83; and life plans, 85; and misaligned ambitions, 108

Educational expectations: and adolescent ambitions, 3–4, 5, 6–9,
257, 261; of parents, 7, 33, 39,
40, 92, 117, 136, 141, 145, 150,
289n4, 293n8, 295n1; and adolescents of the 1950s, 25, 26,
29–30, 59–60; and teachers, 28,
34–35, 254; and college financing, 33–34, 54; and occupational aspirations, 36–38, 47–
48, 79–81, 262, 288n1, 288–
89n2, 289n3; and wages, 74; and
aligned ambitions, 79–81, 99–
100, 289n3; and community
colleges, 130; and four-year institutions, 130, 217, 306n3; and
parental support, 143, 297n5;
and parental challenge, 145,
146, 297n6; and adolescent-parent relationships, 149–50, 160–
61, 165–66, 298n9; and two-
year institutions, 216, 218, 231–
32, 306n3; and ambition paradox, 219, 227, 228, 238; and
college preparation, 222–23;
and transfers from two-year to
four-year institutions, 232, 233–
34; and educational requirements, 234, 283n23; and Sloan
study, 267
Educational requirements: and occupational aspirations, 79; and
aligned ambitions, 109; and misaligned ambitions, 164; and educational expectations, 234,
283n23
Employment: and adolescent ambitions, 5, 6, 11; and adolescents of

the 1950s, 6, 16, 27, 56, 61; stability of, 6, 35, 40–43, 56, 58,
61, 88, 91; and parents' educational expectations, 7, 141; and
college financing, 28, 43; and
dual-career couples, 31; and
counselors, 138, 148; and misaligned ambitions, 162–63; and
work programs, 178, 259; and
community colleges, 222–27,
240, 242; and two-year institutions, 232; and four-year institutions, 250; and aligned ambitions, 263; and Sloan study,
282n21. See also Career choices;
Labor market; Teenage work
Encapsulated work experiences,
175–81, 261
Experience sampling method
(ESM), 10–11, 172, 175, 267
Extracurricular activities, 181, 225,
301n9

Families: and adolescent ambitions,
5, 43, 45–46, 252; and aligned
ambitions, 7, 107, 108–9, 158,
169; and life plans, 7, 95–96,
109–10, 168, 169; and adolescents of the 1950s, 16, 17, 21,
24, 26–27; one-parent families,
31, 191; and social capital, 147,
148; and misaligned ambitions,
164; and teenage work, 181–83;
and friendships, 197; and community colleges, 239; and college
preparation, 247. See also Adolescent-parent relationships; Parents
Farr, Eleanor, 114

Financial aid: and adolescents of the 1950s, 28, 54, 281–82n15; and adolescents of the 1990s, 31; and counselors, 122; and parents, 158; and four-year institutions, 250

Four-year institutions: and college financing, 2–3, 227, 250, 259; and college choice, 8, 11; and high school curriculum, 124–25; and educational expectations, 130, 217, 306n3; success in, 130–31; and community college transfers, 167, 228, 292n5; degree types, 215; enrollment of, 215, 305n3; and bachelor's degrees, 217, 219, 270–73; and race or ethnicity, 218; and aligned ambitions, 221; and counselors, 234; matriculation at, 274–75. *See also* Transfers from two-year to four-year institutions

Friendships: and boyfriend-girlfriend relationships, 8, 190–91, 197, 205–7, 211; and academic performance, 89–90; and drug use, 90, 164, 198, 208–9, 304n14; and aligned ambitions, 96, 101; and norms, 164, 301–2n2; and parents, 164, 211; and peer groups, 190; and activities, 194–97; and motivation, 194, 255; changes in, 203, 205. *See also* Peer groups; Social groups

Gay/lesbian issues, 191, 207–8
Gender: and occupational aspirations, 18, 22–23, 61, 71, 256, 281n14, 285–86n11; and dropouts, 21; and adolescents of the 1950s, 22, 23–24, 56; and adolescent ambitions, 55; and educational expectations, 74; and aligned ambitions, 82, 83, 289n4, 289–90n5; and Sloan study, 266

Gender roles: and adolescents of the 1950s, 22–24, 49, 53, 54, 71; shifts in perceptions of, 49, 54–55, 71; and social roles, 283n28

General education programs, 113, 114, 115

Girlfriends: and time alone, 8; and peer groups, 190–91; and friendships, 197; nature of, 205–7; and aligned ambitions, 211

Guidance counselors. *See* Counselors

Havighurst, Robert, 10, 18, 19–20, 278n1, 279–80n10

High school curriculum: and college preparation, 11, 54, 85, 132, 139, 222, 227, 247; and adolescents of the 1950s, 18, 115, 120, 279n9; and adolescent ambitions, 113–19; and college preparatory programs, 113–15, 127; and graduation requirements, 114–15, 138; and course difficulty, 115–16, 120–21, 135; and counselors, 116, 120–26; and life plans, 117; and uniform curriculum, 118, 134–35; and advanced-placement courses,

High school curriculum
(continued)
120–21, 128, 129, 135, 260;
organization of, 120, 128–29,
260; and college admissions,
123–24, 129–30; curricular
maze of, 125, 139–40, 259,
260; and college entrance examinations, 128; and curricular differentiation, 133, 134; and community colleges, 135, 137–39;
strategies for, 135; and occupational aspirations, 136–37, 260–
61; and friendships, 203

High school diploma: and labor
market, 21, 23, 51–52, 56–57,
72, 81, 261; and occupational aspirations, 42–43, 58; and adolescents of the 1950s, 43, 51–
52, 58–62, 71–72; and wages,
57, 70–76, 81, 261, 286n14;
and adolescents of the 1990s,
58, 62–70

High schools: and adolescent ambitions, 5; and aligned ambitions,
7, 117, 118, 259–61; and ambition paradox, 9; and adolescents
of the 1950s, 18, 20; and life
plans, 39, 110, 117, 119–26,
145, 293–94n9; role of, 39, 49;
and college preparation, 53–54,
106; and misaligned ambitions,
103, 117–19; as comprehensive
high schools, 113–19; vocational high schools, 113; graduation requirements of, 114–15,
122, 138; case studies of, 116,
119–39, 293n8; and college ad-

missions, 117, 126–33, 260; and
student success, 118, 133–39;
size of, 127, 190, 260; and career
choices, 156, 160, 165; schedule
of, 171–72; and teenage work,
171–72, 178; and cooperative
work programs, 178; and internships, 184–85; social organization of, 203

Honors courses, 54, 120–21, 128,
129, 135

Human capital: and labor market,
55; education as, 147; and adolescent ambition, 245

Intergenerational mobility, 277n2
Internships: and occupational aspirations, 37, 48; and teenage
work, 183–87; and aligned ambitions, 187–88, 261; and parents, 259

Junior colleges. *See* Community colleges; Transfers from two-year to
four-year institutions; Two-year
institutions

Labor market: and educational credentials, 4, 5, 6, 7, 21–22, 33;
volatility of, 11, 48, 55, 256,
257, 261; and adolescents of the
1950s, 18, 56–62; and high
school diploma, 21, 23, 51–52,
56–57, 72, 81, 261; and adolescents of the 1990s, 33, 44, 48,
57, 62–70; and occupational aspirations, 35, 77–78; competitiveness in, 42–43, 44, 47, 52;

and human capital, 55; and counselors, 148; and teenage work, 173–75. *See also* Employment

Larson, Reed, 10

Legal Outreach Corporation, 186–87

Liberal arts education, 30, 162, 215, 282n16

Life plans: and adolescent ambitions, 4, 7, 12, 43–44; and families, 7, 95–96, 109–10, 168, 169; and motivation, 7, 91, 107–8; and resources, 7, 39, 84, 107, 108–10; viability of, 38; and high schools, 39, 110, 117, 119–26, 145, 293–94n9; and educational requirements, 79; and aligned ambitions, 83–84, 86–87, 106–7, 110, 263–64; and strategic process, 84, 95–96; and academic performance, 85; and counselors, 86, 123–26; and parents, 86, 146; and teachers, 86, 115, 160; and misaligned ambitions, 95–96, 106–7; advantages of, 106–10; case studies of, 117; and adolescent-parent relationships, 148–49; and activity-based groups, 202; and ambition paradox, 219–20, 222

Marriage: and adolescents of the 1950s, 5, 16, 21, 22–24, 25, 29–30, 52, 53, 61, 280–81n12; and adolescents of the 1990s, 5, 31, 37, 48–49, 70, 191, 207; and career choices, 31, 253

Military service, 24–25

Misaligned ambitions: nature of, 7; and ambition paradox, 8–9, 219; distribution of, 81; and parents' educational level, 82; case studies of, 91–96, 101–6, 159–68, 293n8; and academic performance, 93–94, 105, 108, 163; and adolescent-parent relationships, 94, 149–50, 159–68, 298n9; and life plans, 95–96, 106–7; and career choices, 103–4, 159–63, 222, 228–38; and high schools, 103, 117–19; and college financing, 104–6; and college preparation, 105, 106; and transfers from two-year to four-year institutions, 109, 167, 242–43; and high school curriculum, 139; and college choice, 159, 163–68; and employment, 162–63; and time alone, 194; and peer groups, 211; and two-year institutions, 221–22, 228–38, 242; and educational expectations, 289n3; and parental support, 297n5

Motivation: and life plans, 7, 91, 107–8; and aligned ambitions, 79, 90, 91, 107; and academic performance, 93, 107; and high school curriculum, 120; and internships, 183, 184; and friendships, 194, 255

Music tastes, 16, 210–11

National Commission on Excellence in Education, 114

Nation at Risk, A, 114

Norms: and social capital, 147; and academic performance, 158, 164; and friendships, 164, 301–2n2; and aligned ambitions, 169; and peer groups, 197–98, 200

Occupational aspirations: and adolescent ambitions, 3, 5, 6, 75–78, 251–52; and life plans, 7; and gender, 18, 22–23, 61, 71, 256, 281n14, 285–86n11; and adolescents of the 1950s, 22–23, 25–27, 58, 281n14; and labor market, 35, 77–78; and college choice, 36–38, 42; and educational expectations, 36–38, 47–48, 79–81, 262, 288n1, 288–89n2, 289n3; and internships, 37, 48; and high school diploma, 42–43, 58; and educational requirements, 79; and resources, 95; and high school curriculum, 136–37, 260–61; and two-year institutions, 218, 228–38, 242; and ambition paradox, 219, 226–27, 228, 238; changes in, 251–52, 254, 255–56, 264; and aligned ambitions, 264, 289–90n5; and Sloan study, 267, 288n1. *See also* Career choices

Parents: and college choice, 1–2, 89, 101, 109–10, 129, 157–58, 161–62, 223; and adolescent ambitions, 7–8, 141, 256; educational expectations of, 7, 33, 39, 40, 92, 117, 136, 141, 145, 150, 289n4, 293n8, 295n1; and ambition paradox, 9; educational level of, 21, 32, 39, 82, 83, 117, 148, 293n8; and career choices, 45, 88–89, 92–93, 98, 102, 168, 258–59; and life plans, 86, 146; and teenage work, 87–88, 102, 174, 178, 258–59; and academic performance, 96, 97, 161; and college financing, 101, 149, 158, 166, 217–18, 223, 227, 248, 257, 259, 298–99n12, 307n13; support of, 106; and high school curriculum, 120–21; and counselors, 136; and aligned ambitions, 141, 143, 145, 256–59, 297nn5–6; and parental challenge, 143, 144–45, 146, 296n4, 297n6; and parental support, 143, 296n4, 297n5; and adulthood transition, 144–45, 257, 296n4; strategic actions of, 146, 168, 258; and time alone, 147, 258; and friendships, 164, 211. *See also* Adolescent-parent relationships; Families

Peer groups: and adolescent ambitions, 8, 191, 211; and popularity, 52–53, 189, 190, 198–99; changes in, 190, 205, 208–9; and Sloan study, 190, 197–98, 303–4n10; composition of, 197–99; fluidity of, 198, 199, 202–3, 211; activity-based groups compared with, 199–202, 205, 260; influence of, 202–3, 211, 304n12. *See also* Friendships; Social groups

Planful competence, 290n6
Powell, Arthur, 114
Proprietary institutions, 215
PSAT, 49, 253

Race and ethnicity: and adolescent
    ambitions, 3; and drifting
    dreamers, 7; and Sloan study, 9,
    116–17, 265, 266, 293n8; and
    educational expectations, 74;
    and aligned ambitions, 82, 83,
    289nn4–5; and high schools,
    119, 127, 134; and suburbaniza-
    tion, 119–20; and college
    choice, 126; and romantic rela-
    tionships, 191, 207; and activity-
    based groups, 200; and four-year
    institutions, 218
Resources: and life plans, 7, 39,
    84, 107, 108–10; for aligned
    ambitions, 86, 108–10; and oc-
    cupational aspirations, 95; and
    educational attainment, 148;
    and adolescent-parent relation-
    ships, 161. See also College fi-
    nancing; Families; Parents;
    Teachers

SAT: and college choice, 1, 2, 253;
    preparation courses for, 89; sub-
    ject examinations, 128; and ado-
    lescent-parent relationships,
    148, 150, 165
Scholarships: eligibility for, 4, 34;
    and college financing, 28, 34;
    and athletics, 63–64, 222, 236–
    37; and counselors, 122; and
    two-year institutions, 230

Self-esteem, 193, 194, 303n7
Sexual preference, 191, 207–8
Shadow education, 157
Single-parent families, 31, 191
Sloan study: description of, 9–11,
    265–67; and race and ethnicity,
    9, 116–17, 265, 266, 293n8;
    adolescent case studies from,
    32–51, 278n1, 282–83n22;
    and aligned ambitions, 79–80;
    high school case studies from,
    116, 119–39, 293n8; and ado-
    lescent-parent relationships,
    142–46; and peer groups, 190,
    197–98, 303–4n10; and alco-
    hol use, 210; and occupational
    aspirations, 267, 288n1; and
    employment expectations,
    282n21
Social capital: and adolescent-par-
    ent relationships, 146, 147, 148;
    and aligned ambitions, 147–51;
    and academic performance, 148,
    297–98n8
Social groups: fluidity of, 8, 198,
    199, 202, 211, 259–61; peer
    groups compared with, 190; and
    activity-based groups, 199–202,
    259–60; choices in, 264. See also
    Peer groups
Social mobility, 4, 5
Social roles, 283n28
Solitude. See Time alone
Suburbanization: and adolescents
    of the 1950s, 16–17, 19, 29, 53;
    and race or ethnicity, 119–20;
    and voluntary organizations,
    283n26

Teachers: and educational expectations, 28, 34–35, 254; and college choice, 43; students' judgments of, 47; and academic performance, 66, 93, 97; and life plans, 86, 115, 160; and college preparation, 97, 115; and high school curriculum, 120; and advanced-placement courses, 155; and adolescent ambitions, 256; and aligned ambitions, 257

Teenage Life Survey, 267, 295n1, 302n5

Teenage work: nature of, 5, 62, 170–71, 173–75, 285n8; role of, 8; and adolescents of the 1950s, 22, 24; and life plans, 85; and parents, 87–88, 102, 174, 178, 258–59; and aligned ambitions, 90, 96, 107, 152–53; and misaligned ambitions, 167; and adolescent development, 170; prevalence of, 170, 300n2; and high schools, 171–72, 178; and encapsulated work experiences, 175–81, 261; and families, 181–83; and time alone, 181, 301n9; and internships, 183–87; and gender, 286n11

Television, 16, 17

Time alone: and adolescent ambitions, 8; and parents, 147, 258; and teenage work, 181, 301n9; as percentage of time, 190, 191, 192–93, 302nn3–5, 302–3n6; and aligned ambitions, 193–94, 211

Transfers from two-year to four-year institutions: and college financing, 105, 241; and misaligned ambitions, 109, 167, 242–43; and community colleges, 167, 228, 292n5; and time to obtain bachelor's degree, 217; rate of transfers, 219, 235, 307n11; and credit transfer policies, 220, 222, 262, 263; and course choices, 222, 230–31, 233; and occupational aspirations, 228; and educational expectations, 232, 233–34; and counselors, 233, 234–35; and athletics, 236–38; and persistence, 238–42; and academic performance, 307n12

Two-year institutions: and college choice, 8, 11, 215, 305n2; enrollment of, 215, 219, 305n3; and adolescent ambitions, 216–22, 307n11; and educational expectations, 216, 218, 231–32, 306n3; and bachelor's degrees, 217, 218, 219, 242–43, 270–73; and college financing, 217, 221, 223, 224, 226, 227, 229–30, 237, 243, 259; and ambition paradox, 218–19, 221, 222, 244, 263; and aligned ambitions, 221, 222; and career choices, 228–38; matriculation at, 274–75. See also Community colleges; Transfers from two-year to four-year institutions

University of Chicago, 10

Values, and adolescent-parent relationships, 161, 164
Veterans' education benefits, 28,
  54
Vocational programs: and adolescents of the 1950s, 113, 279n9;
  enrollment of, 114; and academic performance, 115; and
  community colleges, 115,
  215; reorganization of, 115,
  128–29, 292n5; decline in,
  127, 139

Wages: and adolescent ambition, 5,
  33, 70–76, 231; and high school
  diploma, 57, 70–76, 81, 261,
  286n14; and career choices, 98;
  and teenage work, 173, 174–75,
  176, 178–83; and adolescent-
  parent relationships, 257